CHALLENGES TO ACADEMIC FREEDOM

CHALLENGES TO

ACADEMIC FREEDOM

EDITED BY

JOSEPH C. HERMANOWICZ

JOHNS HOPKINS UNIVERSITY PRESS | *Baltimore*

 Published 2021
Printed in the United States of America on acid-free paper
9 8 7 6 5 4 3 2 1

Johns Hopkins University Press
2715 North Charles Street
Baltimore, Maryland 21218-4363
www.press.jhu.edu

Library of Congress Cataloging-in-Publication Data

Names: Hermanowicz, Joseph C., editor.
Title: Challenges to academic freedom / edited by Joseph C. Hermanowicz.
Description: Baltimore, Maryland : Johns Hopkins University Press, 2021. | Includes bibliographical references and index.
Identifiers: LCCN 2020057376 | ISBN 9781421442198 (paperback) | ISBN 9781421442204 (ebook)
Subjects: LCSH: Academic freedom—United States.
Classification: LCC LC72.2 .C527 2021 | DDC 378.1/21—dc23
LC record available at https://lccn.loc.gov/2020057376

A catalog record for this book is available from the British Library.

A good university, like Socrates, will be upsetting.

—*Kalven Report*, University of Chicago

I should say to you, "Men of Athens, I respect and love you, but I shall obey the god rather than you, and while I live and am able to continue, I shall never give up philosophy or stop exhorting you and pointing out the truth to any one of you" . . . This I shall do to whomever I meet, young and old, foreigner and citizen . . . For know that the god commands me to do this, and I believe that no greater good ever came to pass in the city than my service to god.

—Socrates, in *The Apology*, 29d–30a

CONTENTS

CHALLENGES TO ACADEMIC FREEDOM

INTRODUCTION

Problems and Perspectives

Joseph C. Hermanowicz

Properties of Academic Freedom

The American Association of University Professors (AAUP), which was formed in the early twentieth century, partly in response to a cumulative history of threats to academic freedom, set forth a framework by which to understand and uphold (as well as debate) academic freedom as a principle that guides inquiry in colleges and universities. This framework was first articulated in the association's 1915 "Declaration of Principles on Academic Freedom and Academic Tenure," repeated in a more succinct version in its 1940 "Statement of Principles," and refined in 1970 in the midst of a free speech movement. The association's statements on academic freedom are contained in its *Red Book*, an anthology of policy statements pertaining to the work and welfare of faculty members at US institutions of higher education (AAUP 2015). Most colleges and universities and professional associations in the United States subscribe to the tenets of academic freedom espoused by the association.

Since 1915, these tenets are:

> 1. Teachers are entitled to full freedom in research and in the publication of the results, subject to the adequate performance of their other academic duties . . .
> 2. Teachers are entitled to freedom in the classroom in discussing their subject, but should be careful not to introduce into their teaching controversial matter which has no relation to their subject . . .
> 3. College and university teachers are citizens, members of a learned profession, and officers of an educational institution. When they speak or write as citizens, they should be free from institutional censorship or discipline, but their special position in the community imposes special obligations. As scholars and educational officers, they should remember that the public may judge their profession and their institution by their utterances. Hence they should at all times be accurate, should exercise appropriate restraint, should show respect for the opinions of others, and should make every effort to indicate that they are not speaking for the institution. (AAUP 2015, 14)

The third of these tenets has been the most problematic aspect of academic freedom from the beginning (Finkin and Post 2009), a subject to which select chapters in this volume shall return.

At the same time, scholars have been called upon to explain—for reasons that most likely have been self-demonstrating—the purpose of higher education institutions. Edward Shils, in his *Academic Ethic*, put it this way:

> Universities have a distinctive task. It is the methodical discovery and the teaching of truths about serious and important things . . . The discovery and transmission of truth is the distinctive task of the academic profession, just as the care of the health of the patient is the distinctive task of the medical profession, and the protection, within the law, of the client's rights and interests is the distinctive task of the legal profession . . . That truth has a value in itself, apart from any use to which it is put, is a postulate of the activities of a university. It begins with the assumption that truth is better than error, just as the medical profession

> accepts that health is better than illness and the legal profession begins with the belief that the assurance of rights under the law is better than to be at the mercy of arbitrary power. (Shils 1983, 3)

The faculty committee charged with producing the association's 1915 statement on academic freedom spoke of a college's or university's purpose in an increasingly familiar passage—namely, as "an intellectual experiment station, where new ideas may germinate and where their fruit, though still distasteful to the community as a whole, may be allowed to ripen until finally, perchance, it may become a part of the accepted intellectual food of the nation or of the world" (AAUP 2015, 9). A report on an institution's role in political and social action produced by a faculty committee at the University of Chicago in 1967 spoke of this purpose more succinctly: "The mission of the university is the discovery, improvement, and dissemination of knowledge" (Kalven Committee 1967, 1).

And yet there endures confusion about what professors have a defensible right to say or publish (particularly, as noted above, in extramural forums). At least one source of the confusion in the United States is found in the way in which academic freedom is often intertwined with a constitutional freedom of speech. Though related, the freedoms are distinct. We may construe academic freedom, as the historian Joan Scott has observed, as a "protection of faculty rights based on disciplinary competence," whereas freedom of speech involves a right "to express one's ideas, however true or false they may be" (Scott 2017, 1). More specifically, academic freedom defends the pursuit of *knowledge*; constitutional free speech entails a right to an opinion, however unfounded or ungrounded (Scott 2017).

Echoing the points above, the pursuit of knowledge, not the doling out of opinion, is the province of higher education institutions. What counts as defensible speech in an academic context is speech (and writing) that satisfies professional standards:

> The scope of academic freedom is not determined by First Amendment principles of freedom of speech, but by the metrics of professional competence. Professors are free to teach in ways that are regarded as

> professionally competent. Disciplines are grounded on the premise that some ideas are better than others; disciplinary communities claim the prerogative to discriminate between competent and incompetent work. Disciplines do not create expert knowledge through a market place of ideas in which content discrimination is prohibited and all ideas are equal (Post 2017, 13, 16, 17).

Academic freedom is a freedom constrained by professional norms. Scott (2017) notes that fields evince tensions about what constitutes acceptable work, but it is academic freedom, not freedom of speech, that informs such debate. In other words, this is the prime way by which knowledge is advanced—as possessing truth and certified by a learned community.

It is for these reasons that students are generally understood not to possess academic freedom in the American context. They lack expertise in an academic discipline or applied field, are not certified members of an academic profession, and thus are deemed incapable of rendering sound judgments about acceptable speech and writing in accord with a set of professional norms. This, however, is not to say that students on American campuses have free rein of speech, for their speech, too, is constrained, or so it is generally viewed.

Outside of classrooms, constitutionally protected free speech prevails on the American college campus—to the extent that institutions do not limit this freedom through prescriptions about where, when, and under what conditions students may speak, such as through the use of designated speech zones; and excepting, perhaps, at some religiously affiliated colleges and universities that impose particular rules on behavior, constraining the exercise of free speech. While there generally are no such ordinances as "speech codes" inside classrooms, many institutions utilize codes of student conduct that may sometimes pertain to speech in a very broad sense. More significantly, students' speech is generally thought to be uttered in accord with the disciplinary and field norms that they learn in the course of acquiring an education. "Student free speech is appropriately limited in the university classroom, subject to the disciplinary tutelage of the professor in charge," and this entails learning critical evaluation and "how to question orthodoxy and challenge it from a position of knowledge rather than . . . unexamined belief" (Scott 2017, 8). Student voices, she maintains, can be "angry, insistent, [or] condemnatory" in classroom discussion and debate, so long as outrage is guided by reason (Scott 2017, 8). This view is consistent with the AAUP's "Joint Statement on the Rights and Freedoms of Students," which emphasizes, "Students should exercise their freedom with responsibility" (AAUP 2015, 381). Thusly understood, the freedoms enjoyed, and responsibilities borne, by teachers and students in the classroom express their German derivatives *Lehrfreiheit* ("freedom of professors to teach") and *Lernfreiheit* ("freedom of students to learn").

More to the point, *quality* becomes the key differentiating ingredient between academic freedom and free speech. Freedom of speech makes no distinction in the quality of utterances; academic freedom does. Stanley Fish, in his essay "Free Speech Is Not an Academic Value," provides guidance on the matter: "Freedom of speech is not an academic value. Accuracy of speech is an academic value; completeness of speech is an academic value; relevance of speech is an academic value. Each of these values is directly related to the goal of academic inquiry: getting a matter of fact right" (Fish 2017, B10)—that is, establishing truth. Accuracy, completeness, and a demonstrated relevance operate on behalf of quality academic work in teaching and research.

Nonetheless, accuracy, completeness, and relevance—by design—are difficult standards to satisfy on social media platforms. Consequently, utterances on social media, including those made by academics, are generally of lesser quality than we may expect to find in peer-reviewed publications and carefully produced course material. Compromised quality opens itself up to criticism, as well it should in keeping with the goals of science and scholarship. Here again we meet up with problems in what academic freedom does and does not protect in the digital age. If, however, many take the AAUP's 1915 statement as one that cloaks academic freedom as a principle, let us recall that *accuracy* and *restraint* are guiding precepts in the association's statement of defensible extramural speech. Further, if we can discern these several fundamental properties of academic freedom, why do threats to it recur? That is the subject to which I now turn.

The Structure of Recurring Threats to Academic Freedom in the United States

Academic freedom is so centrally configured in the academic profession in the United States that when it is threatened, it always feels as though we—academics, students, legislators, and the public—have finally lost our minds. There is, however, some good news: history has demonstrated that we have not done so permanently. Rather, we recover, and eventually the feeling returns, brought about by situations that incite the sensation of a crisis. By no means is this meant to trivialize those situations that have caused a sense of breakdown, for it has been by responses to them that academic freedom—arguably in a flexible form—has endured. Crisis is what inspired the AAUP to form and adopt its first set of principles on academic freedom in 1915, and then again in 1940. Every decade since has seen academic freedom tested, from writings on the McCarthy period and its effects in the 1940s and 1950s (Schrecker 1986); race relations and sexual harassment in the 1960s (Downs 1999); purity and ideology in social science research in the 1970s (Mata 2010); political correctness, speech codes, multicultural curricula, and affirmative action in the 1980s and 1990s (Menand 1996a); and conflicts of interest and corporate influence in the 2000s (Aby 2007); Present concerns deal with such issues as trigger warnings, safe spaces, and speech zones; renewed concerns about the disinvitation of campus speakers; the language of sexual harassment; trustee and politician interference in curricula; the demands of administrative law; restrictions on research (imposed by, among other entities, institutional review boards); and a growth in contingent faculty whose academic freedom is precarious. Long ago, Richard Hofstadter and Walter Metzger (1955, ix) wrote, "Academic freedom has become one of the central issues of our time." In reality, it is *always* central—if not by calls for its defense in times of conflict, then for its principle through periods of relative calm.

While there is always a context and a situatedness to episodes of contestation, there is also a structure by which perceived crises over academic freedom recur. We are not, in these times, on the cusp of the end of the world, though it may feel that way. Rather, we are part of a repeating historical pattern. To write about such a pattern is perhaps a way to calm the waters, relieve the panic, and quiet the screaming, as well as—perhaps more importantly—to cast some light on the larger social context in which academic freedom resides in the United States. Here I identify main pressure points found in the principle and practice of academic freedom in this country that establish conditions for its periodic tumult.

First, in building on John Stuart Mill ([1859] 1975), Louis Menand (1996b) has explained that freedom, on the one hand, always entails restriction, on the other. In his essay "Two Concepts of Liberty," Isaiah Berlin (1969) distinguishes negative and positive freedoms. "Negative freedom" consists of a *freedom from constraint*. People shall *not* be physically or intellectually barred from activities. By contrast, "positive freedom" consists of the active *capacity to do good things*. People *shall* be able to do what they want, which leads to constructive ends. Two people can favor different ends—that is, different concepts of freedom. If we take academic freedom as freedom from constraint in teaching and scholarly inquiry (a negative freedom), then we collide with those who, for example, favor "trigger warnings" and "safe spaces" or who wish to designate all faculty members as "mandated reporters" of sexual harassment (a positive freedom). Accepting the first while rejecting the second is freedom alongside restriction. Attempting to accept both is irreconcilable without compromising some sense of academic freedom.

As Menand (1996b, 5) states, "A . . . deeply misleading assumption . . . of the university is the notion that there exists some unproblematic conception of academic freedom that is philosophically coherent and that will conduce to outcomes in particular cases which all parties will feel to be just and equitable." "Freedom," he continues (1996b, 7), "is always at the expense of something." Freedom for one thing is a limit on something else. Like the question of when life begins, the line where freedom ends and restriction starts is subject to debate and, historically, is always a moving target.

By recognizing that we are dealing with a target that shifts over time, we can identify a second source of pressure on academic freedom—namely, a tension between the historical contexts in which threats to academic freedom arise, and claims of a universal definition and deployment of academic freedom. The AAUP's 1915 declaration of what academic freedom protects would seemingly give the principle a clear definition. So what is the problem? It is a difficulty that, in considering academic freedom, inheres as an enduring universal ideal versus a principle that is historically circumscribed by the political and social conditions in which it exists. Scott (1996, 165) has written of this tension: "The concept of academic freedom carries many meanings (the defense of individual rights of inquiry, of unpopular ideas, and corporate autonomy), and . . . these meanings are (and have been) developed differently in different relationships of power and in different historical circumstances."

In points parallel to those of Menand (1996a; 1996b), others have described academic freedom as "neither a philosophical absolute nor a tangible entity, but a relational and contextual practice that takes shape in opposition to whatever is locally and ideologically conceived as unfreedom" (Brown 1995, 6, quoted in Scott 1996, 165). But, at the same time, the idiom of academic freedom projects universality, independent of its context, so it can be invoked against any abuse, irrespective of the time or situation. Needless to say, situations are often complex, with different viewpoints and interpretations of behavior and events. For example, does academic freedom protect extramural speech, including posts by academics on social media? The subject of extramural speech is the most ambiguous of the tenets that academic freedom protects. It has always been problematic. Extramural speech was among the chief reasons that brought about the AAUP's "Declaration" in 1915, and the development of the digital age has only rendered this matter more complex (O'Neil 2008). Even though the AAUP—in 1997, in 2004, and again in 2013—issued reports on and recommendations for how to treat electronic communications, cases have presented a complexity that belies definition (AAUP 2015).

Thus academic freedom exists as a universal ideal and, simultaneously, as a malleable principle in applied practice. Though we may invoke some definition of it, the content of academic freedom is never clear cut. This continual tension between a universal ideal and a historical context exposes academic freedom to timely (and timeless) debates about what it should and should not protect.

This ongoing tension is reinforced by a third condition, which structures the recurrence of threats to academic freedom in the United States: limited law. Academic freedom in America is not clearly established in law; it has no substantial presence. Professors have a highly ambiguous legal recourse for alleged violations of their academic freedom. Eric Barendt (2010, 162), a scholar of comparative legal issues, has observed that academic freedom in the United States "is a much more complex subject than it is in the United Kingdom or Germany, where the freedom is based respectively on a statutory right (the U.K. Education Reform Act 1988) or a constitutional right (the German Basic Law)." Untethered to any legal authority in the United States, academic freedom debacles arise episodically and routinely raise questions about what academic freedom actually is, as well as who and what it protects (Fish 2014, x). Rather than being codified in law, academic freedom in America "floats in the law," as J. Peter Byrne has remarked, "picking up decisions as a hull does barnacles" (Byrne 1989, 251). To the extent that courts have reached decisions about academic freedom, they have customarily done so via other grounds, such as tax law, contract law, and public employee law (Fish 2014, x).

Consequently, "academic freedom is rhetorically strong but legally weak" (Fish 2014, x). Despite the successive decades of tumult involving academic freedom, it remains unclear whether it is a constitutional *right*, with its own actionable protections, or simply a *value*, to be taken into account by courts when they apply other laws (Barendt 2010). Even US colleges and universities themselves have ambiguous and inconsistent bodies and procedures for handling cases involving academic freedom. Here, too, people operate without an established legal statute to determine whether a line has been crossed. The US academic profession has routinely had trouble handling this problem. With limited laws to guide an understanding of academic freedom and, consequently, few tribunals capable of adjudicating claims that are directly about academic freedom, cases are left largely to the court of public opinion. When problems arise, they become public spectacles, and the whole of society is called upon to sort out the fate of American higher education. It is strangely ironic that, for its many claims to self-regulation, the academic profession—the ideal-typical profession from which all others derive—relegates challenges to this vaunted principle to the likes of newspapers, trade magazines, and social media.

Finally, I turn to a fourth key condition of recurrent threats to academic freedom. This may be thought of by some as a function of the first three, in that they—alone and together—yield considerable ambiguity. The principle of academic freedom is *taught* virtually nowhere and is otherwise little discussed (except when perceived to be under significant threat). Again, for a principle taken as sacrosanct, this professional omission is remarkable.

Academics concern themselves with many ambiguous things. Over the course of their careers they preoccupy themselves, their students, and other audiences with matters of great complexity. Many of these topics undoubtedly out-compete academic freedom in their ambiguity. Yet without formal (or even informal) teaching, it is as though we return to square one when threats to academic freedom arise. Questions about this issue from those outside higher education institutions—and, more especially, from those on the inside—expose a tolerated ignorance. What is this thing people are calling "academic freedom"? Why does it exist? When and where did it come from? What evidence can we marshal to discern what academic life is like without it? How is it distinct from freedom of speech? Why should both freedoms matter to students? If academic freedom is important, everyone in the academy should be conversant with these types of questions. In addition, they can be more-systematic and -deliberate actors in educating others. On balance, however, they are not.

Legal scholar Geoffrey Stone (2016, 1, 3) has beseeched colleges and universities to educate students "to understand that academic freedom is not a law of nature. It is not something to be taken for granted. It is, rather, a hard-won acquisition in a lengthy struggle for academic integrity... We live today in an era of political correctness in which students themselves demand censorship, and colleges, afraid to offend those students, too often surrender academic freedom."

His points have empirical merit. According to a survey of over 2,000 undergraduates at institutions across the United States conducted by the Foundation for Individual Rights in Education (FIRE), 60 percent of students think promoting an inclusive environment that is welcoming to a diverse group of students should be a more important priority than protecting students' free speech rights. Yet 57 percent think colleges and universities should be able to restrict student expression of political views that contain hurtful or offensive viewpoints. Moreover, 70 percent feel students should be excluded from extracurricular activities if they publicly express intolerant, hurtful, or offensive viewpoints. Nonetheless, 96 percent consider it important to have their civil rights or liberties protected, and 30 percent believe that freedom of speech is the most important civil right or liberty (FIRE 2019). These patterns suggest merely a surface-level understanding of the principle of free speech and the related one of academic freedom, and an unwillingness to see the principles applied to the protection of expression some find offensive or objectionable (FIRE 2019).

While freedom of speech and academic freedom are indeed distinct, distortions of one can affect the other. A culture in which freedom of speech is constrained adversely affects the climate in which people exercise academic freedom. "It is an illusion for... groups to believe that they can censor the speech of others today without having their own expression muzzled tomorrow" (Herbst and Stone 2017, 1). This muzzling is applicable both to academic freedom and to a broader freedom of speech. Disputes about academic freedom would not be as controversial if there was a reduction of ignorance about it. The more enlightened the citizens of the academy are, the more likely the purposes of higher education institutions will be fulfilled.

It is perhaps tempting to search the immediate historical moment for a *root cause* of threats and disruptions to academic freedom. In the present period, for example, it has become popular to identify the *corporatization of higher education* as the source of many ills (Woodhouse 2009). One may question whether academic freedom and academic capitalism are irreconcilably incompatible. Indeed, several of the authors in this volume attribute a present weakening of academic freedom to market forces that have overtaken the intellectual functioning of colleges and universities.

The corporatization of higher education very likely is a key factor in the threats that currently confront academic freedom, and it is critically important to sort out how an element such as this instigates problems for colleges and universities in fulfilling their socially mandated purposes. It is argued that market logics make actors in higher education (especially administrators and governing boards) sensitive to the protection of a "brand" as institutions compete for scarce resources, including students, money, and prestige. It is argued further that this sensitivity sows a "culture of comfort" in which people should not be exposed to offensive verbal utterances or visual displays. Instead, they should be protected from purportedly harmful stimuli and served by such deployments as censorship and self-censorship; pleasant teaching and correspondingly innocuous course evaluations; a curriculum that deigns to make people *feel good*; luxurious living accommodations; lavish dining facilities; and countless outlets for recreation, leisure, and fun. Corporatization is also argued to play a central role in the proliferation and poor treatment of non-tenure-eligible faculty members, in constraints on research imposed by institutional review boards, in changes in the valuation of forms of scholarship and other faculty activities, such as the acquisition of grants—indeed, in myriad aspects of institutional life.

The widespread, institutionalizing corporatization of higher education is a significant development that entails serious implications for academic freedom. Yet corporatization is situated in a specific historical moment. Such influences, albeit in differently permutated ways, have arisen in previous historical episodes, not least of which included cases that gave momentum to the creation of the AAUP. Here we may recall the writings and speeches of Stanford University economist Edward Ross, whose outspoken criticism of immigrant labor and the Southern Pacific Railroad led Jane Stanford—protective of her late husband, railroad magnate Leland Stanford—to call on the university's president, David Starr Jordan, to fire Ross. Jordan obliged and, by doing so, demonstrated a clash between business and academic interests, on the one hand, as well as an administrative behavior of disguising reasons for dismissal, on the other—fact supplanted by fiction.

To be certain, such clashes were also on hand in the observations of Thorstein Veblen in the early 1900s, whose critique of the ascendancy of business values led him to contend that the pursuit of knowledge had become secondary to the intervening interests of corporations and trusts (Veblen 1918). In other historical periods, still different problems posed threats to academic freedom. Such was the situation, for instance, in the mid-twentieth century, when, following the lead of US Senator Joseph McCarthy, agents working on behalf of the federal government employed a political agenda to rid the academy of enemies from within. Richard Hofstadter (1962) asserted a more fundamental explanation: an anti-intellectualism that strangled American civic and social life.

If we imagine, though it might be a strain at present, that the corporatization of higher education was corrected and the influence of market logic on higher education subdued, *we would still face threats to academic freedom* from any number of factors that had arisen situationally in historical time. Corporatization—like McCarthyism or anti-intellectualism—is not the root cause of threats. Such conditions are better understood, important though they remain, as historically situated factors that enable a perpetually underlying threat to academic freedom to be able to express itself.

For a root cause of academic freedom's volatility, we return, insofar as the United States is concerned, to the contest between freedom and restriction, the tension between historicity and universality, the reality of limited law, and, heretofore, an absence of teaching about academic freedom and a related, though separate, concern for freedom of speech. It is *for these reasons* that threats to academic freedom recur and demonstrate why we find ourselves in a troubled time. Were we to somehow correct for these causes (as John Thelin's chapter in this volume proposes in its own way), then—and only then—might academic freedom form a more secure principle in the US academy. Short of such an evolution, threats recur. As such, thoughtful responses to them must arise.

On this crucial matter, is the professoriate dependable? The answer is far from clear. Robert O'Neil, the First Amendment scholar who, during his career, was both a member of the law faculty and a provost and president at three major public universities in the United States, observed what he called "elusive truths" from this experience: that "most university professors are indifferent to academic freedom, which they typically view as someone else's problem," and that "the defense and survival of academic freedom depends most upon the commitment of those faculty who are least likely to need its protection for their own careers" (O'Neil 2008, vii). This may seem like a tall and intrusive order to some, until perhaps one's own individual freedom is the target.

In her extensive work on the McCarthy period and its consequences for American higher education, historian Ellen Schrecker discovered a striking finding in talking with those who had suffered blacklisting and dismissal at the hands of this movement. It was not the congressional committees, boards of trustees, or academic administrators that they found so problematic. All of these bodies behaved in ways that were expected and, indeed, understandable in terms of their desire to protect a status quo. Rather, professors reserved their "bitterest condemnation for those of their colleagues who failed to support them, those colleagues whose 'speed of light' . . . 'was hotter than their love of liberty' . . . It was the behavior of their fellow academics, especially the self-professed liberals among them, that really rankled. In most cases, it was not so much what these people did that upset the blacklisted professors as it was what they did not do. They did not organize; they did not protest; they did not do anything that reversed the tide of dismissals" (Schrecker 1986, 308).

If faculty apathy was problematic then, it most likely has become more so over time. Two forces work against faculty involvement in institutional life. One consists of growth in the size of institutions, and the other of heightened expectations for research and publication productivity across many different institutional types. Increased size breeds a feeling of anonymity among faculty (and students), where they perceive little, if any, stake in the operation and governance of an institution. The institution is something "outside" and generally alien to themselves. It is a place of employment, more than a special community that requires its members' investment and protection. Many colleges and universities (perhaps, especially, large public ones) may be thought to have evolved into bureaucratic behemoths. Few people want much to do with leviathans, because they think there is little such goliaths can meaningfully do for them.

Heightened research and publication expectations, while socially manufactured, are highly individualizing. In general, behavior will be channeled according to reward systems, and, increasingly across higher education institutions, reward systems strongly favor research. While universities embark on quests for research developments, publications, and grant monies to outcompete other institutions for distinctions, faculty members experience this pursuit as an individual contest—to outcompete colleagues in their departments and larger fields—and reap rewards conferred individually by those groups. Both of these forces galvanize an individualist, rather than a collectivist, mindset among academics. The biggest concern of faculty members is for themselves. This may ultimately always be a true statement, but conditions appear to favor its intensification.

Academic *freedom* is both an individual and a collective condition of academic *work*. Defenses of academic freedom would be more readily articulated by the professoriate if institutions had explicit structures and processes through which to handle situations specifically implicating it. Faculty senates and other governing bodies, to the extent they may play a role in disputes over academic freedom, have only a tenuous connection to them. Faculty members are left largely to themselves in organizing and voicing their claims in defense of this principle. This, too, is a recurrent pattern.

Hanna Holborn Gray, notable for her counterexample as an exemplary academic citizen and a former president of the University of Chicago, has put the matter in the perspective of her field, history:

> The air today is filled with melancholy diagnoses of the state of higher education and still gloomier prognostications about the future . . . Once again the fundamental principles of the academic universe—the commitment they require to freedom of thought and expression—are under scrutiny and debate . . . I have experienced the university world today as one that has undergone a profound transformation in my lifetime, but also one that has demonstrated the same basic struggles of self-definition and freedom as those of the past, and those struggles continue . . . It is disturbing to see so much disregard for freedom of expression on campuses (not only in the United States) and dismaying to observe the extent to which its meaning is not only misunderstood but even distorted to justify disruptive behavior or defend rules outlawing speech deemed offensive . . . The belief that universities should be, above all, the homes of searching and critical intellectual vigor and thought needs recurrent renewal and reaffirmation. Universities have always been vulnerable to outside influence and to the threat of control and manipulation, and they have been vulnerable, too, to conformities imposed from within. (Gray 2018, 297–98)

Members of a profession are both beneficiaries and guardians of the conditions under which they work. Without the two operating in tandem, there is little benefit in an activity whose underlying principle has been lost or severely weakened and not much worth guarding, aside from the benefits that come by virtue of protecting a principle that operates on behalf of seeking truth. In theory, if not always in practice, professors cultivate, while also protecting, the institutions in which they work. Under threat—even in times of relative calm—they are called upon to act, but also (and more generally) to discern, discuss, and debate this crucial foundation of higher learning. That is what colleagues, in the following chapters, have been called upon to do.

Organization of the Book

This volume is divided into four parts, although issues arising in a given chapter (e.g., faculty dismissal or extramural speech) communicate with the concerns of others (e.g., contingent faculty or law). Throughout the book, chapters reference events in order to illustrate threats, damage, and change in academic freedom in the United States. In Part I, the discussion begins with a fulsome illustration of the times in which we find ourselves. This account helps set the stage for much of the ensuing discussion about the character of threats to academic freedom in contemporary times.

In December 2013, Professor Patricia Adler was asked to leave her job for having used a pedagogical device deemed too risky by her university. She and her co-author, Peter Adler, discuss how teaching turned into an event where her university's administration denied her due process and academic freedom in making their closed-doors decisions. With a speed foreign to university operations, academic life turned Kafkaesque, and we see up close the signal qualities of this transformation: fear-mongering; the silencing of speech, interchanges among colleagues, and even humor; illogic amid suspended rules and made-up-as-we-go processes; formal decrees rendered with great consequences but which were nightmarishly bizarre; hypervigilance in what was once understood as ordinary existence. The chapter concludes by discussing how this case may be representative of larger, disturbing trends in academia, including a culture of fear, risk aversion, pandering to helicopter parents, administrative bloat, retreat from discussing disturbing topics, the rise of trigger warnings, and the overreach of administrative offices. The Adlers' recounting conveys that this is not a staid academic matter, but, rather, is real and merits serious attention.

Part II of the book, "The University and the External World," examines several aspects of the troubled relationship between academic freedom, articulated both from within the academy and by those outside its walls, on whose beneficence universities depend, be they legal entities, government officials, or the public. (Note that throughout, the term "university" is used in its broad sense and applies to 2- and 4-year colleges as well as universities per se.) In Chapter 2, Stephen Turner asserts that academic freedom is increasingly restricted by regulations implemented by higher education institutions themselves—for example, in the form of institutional review boards, research misconduct tribunals, and Title IX enforcement. Turner argues that these are not normal parts of legislative law, but are the indirect product of what is referred to as "administrative law": a massive category of federal regulation only lightly policed by the courts. Because these types of regulations are vague and broad, they create discretionary power over those in the academy that is inimical to the traditional notion of academic freedom as a well-defined right.

In Chapter 3, John Thelin observes that for over a century, professors have presumed academic freedom is something that is, or would be, protected by the US Supreme Court. He shows, however, that the historical record belies this belief. What is more, new factors associated with intellectual property, corporate investment and involvement in academic programs, and the frequent tension between boards of trustees and faculty scholarship cast doubt on the efficacy of traditional protections of academic freedom. The chapter connects past and present data to contend that new strategies, such as the use of regional accreditation standards, are needed to redefine and protect academic freedom in the twenty-first century.

Turning to the highly contested arena of extramural speech, Hans-Joerg Tiede begins Chapter 4 with a foundational principle: the conception of academic freedom that has developed in the United States since the late nineteenth century, which includes, as one of its constituent elements the freedom to speak as a citizen outside of one's college or university. Tiede explains that this freedom of extramural utterance is both conceptually puzzling, since it is not necessarily related to the role and expertise of faculty members, and frequently challenged from within the academy and outside it. He makes it plain that since its founding in 1915, the AAUP has advocated for the recognition of freedom of utterances made outside of the academy and has investigated many cases of faculty members' dismissals because of their extramural speech. Tiede notes that some accounts of the development of the AAUP's position on limits to the freedom of such utterances have claimed that it has undergone significant change during that time. Instead, the chapter provides historical evidence for its constancy.

In Chapter 5, "Attacks on Tweets," academic freedom is cast in relation to *money*—the monied interests of universities. Gaye Tuchman argues that the phenomenon of "branding" and the rise of the "commercialized university" impede academic freedom. She examines the Twitter and Facebook posts of three professors that deal with colonialism and race. Paying specific attention to the inner workings of corporate universities, Tuchman contends that administrators' adverse reactions to this extramural speech are a specialized case of a more general practice—protecting the brand—that is part and parcel of "accountability regimes," or organizational devices, designed to control faculty activity on an institution's behalf.

Part III, "The University and Its Internal World," considers ways in which academic freedom is contested by practices inside the academy, both in formal arrangements (e.g., the hiring of adjunct faculty and the functioning of institutional review boards) and by less-standard activities (e.g., student protests). Gary Rhoades, in Chapter 6, focuses on three categories of precarious academic workers—adjunct faculty, graduate assistants, and postdoctoral employees—and analyzes the extent to which academic freedom protections are embedded in collective bargaining agreements. The chapter's findings illuminate the success of contingent academic appointments, especially for adjunct faculty and graduate student employees, in negotiating traditional aspects of academic freedom in teaching, research, and extramural speech into their contracts.

Chapter 7 builds on this discussion. Eve Weinbaum and Dan Clawson boldly state that the future of academic freedom depends above all on the situation of contingent faculty, as they constitute a growing majority of faculty labor. The chapter argues that the structural position of faculty members shapes how academic freedom cases unfold. The authors advocate the role of unions, arguing that non-tenure-line faculty positions are fortified by such arrangements.

In Chapter 8, Laura Stark focuses on institutional review boards (IRBs) and critics' claims that their operation infringes on academic freedom. The chapter proposes a framework to characterize and, in practical terms, better manage threats to academic freedom that arise in the process of research review. She applies the concept of "expert professional speech" to this process, which positions the relationship between researchers and IRB members as one of peer review.

In Chapter 9, Philip Lee provides an account of Harvard Law School students occupying a campus building in 2016 and calling for the removal of a slaveowner's family crest from the law school's shield. The chapter explores the intersection of these students' activism and what Lee purports to be their academic freedom rights. It argues that the First Amendment is inadequate to safeguard the students' right to protest and urges an alternative foundation of protection that develops the principle of "student academic freedom."

In Part IV, we conclude with a chapter by Timothy Reese Cain, "Academic Freedom and Its Useful Past," to help understand and navigate the present by drawing out lessons from earlier times. With a scope that extends back to the turn into the twentieth century, when the modern era of academic freedom in the United States began, the chapter encapsulates critical points in this history to highlight perennial issues related to protecting academic freedom. In so doing, we glean, on the one hand, the substance of threats to academic freedom and, on the other, the non-assured, non-guaranteed imperative of faculty attentiveness to its care.

As a collection, the chapters are differentiated not only by topic, but also, deliberately, by approach and perspective. These factors are numerous and traverse a conceptual range. The authors adopt varied epistemological bases to engage their subject matter. The chapters demonstrate perspectives that are, by turn, case study analyses (Adler and Adler, Tuchman); historical (Thelin, Tiede, Cain); legal-analytic (Turner); formal-empirical (Rhoades, Weinbaum and Clawson); and analytically policy oriented (Stark, Lee). In accord with this diversity, the authors call upon different types of evidence and follow varying courses of argumentation to make their points. In so doing, they demonstrate the imperative of academic freedom amid its entanglements in the twenty-first century.

References

AAUP (American Association of University Professors). 2015. *Policy Documents and Reports* [aka the *Red Book*], 11th edition. Baltimore: Johns Hopkins University Press.

Aby, Stephen H. (ed.). 2007. *The Academic Bill of Rights Debate.* Westport, CT: Praeger.

Barendt, Eric. 2010. *Academic Freedom and the Law*. Oxford: Hart.

Berlin, Isaiah. 1969. "Two Concepts of Liberty." In Isaiah Berlin (ed.), *Four Essays on Liberty*, 118–172. Oxford: Oxford University Press.

Brown, Wendy. 1995. *States of Injury: Studies in Power and Freedom in Late Modernity.* Princeton, NJ: Princeton University Press.

Byrne, J. Peter. 1989. "Academic Freedom: A 'Special Concern of the First Amendment.'." *Yale Law Journal* 99(2):251–340.

Downs, Donald Alexander. 1999. *Cornell '69: Liberalism and the Crisis of the American University*. Ithaca, NY: Cornell University Press.

Finkin, Matthew W. and Robert C. Post. 2009. *For the Common Good: Principles of Academic Freedom*. New Haven, CT: Yale University Press.

FIRE (Foundation for Individual Rights in Education). January 30, 2019. "Survey: What Students Think about Expression, Association, Student Fees, and Charlottesville." Foundation for Individual Rights in Education, https://www.thefire.org.

Fish, Stanley. March 31, 2017. "Free Speech Is Not an Academic Value." *Chronicle of Higher Education*, B10–B11.

Fish, Stanley. 2014. *Versions of Academic Freedom*. Chicago: University of Chicago Press.

Gray, Hanna Holborn. 2018. *An Academic Life: A Memoir*. Princeton, NJ: Princeton University Press.

Herbst, Jeffrey and Geoffrey R. Stone. June 5, 2017. "The New Censorship on Campus." *Chronicle of Higher Education*, https://www.chronicle.com.

Hofstadter, Richard. 1962. *Anti-Intellectualism in American Life*. New York: Alfred A. Knopf.

Hofstadter, Richard and Walter P. Metzger. 1955. *The Development of Academic Freedom in the United States*. New York: Columbia University Press.

Kalven Committee. 1967. "Report on the University's Role in Political and Social Action." Chicago: University of Chicago.

Mata, Tiago. 2010. "The Enemy Within: Academic Freedom in 1960s and 1970s American Social Sciences." *History of Political Economy* 42(annual supplement): 77–104.

Menand, Louis (ed.). 1996a. *The Future of Academic Freedom*. Chicago: University of Chicago Press.

Menand, Louis. 1996b. "The Limits of Academic Freedom." In Louis Menand (ed.), *The Future of Academic Freedom*, 3–20. Chicago: University of Chicago Press.

Mill, John Stuart. [1859] 1975. *On Liberty*. New York: Norton.

O'Neil, Robert. 2008. *Academic Freedom in the Wired World: Political Extremism, Corporate Power, and the University*. Cambridge, MA: Harvard University Press.

Post, Robert. 2017. "The Classic First Amendment Traditions under Stress: Freedom of Speech and the University." Unpublished manuscript.

Schrecker, Ellen W. 1986. *No Ivory Tower: McCarthyism and the Universities*. New York: Oxford University Press.

Scott, Joan W. 2017. "On Free Speech and Academic Freedom." *AAUP Journal of Academic Freedom* 8, https://www.aaup.org/reports-publications/.

Scott, Joan W. 1996. "Academic Freedom as an Ethical Practice." In Louis Menand (ed.), *The Future of Academic Freedom*, 163–180. Chicago: University of Chicago Press.

Shils, Edward. 1983. *The Academic Ethic*. Chicago: University of Chicago Press.

Stone, Geoffrey R. August 26, 2016. "Free Expression in Peril." *Chronicle of Higher Education*, https://www.chronicle.com.

Veblen, Thorstein. 1918. *The Higher Learning in America*. New York: B. W. Huebsch.

Woodhouse, Howard. 2009. *Selling Out: Academic Freedom and the Corporate Market*. Montreal: McGill-Queen's University Press.

PART I

AN ILLUSTRATION

CHAPTER 1

Administrative Interference and Overreach

The "Adler Controversy" and the Twenty-First-Century University

Patricia A. Adler and Peter Adler

"Curiouser and curiouser!" cried Alice, in Lewis Carroll's ([1865] 2000) *Alice in Wonderland* classic. This observation is apt today. Colleges and universities around the world are undergoing a period of turbulence and turmoil, battered from both the Right and the Left, from within and without. How they are transformed and weather this storm remains an open question. We write now to discuss, from the inside, one particular incident that had occurred to the lead author, Patti Adler, at the University of Colorado from the fall of 2013 through the spring of 2014. It has been cited by the American Association of University Professors (AAUP) as one of the most egregious violations ever of Title IX and academic freedom (AAUP 2016). All of the events, including institutional and individual identities, are a matter of public record (see Schmidt 2013; Ferner 2014). Drawing from this case and events since then, we discuss and analyze developments that threaten North American institutions of higher education. Though a co-authored piece, for convenience we use the "I" form in presenting this story.

As some readers will know, I have joined the ranks of an elite group: the tiny number of tenured faculty members terminated or "asked to leave" their jobs. A 2005 *Wall Street Journal* article estimated that only 50 to 75 tenured professors out of 280,000 are fired each year (Lubin 2005). My exit from academia resulted from a controversial decision made by my university in December 2013 that resounded globally. It concerned a pedagogical device I had used in my class for over twenty-five years. In the climate at that time, however, it was deemed too great a risk to the university.

Peter and I moved to Boulder in 1987, when I started working at the University of Colorado. I began teaching "Deviance in US Society" that first semester, and it quickly grew into the most popular class on campus, specifically mentioned in several college guidebooks. It enrolled 500 people every semester, so that, over twenty-seven years, I'd taught this class to around 25,000 students. In one of the course lectures, I used a role-play exercise ("the skit") to outline the eight features of a deviant subculture and illustrate one of them: a system of status stratification. I used the example of prostitution (now preferably called "sex work") to portray six strata of prostitutes: sexual slavery; crack-addicted prostitutes; male and female streetwalkers and their pimps; sex workers in bars; brothels; and escort services. One of the didactic purposes of the skit was to open students' eyes to the wider array of life options, lifestyles, motivations, living conditions, working conditions, careers, violence, and degradation that exist among the different categories of prostitutes. Twelve participants joined me in performing the skit each time, role playing their parts from scenarios that I continually updated for use in my questions and narratives, drawing on academic research, investigative journalism, first-person accounts, and documentaries. Over the twenty-seven years that I've featured this role-play exercise in my class (twice annually), there have been over 500 people portraying various roles. In all of this time, there has never been a complaint.

To personalize my larger group class, I used both grad student teaching assistants (TAs) and assistant TAs (ATAs). The latter were outstanding undergraduate students I recruited from the previous semester to help me write and, with the TAs, grade non-standardized exams. They also enabled me to personalize the class beyond what the TAs could offer, since the latter were stretched thin with so many students in the class. The ATAs were offered the first right of refusal to play roles in the skit, and after that I opened it up to volunteers from among former ATAs, friends, publishers' reps, and others. These were prized roles, and some former ATAs even drove or flew back to Boulder to participate in the skit. It was the highlight of the semester, and there was never a paucity of volunteers.

In the fall of 2013 the skit ran on November 5. The next day I heard that one of my second-year TAs, Vanessa Roberts, had been badmouthing me after the skit in her discussion section. On November 7, after our weekly TA meeting, I asked Vanessa if she could stay afterward to talk for a few minutes. She had two concerns: (1) that evolving cellphone technology and social media might cause participants to worry about being embarrassed by students posting pictures of them; and (2) that participants might feel uncomfortable portraying their roles but not want to tell me, for fear of retribution. We brainstormed about how to ameliorate this, and I thought we had a productive meeting, coming up with new recruitment strategies and precautions.

Nonetheless, five days later, on November 12, Vanessa sent me an email confessing that she had brought her concerns about the ATAs to the department chair earlier in the semester. She explained her motivation for this by saying that she was just trying to protect the ATAs from feeling uncomfortable. But as I later learned, this account was spurious, because she had surreptitiously begun trying to usurp my role from the beginning of the semester, undermining me and empowering herself. She held a meeting with my incoming staff while I was away at an international conference and told them that I was scary and standoffish, encouraging them to come to her with complaints about me behind my back.

Apparently, after hearing of Vanessa's concerns, departmental chair Joanne Belknap immediately referred the case to the Office of Discrimination and Harassment (ODH). In so doing, she violated formal and informal departmental policies by failing to discuss it first either with me or with the Executive Committee. This raises the question of why Belknap took this case—a "concern" and not an actual "complaint"—right away to the ODH. Several possible explanations can be conjectured.

First, as an ardent feminist, she had never liked the skit and saw this as her chance to do something about it. Perhaps that's because she has a degree in criminal justice and teaches courses on "Violence Against Women," while I'm a sociologist who teaches "Deviance in US Society." Criminal justice is an applied, ameliorative, value-laden discipline, while I come from an ethnographic, inductive, value-neutral tradition. She told me that I should have infused the material with more of a victimization perspective.

Second, it's hard to talk about a critique from the Left, but some feminists view sex workers as victims of their traffickers, pimps, johns, the criminal justice system, and a patriarchal system more generally, and they want to save them. In contrast, there are people who view sex workers as women who have rights, free will, and agency and want to support their rights. My skit philosophically challenged the orthodoxy of both sides.

Third, some people believe that political correctness—a vital concept—has overreach. We all probably agree that words have power and should be wielded sensitively, but does that leave no room for role play or for different pedagogical devices?

Fourth, Belknap, a new and inexperienced chair that semester, was apparently sending every concern she received to the ODH, in a knee-jerk manner. In her first three months on the job, she referred a total of three cases to that office. This contrasts with the ten-year tenure of the previous three chairs, during which no cases were referred to that office. With the report filed, the ODH opened their investigation. For one month, no one came forward. Vanessa did not qualify as a complainant herself, because she had never been a skit participant. With no complainant, the ODH did not have a case.

Thus stalled, that office then decided to examine the *content of the skit*. On November 5, uninvited and unannounced, two ODH investigators violated their office's policies and procedures and attended the skit. This represents a *key turning point*, because they expanded their focus from the issue of a power imbalance (professor-staff) to one of classroom content, a *violation of my academic freedom*.

After the skit, they more actively tried to drum up complainants from actual skit participants. Vanessa called each of my then current ATAs, as well as the graduate (Janet Jacobs) and undergraduate (Hillary Potter) chairs, both ardent feminists, and tried to solicit complaints from current and former (going back several years) TAs and ATAs. It was a witch-hunt!

Meanwhile, I didn't know what to do. Should I contact the ODH preemptively? Should I wait for them to finish their investigation and be in touch with me? I wanted an opportunity to present the didactic value of the skit and see what they thought. I figured I could always stop using ATAs or just drop the skit if they informed me that it was a problem. So I waited. I didn't worry too much about it. After all, what could they do to me? I headed off to Thanksgiving break thinking maybe the whole thing would just die.

Wrong! On December 5, the week after Thanksgiving and the second to last week of classes, the ODH investigators decided to take action. Without ever communicating with me, they called an emergency meeting with the dean and associate dean of arts and sciences, the chief university counsel, the head of the ODH, and the chair of the sociology department. I was not invited to this meeting, and, at this point, I had still never been officially notified that there was an investigation. The investigators presented a case to the administrators, indicating that they thought the skit was a "risk" to the university. The lawyer was concerned. This alarmed the deans. They brainstormed about what they could do to avert this dire threat. On the advice of the lawyer, Dean Steven Leigh made his dynamic decision: I had to be removed from teaching "Deviance in US Society" immediately.

Apparently this was not enough. What else could they do to deal with this problem? How could they make it disappear? What if they could "convince" me to *retire immediately*? If this could happen, the lawyer and dean asked the ODH, what would happen? They said they do not investigate retired faculty, and the case would go away. A plan was hatched.

That afternoon, departmental chair Belknap called me into an emergency meeting. As she delivered the verdict, she told me that she had "good news" and "bad news." The good news was that they were offering me an early retirement buyout (known around campus as the "cash for clunkers deal," a term apparently referring to its use to encourage the retirement of "deadwood" faculty). This deal, for which I had previously applied and been denied (because, they told me, of my outstanding value to the university), consisted of two years' salary, spread out over five years. The bad news was that I had to take it *immediately*. I would have one week to finish up my classes, empty my office, and get out. If I declined to accept this offer, there would be severe consequences. First, I would be removed from teaching "Deviance in US Society," my signature course. Second, even if I no longer taught it, if just one person ever came forward at any time in the future to complain about having felt uncomfortable (not only a skit participant, but also any one of the 25,000 plus students who had ever taken the class), I could be found guilty of violating the university's sexual harassment policy and fired for cause. Third, if fired for cause, I would lose my retirement benefits, which included supplemental health insurance for my family for life.

The next day (December 6) the contract appeared in my box. I was amazed! Normally the wheels of bureaucracy grind exceedingly slow, but in less than twenty-four hours, this paperwork was issued and signed by the chair, the dean, and the associate vice chancellor for faculty affairs.

What to do? On the advice of the faculty ombudsperson, I scheduled two meetings for Tuesday of the last week of school, December 10. In the morning, a colleague who sat on the ODH board and I met with the ODH investigators. They first confirmed for us that this whole ruckus was completely confined to the skit. Despite their efforts, they had found no complainant, so they technically had no investigation and no case. But they pointed out three risk factors. First, the student portraying the slave role, using a fake accent, talked about how she had been trafficked from Latvia to America. This might have offended students from that nation (protected class: national origin). Second, the student playing the role of a straight male streetwalker used the street vernacular "faggot" to refer to his customers (protected class: sexual orientation). Third, the student playing a pimp bragged about how he used a combination of love and fear to manipulate his women and mentioned beating a woman who held out on him (protected class: gender). They confirmed one other thing: there had never been a complaint made against me in my twenty-eight years of teaching this course. I offered to drop the skit, but they said it was out of their hands.

Next, another colleague and I met with the dean and associate dean. They made the following points. First, I was in violation of the university's institutional review board (IRB) policy, because I had used students in a skit without institutional approval. Really, we thought? Using the IRB for a classroom exercise? My colleague, who served on the IRB, pointed out that IRB approval is only required for research, which this classroom role play wasn't. My dean, an anthropologist by training, assured us three times that he knew better and that we were wrong. Second, the dean also said that in this "post–Penn State environment," if he knew about a "problem" and didn't "do anything about it," then the university could be at too much risk. Was I being analogized to Jerry Sandusky, the repeat child molester who had coached at Penn State? I argued that my dean *was* doing something about it: he was talking to me and I agreed to drop the skit. But it didn't matter. It was too late! Third, if I did not sign the early retirement agreement and retire immediately, the dire consequences that the dean and lawyer mentioned would ensue. I asked the dean for a one-year extension, so I didn't feel like I was being ignominiously and unceremoniously kicked out of my job on one week's notice, but he said, "Absolutely not." Moreover, he stated that if I tried to delay my retirement for one year and a retroactive complaint came forth, even after I had signed the document, it would "damage the deal" and I would lose the buyout. The pressure to make a decision was intense. Fourth, if I signed the agreement, I would have to relinquish my tenure, my right to due process, and my right to file a grievance through the Tenure and Privilege Committee of the University of Colorado system. That sounded kind of scary. I didn't think that a full professor could be pressured to leave so quickly without being notified, at some point, that there had been a problem and given the opportunity to fix it. When I asked about where my *due process* had been in this decision so far, the associate dean said, "What do you mean? You're getting it now!"

Shell-shocked, I went back to my department and told my colleagues, who were standing in the hall, what had happened. I said goodbye. I cried. They were stunned. And scared. The situation resonated with them personally and had a chilling effect. Could the ODH walk into any classroom unannounced and uninvited and, in the absence of a complaint, go to the administration and pressure a tenured faculty member to resign? Every single person to whom I spoke brought up some topic they had discussed or lecture they had given that could potentially cause offense: racial privilege, immigration, sexism, theory, environmental politics, inequality, and more.

On the last Thursday of the semester, December 12, I went to class. I said goodbye to my students, tearfully thanked them for being such an amazing group, and told them that this would be the last class I would teach, ever. Most of the 500 people arose three times to give me standing ovations, and then 200 of them came down to the front to hug me, to cry with me, and to tell me how much they had loved the class. By the time I got back to my office, the shit storm had begun. Students were rampaging all over campus and calling their parents.

Then the students went to the media. They began with social media, where they started a Change.Org petition that received over 3,500 signatures and comments, as well as a "Help Save Patti Adler's Job" Facebook page that got over 500 postings and members. Next, the mainstream media joined in. The following day (December 13), the first article came out in the local Boulder newspaper. *Inside Higher Education* published an article three days later (December 16). The *Chronicle of Higher Education* carried the story on December 17. I was deluged with hundreds of emails a day, along with phone calls and media inquiries. The story was carried on CNN, MSNBC, the Associated Press, Reuters, the *Huffington Post*, and others. The University of Colorado (CU) became the butt of a joke on the Jay Leno show.

Back at CU, protests erupted. Even though classes had ended, students held a rally. Faculty members on my campus freaked out. My department held an emergency meeting on December 17. The Boulder Faculty Assembly held an emergency meeting on the 18th.

Support poured in from all over the country and the world. Numerous letters and emails were written to the chair, dean, provost, chancellor, and Board of Regents. Public letters and statements denouncing the university and supporting me were made by the state and national branches of the American Association of University Professors, the American Sociological Association, the Midwest Sociological Society, the Society for the Study of Symbolic Interaction and its European branch (the EU SSSI), the Society for the Study of Social Problems, the Foundation for Individual Rights in Education, the National Coalition Against Censorship, the American Civil Liberties Union, and a lot of other organizations. I was still freaking out, but I was buoyed by this amazing support.

The university then tried to respond to the waves of negative publicity that were released. Each reply seemed more bungled than the last. They first had to address queries about the dean's IRB allegation. Mark Miller, a university spokesman, initially answered inquiries from the press by reiterating Dean Leigh's statement that this classroom exercise violated the university's human subjects policy. But by the next day, they backed off that explanation when members of the institutional review board and others pointed out that IRBs focus on research, not classroom activities. A week later, spokesman Mark Miller, who had recently been hired, "left the job to spend more time with his family."

Next, questions were raised about the post–Penn State allegation. How were volunteer students, acting out roles in a classroom exercise, equivalent to the forcible violation of underage boys in a locker room by a retired coach? The answer, I think, is that what the dean had in mind with regard to the Penn State affair was not the sexual abuse of young boys, but, instead, what happened to the university officials who covered up that abuse. Penn State's ex-athletic director, the former vice president, and the former president all faced very serious criminal charges. So I suggest that what motivated CU's lawyer and the dean was the fear that if they failed to act very quickly and extremely vigorously to deal with any occurrence at the University of Colorado that some (however unreasonably) might think was problematic, they both might very well wind up facing grave charges themselves. This allegation, therefore, was never retracted.

On December 16, Provost Russell Moore sent out an email blast to all University of Colorado faculty, staff, and students. In it, he suggested that I had violated the university's sexual harassment policy and possibly created a "hostile environment." He then added that CU had heard from "a number of concerned students" who said they believed there would be retribution if they did not participate in the skit. He closed by affirming that anyone found in violation of these policies was subject to "discipline up to and including termination." The AAUP demanded that he withdraw these allegations, but he declined.

Then, several days into the controversy and shortly after a closed-door meeting with faculty representatives, the university suddenly raised a new issue, which it now stated was the main concern: the photo-consent allegation, claiming that students were being photographed or filmed without their consent during the skit. "With any course involving something unusual, like photographing students, we ask for consent forms to be signed," Dean Leigh said. By this time, it was clear that they were clutching at straws.

In response to attacks from the AAUP and other organizations about violations of academic freedom, the dean then lied, claiming that there had been ongoing concerns over the "Deviance in US Society" course for years, which had not been dealt with in an effective manner. To save face, given all of the negative publicity, the university had to reverse course about their insistence that I be removed from teaching this course. They deflected the decision by calling for an examination of the course by the sociology faculty. An ad hoc committee of senior full professors was assembled, despite the fact that the university was closed for the holidays, to review the course. The AAUP rejected this suggestion, arguing that this course, taught successfully for over twenty-five years, had no business being subjected to this extraordinary level of scrutiny.

Over winter break, things continued to churn, with accusations and allegations flying and being aired in the media. I had to hire a lawyer (at $400 per hour). The stress my husband and I were under was intense, and high blood pressure and palpitations drew him to the emergency room at one point. The sociology committee approved the course without change, except to suggest that I should consider using consent forms for skit participants. Because of all the support and the public relations debacle, the university had to offer me the one semester transition option I had requested, while still keeping to the buyout. At the same time, they offered to pay me that final spring semester's salary if I didn't return.

Now I had a decision to make. I could just take the buyout and leave, or I could reject the buyout and stay. After all, I was still a tenured faculty member. And since I could continue to teach my class, that made it a lot more attractive. If I were forty-five years old, I'd definitely have done that. But I wasn't forty-five, and I had been starting to think about retiring. Remaining at CU for the long term might not be good. Maybe I should take the modified buyout. My husband and I tossed and turned over the decision. Should I just accept the retirement agreement and leave, or should I shoulder the risk and come back? How would these decisions affect others? Would I make the university look good by returning, letting them say that they had given me academic freedom? Or would I make them look bad by doing so, forcing them to retract their decision? There seemed to be good arguments on both sides.

On the one hand, there were several reasons why I was afraid to return. First, the threats against me still stood. If anyone came forward to complain, I could be fired for cause and lose both the retirement deal and my future health insurance. Since the situation had gone viral and those involved in the decision had made fools of themselves, I thought CU would be motivated to pull people out of the woodwork to support their claims, even though they still hadn't found any actual complainant. Second, my department was roiling, torn apart between the chair, who had pushed me out; the people who had stood behind me; and the junior faculty, who were too scared to take a stand. Threats, intimidation, yells, and curses were being thrown around through the faculty email list and in person. I would definitely be going back to a hostile working environment. Would doing so be even more stressful?

Despite this, I wanted to return. First, I didn't want to feel like I was being pushed out on a moment's notice. I thought that one more semester at CU would help me adjust my life and my identity. Second, I was devastated by the sadness I would feel from losing my classroom and my students. I wanted to experience the joy and passion I felt for teaching one more time. Third, many people and organizations had supported my rights of academic freedom and due process, and I felt that if I was given the chance to return, I ought to take it for them. Finally, I was motivated to stand up for principles. I didn't want the university to be able to just push me out, or to set this as a precedent for what they could do to other people. And the Boulder Faculty Assembly was forming a Patti Adler Committee to look into how my case was handled by the university.

In the end, I decided to come back, even though I knew it would be more stressful. I felt that whatever anxiety I had to undergo, it was important for me to fight. I ended up taking the early retirement deal, but on my own terms and in my own time. I retired at the end of the next semester, and my husband, also shaken to the core by this stress, did the same.

The last semester was as awful as I had imagined. I had to pass people in the hall who averted their eyes. The university's legal counsel told my colleagues not to talk to me, for fear of a lawsuit; thus many of them were scared to interact with me. I was stalked and got scary emails from creepy people who were religious fanatics, birthers, and right-wingers. I also received anonymous notes of support slipped under my office door from colleagues within and outside my department, saying how scared they were. Legions of sex worker activists crawled out of the woodwork to tell me how I should teach the course, which now felt like a powder keg. Naturally, they did not agree with each other. I felt afraid to make a joke in my classroom, which I think is a byproduct of the contretemps that continues to this day. Even though I tried as hard as I could to keep the skit, the chilling effects on its participants and me made that impossible, and I ended up dropping it at the last minute. So the victory was small and ultimately Pyrrhic.

Observations

What are some of the take-aways from all of this, in terms of developments in the academy for the twenty-first century?

The Culture of Fear

There was a time when universities, in a free society, ideally were centers of learning, places to experiment with new ideas, and sites of exploration and growth. They existed to challenge people's beliefs and assumptions, including on controversial subjects, such as sexuality. We have not always achieved that ideal, but threats to it are currently on the rise. That has been a change. The *corporatization of the academy* is now well known. Email missives hail the business model under which universities now operate and unabashedly refer to students as "customers." Since the economic downturn in 2008, liberal arts colleges and universities across the country have reshaped their curricula. They have narrowed their fields of study, preparing students for vocational work geared toward quantification and statistical analysis, and sheared away the arts and humanities from the intellectual model that has underpinned students' critical thinking in the United States over the past century. As many as 50 percent of private universities may be out of existence in the next fifteen years, and these institutions have turned to anything they can do to stay alive, including dropping departments or colleges and pampering to whining students and overinvolved parents. *Risk aversion* and *fear of lawsuits* now dominate decision making, and the role of the university's counsel has grown. Administrative decisions are commonly made that violate core principles of academic freedom, autonomy, and policy in naked attempts to placate irate students and their tuition-paying, helicopter parents. We have come to an age when campus administrators view unhappy students as consumers who are always right, and faculty are seen as potential lawsuit risks whose careers can be threatened without due process.

Learning and Comfort

Does a discussion of uncomfortable topics constitute harassment? Many students come to colleges and universities, especially large state institutions, from sheltered home environments, where few challenges to existing norms and values are present. Many disciplines, but especially sociology, have the potential to offer new and possibly disturbing perspectives. Sociology was, is, and always should be an unsettling field of research. My friends and colleagues, and perhaps people reading this book, examine some very discomforting topics, and many work to humanize the dehumanized, normalize deviance, question the powerful, give voice to those without a platform, and challenge the everyday assumptions that we all have held at one time or another. Sharing research such as this is often difficult, but education about uncomfortable issues is not "harassment." Courses with content about white privilege, racism, and deviance present a pedagogical challenge to everyone who teaches these topics. Yet the issues should not be avoided because they are unsettling; they should be tackled precisely *because* they are.

The trend among college campuses across the country—coming from the Left, especially from students—is pressure on faculty to give trigger warnings if they will be discussing sensitive topics in their classes. A trigger warning signals not only the growing precautionary approach to words and ideas within a university, but also a wider cultural hypersensitivity to harm and paranoia about giving offense. Issuing cautions on the basis of potential harm or insult doesn't help us negotiate our reactions. Instead, it makes our dealings with others more fraught. Trigger warnings reinforce a fear of words by depicting an ever-expanding number of articles and books as dangerous and in need of regulation. The question then for us is, Do we dare to be uncomfortable?

Administrative Bloat and Overreach

We have recently been witnesses to the greatest increase in administrative hiring in academia. This is well documented in the report by the

Delta Cost Project (Desrochers and Kirshstein 2014) on labor trends in higher education. Drawing on data collected between 2002 and 2010, the authors found that the growth in administrative jobs has been widespread across higher education, and that most of these jobs have gone to midlevel administrative management positions (business analysts, human resources staff, counselors, and admissions staff), rather than professional executive and managerial positions. The percentage of new faculty hires that went to full-time, tenure-track positions declined, while part-time, adjunct, and instructor jobs increased. The ratio of faculty and staff to administrators decreased by over 40 percent as more administrative units were created, while departments and programs were curtailed and merged. Across all educational sectors, wage and salary expenditures for student services were the fastest growing remunerative expense. While faculty salaries remained relatively flat, increasing portions of university and college budgets have been allocated to student services and dramatically rising administrative salaries. Although college tuition has skyrocketed, this has not been due to the cost of an actual education, but rather to administration. This administrative takeover of academia has gone hand-in-hand with several related trends.

Mission creep has become commonplace, as a number of entities within universities today can now be recognized as having expanded their domain beyond what was originally intended, including institutional review boards, offices of discrimination and harassment, learning disabilities centers, athletic departments, and legal departments.

IRBs

Peter and I (Adler and Adler 2003) wrote an article about IRBs in which we asked if university lawyers defined our research value system. This question is even more apt now. The reach of IRBs has grown every year since their inception. While they were once tasked with monitoring the exploitation of human subjects in medical research and protecting people from being the unknowing subjects of experimental research, they have extended their tentacles into the social sciences and humanities, applying an experimental/medical model of research that is not an appropriate fit for these fields. Rules and policies change regularly, expanding the purview and demands of IRBs. Enormous variability exists horizontally, as the rules and policies are unclear and differ widely between institutions. Members of IRBs mainly serve for three-year periods, and there tends to be little institutional memory over time. To members of the social sciences especially, the demands of these boards often appear capricious and ignorant (see Van den Hoonaard and Hamilton 2016).

Offices of Discrimination and Harassment

Though founded with the ideal of protecting women and students from exploitation due to male privilege and power, these administrative units have continuously redefined their purpose, increasing their jurisdiction and power. They strike fear into the hearts of faculty and administrators alike. To be accused has come to mean "assumed to be guilty." Investigations have taken on a witch-hunt quality, with leading questions asked of respondents, unproven accusations presumed to be true, and stigmatizing judgments rendered. These bodies claim a disproportionate amount of power and have no corresponding checks and balances, answering to no higher body. Academic principles get trampled. This situation has veered so badly away from a neutral presumption of innocence that male graduate and undergraduate students have been getting railroaded. Not surprisingly, this has provoked a backlash from the Right, and it was one of the many factors propelling Donald Trump into office. Once there, his Secretary of Education, Betsy DeVos, set about unwinding the avenues of redress available to women on college campuses. In 2017, the Department of Education (DOE) formally rescinded Obama-era guidelines on how schools should handle sexual assault reporting and investigations under Title IX federal law. Criticizing these ground rules as having gone too far, the DOE raised the standard of proof for school disciplinary proceedings, undermining protections for victims of sexual harassment and assault. Many view this as the beginning of a larger onslaught on Title IX.

Offices of Disability Services

Although established to level the learning environment for students with differential learning abilities, these entities have come to offer enhanced privileges for those whose parents can afford to acquire the expensive documentation required to support diagnoses of learning disabilities. Once students are accepted as clients of disability services units, they are often offered a laundry list of benefits they can ask for, a menu that continues to grow each year. Initially, the required accommodation was for faculty to provide such documented students with extended time when taking exams. Added to this have been mandates that teachers provide "distraction-reduced environments" (no more than three students in any exam room), note takers, tutors, and laptop computers for test taking, as well as turning over their own notes and PowerPoint slides and not enforcing class attendance, among many other stipulations. All of this is demanded of faculty without providing *them* with the necessary support resources. A backlash has begun from non-disability students, who complain about the greatly enhanced privileges of their classmates, which they view as exceeding reasonable benefits. This puts professors in a bind and, once again, impinges on their ability to teach what and how they want.

Athletic Departments

Although athletic programs once struggled to gain the academic help necessary to aid their struggling student athletes, the educational services provided to athletes have similarly expanded. The academic support divisions within athletic departments are enormous domains, employing several full-time coordinators and administrators. They hire undergraduate and graduate students to assist athletes with course preparation, exam preparation, and help in writing papers. They come to professors and ask for differential accommodations for athletes, such as oral exams, take-home exams, and amnesty from exams. Some schools place athletes in different sections of required classes, where faculty (and especially graduate student teaching assistants) are pressured to "dumb down" the curriculum and standards. Sadly, it has become commonplace for scandals to emerge, documenting the extent to which such programs bribe, coerce, and sidestep the *educational* principles and academic freedom of the scholastic side of institutions.

Legal Departments

Finally, the offices of university counsel extend their tentacles into every corner of the institution. They guide decision making. They encourage administrators to cut more and more secret deals. They get rid of individuals through threats and intimidation. They silence people with gag orders and non-disclosure agreements. They represent an intractable force of bureaucracy.

What's Next?

Ultimately, there is a much bigger story to be told here. My case was not isolated. It just received more publicity because of how ludicrous the decisions were; because I was a respected, internationally recognized senior scholar with strong professional support; because I was a popular teacher on campus with enormous student support; and because I didn't shut up. Since my time, the media has reported on many people whose stories are scarily similar, and the number of instances that go unreported are significantly greater. While I was able to fight, although only to win back one semester, I know that those with less experience, especially junior faculty, do not get even that. Most cases get swept under the rug, as faculty are intimidated and disempowered.

This, sadly, has been the harbinger of things that continue to deteriorate. The academy in which many of us have fruitfully spent our careers is changing dramatically and rapidly all around us, in frightening ways. Threats to academic freedom come not only from the Left and the Right, but also also from institutional authority, as university counsel is neither leftist nor rightist per se, but *institutionalist*, in a very limiting, reactive sense. Some, but not all, of the greatest dangers come from "establishments" that are motivated not by ideology, but by more mundane concerns with risk and brand. These trends will have ripples globally, as some of our worst trends have a domino effect overseas and can become exacerbated in the post-COVID era in which institutions increasingly turn toward online and computer-mediated teaching as they fight for their very existence.

We have argued that initially well-intended issues, such as sensitivity to language, in addition to students' abilities, roles, and identities, have a tendency to propel themselves to extremes, where they become destructive and threaten both the integrity of education and academic freedom. It is dangerous to be lulled into complacency because something's original purpose appeared to be beneficial. If one little skit on one day of a class is going to get a full professor fired, in effect, with no due process, something more seriously problematic will receive worse treatment.

The role of classrooms as centers of exploration has ebbed, and faculty find themselves increasingly fearful of being victims of student challenges, complaints, and lawsuits. Potentially sensitive topics are being eliminated from the curriculum, humor as a didactic device is under seige, and professors find themselves much more guarded in their self-expression. Faculty have become disposable as administrators, guided by lawyers, do their cost-benefit analyses and realize that their institution's financial interests do not lie with its teachers. This represents a power shift from once-autonomous faculty to administrators, students, and their parents.

Increasingly, conservative state legislatures are stepping in, implementing loyalty oaths and disciplinary committees, as well as subjecting to scrutiny faculty behavior and social media postings in these individuals' private lives. Firings have occurred that are based on tweets, Facebook postings, civil disobedience, and political activism. The Wisconsin legislature (under Republican governor Scott Walker) instituted policies that weakened tenure protections and gave administrators greater flexibility in closing programs and eliminating faculty jobs. Left-leaning faculty and programs have become threatened, as well as those that show a less direct tie to financial benefits for both students and university budgets.

It is important to be sensitive to students, of course, but it is also imperative to be able to address significant and diverse topics, and to have freedom of expression. At stake are fundamental issues in a war against academic freedom. This freedom is the purpose of tenure, and that is what is being ultimately threatened.

These trends are tied to the increasing *loss of power and autonomy for faculty* in universities. We see this in the institutionalization of the "lumpenprofessoriat," what Alan Greenspan lauded as the class of "insecure laborers" who would inject health into society by not asking for wage benefits or increases. We see this in the rise of internet courses, which have been characterized by some as a means of replacing faculty with cheap online education. This is evident in the plethora of new rules about absences from campus, conflicts of interest, post-tenure reviews, and accountability.

Faculty senates have become reticent about representing the voices of their members; the role of department chairs as advocates for their units has declined. They become lackeys—marionettes of the administration, not defenders of their colleagues. It is surprising how quickly many of them move over to the other side and leave their professorial perspective behind. They become the "office" and protect their institutions. They listen to lawyers whispering in their ears, sidestep political controversy, and have learned that it is easier to dispose of faculty, rather than stand up and advocate for us and what is right.

While we were dozing, no one was paying attention. If we allow these trends to continue unchallenged, the power and position of faculty erode, and due process and academic freedom die.

References

AAUP (American Association of University Professors). 2016. "The History, Uses, and Abuses of Title IX." *Bulletin of the American Association of University Professors* 102(July–August):69–99.

Adler, Patricia A. and Peter Adler. 2003. "Do University Lawyers and the Police Define Our Research Value System?" In Will C. Van den Hoonaard (ed.), *Walking the Tightrope: Ethical Issues for Qualitative Researchers*, 34–42. Toronto: University of Toronto Press.

Carroll, Lewis. 2000. *Alice's Adventures in Wonderland*. Peterborough, ON: Broadview Press.

Desrochers, Donna M. and Rita Kirshstein. 2014. *Labor Intensive or Labor Expensive? Changing Staffing and Compensation Patterns in Higher Education*. Washington, DC: Delta Cost Project.

Ferner, Matt. January 24, 2014. "Patricia Adler, CU-Boulder Professor, Allegedly Forced Out Over Prostitution Lecture [UPDATE]." *Huffington Post*, https://www.huffpost.com.

Lubin, Joann S. January 10, 2005. "Travel Expenses Prompt Yale to Force Out Institute Chief." *Wall Street Journal*, https://www.wsj.com.

Schmidt, Peter. December 17, 2013. "U. of Colorado's Response to a Gritty Lecture Worries Sociologists." *Chronicle of Higher Education*, https://www.chronicle.com.

Van den Hoonaard, Will C. and Ann Hamilton (eds.). 2016. *The Ethics Rupture: Exploring Alternatives to Formal Research-Ethics Review*. Toronto: University of Toronto Press.

PART II

THE UNIVERSITY AND THE EXTERNAL WORLD

CHAPTER 2

The End of Clear Lines

Academic Freedom and Administrative Law

Stephen Turner

In this chapter I will be concerned with the legal structures and quasi-legal regulatory structures that relate to academic freedom, in addition to the basic theory that applies to them. My aim is to explain (1) how changes in them affect academic freedom, (2) the legal properties of the new constraints under which those in the academy operate, and (3) the differences between this current situation and academic freedom as it has traditionally been understood. The primary issues I will be concerned with are discretionary legal and administrative power and the way that regulations, as implemented by universities, have expanded this power, as well as the enlarged role of contract law and employment contracts as protections of academic freedom.

Academic freedom is undergoing a redefinition in the face of new legal circumstances. Its two traditional dimensions are the higher education institutions' autonomy from the state and the individual freedom of scholars. It was traditionally thought that independence from the state and the existence of strong faculty governance were the best guarantors of academic freedom (Tiede 2015). The American

Association of University Professors (AAUP) fought for both. Academic freedom, however, is increasingly restricted by regulations implemented by universities, which can take the form of institutional review boards, research misconduct tribunals, and Title IX enforcement. Because many federal regulations governing institutions of higher education are themselves vague and broad, the specific rules created by these institutions are a result of discretionary power over academics that is inimical to the traditional notion of academic freedom as a well-defined right. The idea of university autonomy, similarly, has undergone important changes. It has been significantly compromised as a result of federal regulation of a kind that did not exist in the first half of the twentieth century. One effect of intensified federal regulation is self-monitoring within higher education institutions (often with the assistance of an internal bureaucratic office) that not only seeks to conform to these externally imposed rules, but also to invent local variations that expand on them.

The Basic Legal Situation

There are several kinds of law that interact in cases of academic freedom: (1) statutory law, or law created by legislation; (2) constitutional law, which authorizes or limits the power of legislatures; (3) case law, which is created by judges through decisions that become precedents for other judicial decisions and follow legal or constitutional principles; (4) contract law, which bears on academic freedom, because the relation between professors and their university is defined by an employment contract; and (5) administrative law, which is the "law" created by bureaucrats that specifies and interprets legislation, as well as regulates the actions of the government itself and (indirectly) the actions of bodies, such as universities, that are expected to conform to administrative regulations. Many federal regulations compel institutions of higher education to produce their own internal regulations and leave them open to sanctions if they do not.[1] Theoretically, these directives are grounded in actual statutory law. But interpretation of the law by the agencies, and by the organizations implementing their own regulations, often strays far from the text and the original intent of the law.

The procedures that directly govern faculty members are those of the university itself. The ones to be discussed here, involving equal opportunity, research misconduct, and a review of research to conform to ethical standards, are responses to federal administrative law—that is, to the law contained in directives, definitions, and "letters of guidance" provided by federal agencies—and are motivated in part by the threat of litigation or a withholding of funds. The procedures for implementing the directives in different academic institutions typically meet neither ordinary legal standards of predictability, transparency, or the equitable treatment of persons, nor are they required to do so. In law, they are viewed as an extension of the rights of employers to govern their employees as they see fit. But the contractual relation between universities and their employees itself has limits, and one of the features of the present situation is that these boundaries are being reached, making employment law the new arena for academic freedom issues.

The historical legal strategy of the AAUP, in its attempts to define academic freedom, was to delineate it as a contractual relation between higher education institutions and individual faculty members, in order to offer protections beyond those of ordinary employment law. The goal was to provide a definition of academic freedom that mimicked the form of law itself, rather than merely specifying an ideal. This meant establishing clear distinctions that could be appealed to by the AAUP to condemn and sanction universities and colleges for administrative actions inconsistent with academic freedom. Clarity in these distinctions served various purposes: it assured the credibility of the actions; provided guidelines for university administrators; protected the AAUP from charges of partisanship and inconsistency; and, perhaps most importantly, linked the notion of academic freedom to the legal idea of due process and the value of legal certainty. Thus this framework also aligned with one way in which courts decide cases—by striking down laws that are "unconstitutionally vague."

But the AAUP does not enact law, and its definitions are not law. The strategy was to assert certain rights for faculty, yet these were rights that went beyond anything codified in law. By describing correct standards, the AAUP could establish what Continental legal theory calls "customary law." Actual courts could defer to these standards in the name of normal and accepted practice when the term "academic freedom" appeared in employment contracts or handbooks. The AAUP standards thus served to provide a definition of the concept and of standard practice with a quasi-legal meaning (i.e., a bright-line rule) and the marks of legality in its own processes (a quasi-judicial process of inquiry). In addition, they carried the mark of law: a regime of sanctions applied by the AAUP itself, in the form of notifications to the scholarly community that a university was not in compliance.

The basic idea of the AAUP statements on the academic freedom of *individuals* (as distinct from the academic freedom of institutions from state interference), which have undergone only minor revision, is that:

> Teachers are entitled to full freedom in research and in the publication of the results, subject to the adequate performance of their other academic duties . . .
>
> Teachers are entitled to freedom in the classroom in discussing their subject, but they should be careful not to introduce into their teaching controversial matter that has no relation to their subject . . .
>
> College and university teachers are citizens, members of a learned profession, and officers of an educational institution. When they speak or write as citizens, they should be free from institutional censorship or discipline, but their special position in the community imposes special obligations. As scholars and educational officers, they should remember that the public may judge their profession and their institution by their utterances. (AAUP 1940)

This definition had two elements: (1) professional autonomy, or freedom of teaching and research within the limits of the professional activities of the faculty member, and (2) freedom of speech and action as a citizen outside the classroom. In the past, virtually all academic freedom issues, including those that motivated the original formulations of these principles in 1915 (AAUP [1915] 2015), fell into two categories: governance issues involving the freedom of colleges themselves (e.g., those regarding the interference of governing bodies), and the rights of academics as citizens (particularly issues of freedom of speech).

Citizen speech had a problematic legal status. Standard employment law *does not* protect free speech in the broad sense envisioned by the AAUP standards. Public speech deleterious to the interests of the employer *can* be sanctioned by employers, more or less at their discretion. They are free to protect their interests, as they understand them, by firing employees within some reasonably limited notion of harm. This contractual right overrides the freedom to speak guaranteed by the First Amendment and directly conflicts with the right to be "free from institutional censorship or discipline," as asserted by the AAUP. This special academic right is something the courts have never directly established, though there are no clear cases rejecting it, either. None of the standard First Amendment cases in employment law concerns professors. A few, notably *Pickering* (1968), relate to teachers.[2] In cases involving professors, courts have typically evaded the issue by deciding the cases on other grounds—for example, by pointing to the violation of a different rule to which the professor was bound as part of the employment relationship (Svrluga 2017), or rejecting the action of the university on the grounds that it was in violation of the employment contract.

In one recent case involving extramural speech, a jury trial found for the university against a fired tenured professor who, on a blog, asserted a conspiracy theory about the Sandy Hook shootings. The institution successfully argued that he had lied to them about his "use of university resources" for his blog and "repeatedly and intentionally refused to file mandatory disclosure forms that require all professors to reveal outside work and activities that could affect their work or the university." Though the trial showed that this policy was inconsistently applied, the professor lost the case (Ramadan 2016; McMahon 2017.). The greater bureaucratization of higher education institutions and the vast expansion of rules of this kind pose new risks for faculty. These rules provide multiple occasions for their violation and many issues of interpretation. Under the law, employers have wide discretion in interpreting their own rules. The proliferation of vague language in them creates greater discretionary power for administrators, who can use them against faculty members they choose to punish, while avoiding overt challenges to academic freedom.

The core of academic freedom—freedom within the classroom and in professional writing—has no direct constitutional standing and no basis in federal law. It does, however, have an indirect existence in employment law. The courts acknowledge it as a "good" that is distinctive to the academic setting and indirectly affirm it as the basis of the contractual understandings governing academics—the thought being that the meaning of an employment contract is determined in part by normal practices in the field in question. But there is sometimes a more direct and stronger legal basis. To the extent that professors are protected, this occurs under the heading of employment law: for doing their job according to their employment contract, as other types of employees are. State law and state university charters also sometime guarantee academic freedom, and faculty handbooks asserting academic freedom have intermittently been held to be legally binding.

Employment cases have not, however, produced a body of case law. Case law is limited in this area, for a simple reason. Academic lawsuits that come before courts and juries tend to produce surprising results, because they are handled in terms of non-academic understandings of the same practices. Those in the professoriate avoid court cases, because they are typically advised that juries react to suits where an employee disobeys an employer by affirming that one should do what the boss says. Precedent-establishing legal cases involving academics are thus rare. Ordinarily, out-of-court settlements are negotiated. Partly, this is to avoid litigation expenses. In addition, it is because the courts have not been terribly respectful of standard academic practices and are consequently unpredictable when cases involving them arise, which poses a risk for both sides. For example, in dealing with publishers, one ordinarily signs a document asserting that one holds the rights to the book or paper one is publishing and that the work was not done "for hire," which would mean that the rights would belong to the employer. A decision involving Brown University, however, addressed this question (*Forasté* 2003), and the judge found that academic publication was "for hire"—contrary to the documents academics routinely sign for publishers. The practice did not change, though some problematic legal documents were created by universities to release these rights to the professorial authors—but not without reserving for themselves final authority over the disposition of the work in question.

The California Oath Case

The University of California loyalty oath controversy was the most important academic freedom case of the twentieth century in the United States. It can serve as a baseline for understanding what has changed in the legal atmosphere of the university. The case began with two incidents that fell under the second area of academic freedom defined by the AAUP. Three professors were fired from the University of Washington in January 1949 for having Communist sympathies: Herbert Phillips, Joe Butterworth, and Ralph Gundlach (Lange 1999; Schrecker 1999). The UCLA Graduate Student Assembly received permission to host a debate featuring Phillips ("Prelude to Controversy" 1949). He was invited to speak at the Los Angeles campus of the university, which was not then a separate institution, as the Berkeley and Los Angeles faculty were nominally one unit. When the invitation was made public, members of the institution's Board of Regents moved to stop it.

The California state constitution "required [the University of California] to be free of all sectarian or partisan influences" (Gardner 1967, 15). This is a formulation of a fundamental principle of liberal democracy: the political neutrality of the state. The rules implementing this provision were understood by the provost to mean that controversial views could be presented, but only if both sides were represented. Despite the fact that the event was structured as a debate, the Regents expressed concern that the university was being used for propaganda purposes (Gardner 1967, 24). In response, the administration was led to "strengthen" both the prohibitions against using the university as a platform for propaganda and the existing loyalty oath. Accepting the oath was already a condition of employment for all state employees.

The oath became the issue. Faculty who were opposed rejected the addition to the existing oath, which was an affirmation that the oath-taker did not believe in and was not a member of an organization advocating the overthrow of the US government. The Communist party was the only relevant example of such an organization (Gardner 1967, 26). The initial skirmish over the oath involved a graduate student instructor. In response, the body representing these non-faculty employees called for the elimination of political tests for appointments. The objections of the faculty, however, hinged on tenure and focused on the slogan "academic freedom does not exist where the right of tenure is not inviolate" (Gardner 1967, 121). There was also a due process objection, because refusals to sign the new oath could lead to firings "without the Regents ever bothering to investigate whether these men are in fact communists or otherwise disloyal" (Gardner 1967, 122).

The controversy ended with a long-delayed censure of the administration by the AAUP (Gardner 1967, 208–10), and a court case in which the California Supreme Court ruled that the Regents had invaded the authority of the legislature by its actions. The court ordered the Regents to appoint the non-signers of the new oath who had already signed the oath required of all state employees (Gardner 1967, 242–44). The principles at stake in this case were eventually affirmed in a decisive federal court case (*Keyishian* 1967), in which the court ruled that requiring faculty to sign a document asserting that they were not and had not been Communists was a violation of First Amendment rights and was also "vague and overbroad." This case produced the standard text on which legal appeals of academic freedom have since relied:

> Our nation is deeply committed to safeguarding academic freedom, which is of transcendent value to all of us and not merely to the teachers concerned. That freedom is therefore a special concern of the First Amendment, which does not tolerate laws that cast a pall of orthodoxy over the classroom . . . The classroom is peculiarly the "marketplace of

ideas." The nation's future depends upon leaders trained through wide exposure to that robust exchange of ideas which discovers truth "out of a multitude of tongues," [rather] than through any kind of authoritative selection. (*Keyishian* 1967)

This is a succinct formulation of what we might dub the "liberal theory of academic freedom,"[3] and the participants in the oath controversy also adhered to it—namely, scholars were independent and beholden only to truth and their conscience in the pursuit of truth. As autonomous scholars, they were protected by the inviolability of tenure and free to make their own choices in the face of actual diversity of thought in a competitive marketplace of ideas (at a time when research was not yet grant dependent). The customs of the university, such as tenure and non-sectarianism, were to serve to protect this freedom. Although the issues in this controversy were complex, they involved statutes and bright lines, such as the inviolability of tenure and due process. The acts of the administrators were simple and objective: the Regents threatened dismissal for failure to sign a piece of paper.

The First Amendment and Employment Law

The liberal theory of academic freedom was thus endorsed by the courts in the *Keyishian* case cited above. The courts, however, did not create a novel right to academic freedom, but instead appealed to the First Amendment as the source of the right to reject the loyalty oath. The First Amendment has also played a role in many subsequent cases, but it is not as helpful as might be expected, because, in general, one gives up many of one's rights in an employment relationship, including much of one's free-speech rights. There is case law in the instance of state institutions, and it is clear: "Statements public employees make as part of their official duties are not protected under the First Amendment; thus, it does not protect employees who make them from disciplinary actions" (Norman-Eady 2006). The concern motivating this ruling comes from the consideration that "without some control over employees' words and actions, a government entity could not provide services efficiently or effectively." Nonetheless, there is an important exception to this general rule. Speech that does not impair services is protected, if it *is* in fact speech as a citizen "about matters of public concern" (Norman-Eady 2006). The difficulty with this rule comes in drawing a line between citizen speech and speech related to duties.

The controlling case law is itself surprisingly narrow in its view of citizen speech. The *Garcetti* case involved a deputy prosecutor who was fired for concluding, as part of his duties, that an affidavit was flawed and testifying for the defense after the district attorney decided to prosecute the case anyway. The employee claimed that his speech was protected citizen speech because it met the test of public concern. The court ruled against this claim. Truth was not a defense. Justice Stevens, in a dissent, commented that this meant there was no protection for speech that "is just unwelcome speech because it reveals facts that the supervisor would rather not have anyone else discover" (*Garcetti* 2006; Kaplin and Lee 2013, 384–85).

Would *Garcetti* apply to professors who are state employees? There is no definitive case involving professors that would protect those who made public statements against the positions taken by a university. Moreover, there is little ground for thinking that an exception would be made. Employment law would protect professors from arbitrary actions by their university in violation of the contract with them as employees, but not from punishment for opposing the will of, or doctrines endorsed by, that institution. We will see an example of the use of this power in a later section (on Title IX). Although such power is not extensively invoked, there are few limitations on its use, and that, in itself, has a potentially chilling effect on speech. There is no clear line between "public" speech critical of a university's policies and speech that is disruptive of that institution's mission and, thus, punishable.

Administrative Law and Academic Freedom

Administrative law is law made in the form of rules and other authoritative pronouncements by bodies that are part of the executive branch and by judicial interpretations that modify these rules. It is not law in the sense of incurring judicial penalties. The penalties are administrative, based on the idea that an agency can regulate bodies with whom they have a contractual relationship. For example, universities enter into this type of relationship by accepting federal funds, directly or indirectly, such as through governmental loans to their students for tuition. The rules implement and specify the legislation on which they are based. The core laws relating to higher education institutions include Title IX (the federal law against sex discrimination, which is implemented through regulations that universities are required to create); federal law relating to the responsible conduct of research (which is governed within the academy by institutional review boards); and laws against research misconduct (which are further specified by university regulations and dealt with by procedures the institutions create). Each will be discussed below.

Federal agencies implement these laws by developing rules that are more specific than the initiating legislation. There is a legislative basis for this practice in the 1945 Administrative Procedure Act, which specifies formal procedures for rule making and public input and requires a degree of transparency. Agencies may have their own courtlike, quasi-judicial structures to try cases involving these rules. The legal basis for this activity is the judicial finding that agencies have "the power to construe" legislation. There is, however, no direct constitutional basis for this kind of law or power, and, indeed, subdelegation of legislative powers is forbidden by the constitution. The courts have evaded this restriction by claiming that the agencies, in their rule making, are merely defining terms in the law. The grounds for permitting agencies to construe the law are that the legislature, by failing to be specific, grants discretion to the agencies to do so (Strauss 1989, 22–23). This is itself an oddity—traditional legal thinking is that ambiguity in the law grants discretion to the *courts*. Thus, in the US context, the doctrine of deference amounts to a grant by the judiciary of *their* authority to agencies. We can leave aside the vexing question of whether this judicial recognition and deference to these agencies is constitutionally justified (Hamburger 2014; 2017), or whether the administrative law "courts" are genuine courts, but it is important to note that there is a fundamental issue here over the nature and legitimacy of authority. Judicial deference to the agencies, except in cases of clear failures of due process or other egregious errors, is a revocable judicial choice, not a constitutionally specified feature of the power of agencies or the executive branch.

The body of rules in administrative law today exceeds the body of federal legislation by a factor of ten. Yet the published rules are only part of the story. There is much more law making by agencies in the forms of "guidance," definitions, and authoritative interpretation of the statutes themselves. These activities are not subject to the restrictions on rule making, and the mere fact of selective enforcement of the rules requires the bodies subject to them to infer "the law" from the practices of the agency. Statute law is subject to legal construction, based on the explicit language of the statute, and, if this fails, on legislative intent. The courts, however, have treated administrative law differently, by introducing the element of "purpose." The discretionary power of agencies to issue rules in accordance with the supposed purpose of the legislation was affirmed in an opinion stating that "Title IX must [be] accord[ed] . . . a sweep as broad as its language" to realize its goals of eliminating discrimination and promoting equal opportunity (*North Haven* 1982; see also *Dickerson* 1983). In the case of Title IX, which merely forbids discrimination, the effect of agency and court decisions is to warrant precisely the opposite of the law. "Affirmative action" (the result of an additional executive order), which evolved, after litigation, into discrimination in the name of "diversity"—a doctrine unmentioned in the law—can be used to justify favorable treatment of historically disadvantaged groups.

Universities are obligated to regulate themselves by issuing rules implementing those devised by the agencies. They are granted discretion, however, in constructing their own regulations to enforce the rules, in accordance with the purpose of the law. A higher education institution is not limited by the law—it can introduce its own, more restrictive rules as part of its rights as an employer. The attitude of universities, to quote one official at my own institution, is that federal regulations are "the floor," or the minimum, and there may be compelling interests in going beyond the minimum in constructing the regulations within a university that academics must follow. This means that university policies implementing the law and the administrative extensions of the law may vary substantially from one university to another and, like administrative law itself, create their own quasi-legal procedures for appeal, sanction, and the like. The role of a federal agency in relation to these internal university regulations becomes one of reviewing policies for conformity to the agency's construal of the law.

Courts may play a role if the approved policy conflicts with other explicit rights, including contractual rights that are part of the employment relationship. One place in which policies based on Title IX have come into conflict with academic freedom concerns anti-harassment policies. In the 1980s and 1990s, courts invoked the principles of free speech and academic freedom to protect the constitutional free speech rights of public university professors and students against encroachments by overly broad anti-harassment policies. For example, in a case brought by a biopsychology graduate student who was concerned that theories he wished to explore could be labeled as "racist" or "sexist" under the policy, a federal court found the University of Michigan's sexual harassment policy to be unconstitutionally vague and overly broad (AAUP 2016). A federal court also found the University of Wisconsin's harassment code to be unconstitutionally broad, notably in its prohibitions against "discriminatory comments, epithets or other expressive behavior directed at an individual . . . [that] intentionally . . . demean the race, sex, religion, color, creed, disability, sexual orientation, national origin, ancestry or age of the individual . . . and . . . create an intimidating, hostile or demeaning environment for education, university-related work, or other university-authorized activity" (AAUP 2016). These cases have turned on the problem of vagueness and illustrate the difficulty of distinguishing discriminatory speech from legitimate academic speech. They also, however, involve a novel assertion of administrators' power over speech.

The rules and procedures of universities in carrying out these laws do not have the usual features of actual law. They do not create visible precedent (as secrecy is the norm for many of these procedures, and no public record is created), nor do they provide guarantees of due process similar to those in courts. Moreover, the responsible officials and committees carrying out these quasi-judicial functions are typically creatures of the administration, serving at its pleasure. Their findings are normally advisory and can be overruled by higher-level administrators. In this respect, they resemble administrative law generally, rather than proceedings in actual courts. Nevertheless, there are some constraints on administrative actions, and it is no coincidence that the issue of vagueness in policy statements plays a role in the relatively rare instances where courts intervene to protect academics from administrators. The policies are intentionally vague: this is what gives administrators discretionary power. These policies create or help define the contractual relation between an institution and its employee under employment law. Even the courts, which normally defer to a policy created to fulfill an administrative rule of the federal government and are reluctant to invoke constitutional considerations, recognize that the policies in question are too vague to support sanctions under employment law. The requirement that the regulations must meet some minimal standard of clarity does impose an important burden on administrators who act to sanction a faculty member in ways that curtail academic freedom.

Three Problem Areas

Title IX

According to the the text of Title IX, "No person in the United States shall, on the basis of sex, be excluded from participation in, be denied the benefits of, or be subjected to discrimination under any education program or activity receiving Federal financial assistance" (US Department of Labor 1972, Section 1681, Sex, (a)). This law has been quite radically extended, both by the relevant agencies, notably the Office of Civil Rights (OCR) of the Department of Education through letters of guidance, and by its implementation in university regulations, particularly in relation to ones involving the concept of "hostile environment," such as those that are understood as warranting restrictions on speech. Although some of the guidance relating to procedures governing student misconduct has recently been rescinded, the university regulations created in compliance with them have not, so this continues to be an important issue. According to the original guidance provided during the Obama administration, which did not go through the procedures necessary to make it an official regulation, there is a specific requirement for universities to educate students about what constitutes sex discrimination.

Title IX does not require a recipient of federal funds to adopt a policy specifically prohibiting sexual harassment or sexual violence. As noted in the "Revised Sexual Harassment Guidance" (2001), however, a recipient's general policy prohibiting sex discrimination will not be considered effective and would violate Title IX if, because of the lack of a specific policy, students are unaware of what kind of conduct constitutes sexual harassment, including sexual violence, or that such conduct is prohibited sex discrimination. The OCR therefore recommends that a recipient's nondiscrimination policy state that prohibited sex discrimination covers sexual harassment, including sexual violence, and that the policy include examples of the types of conduct that it covers (Ali 2011, 7).

This is an intrusion into academic freedom in one of the two meanings of this term: a university's autonomy from the state. It dictates what the students must be taught, even though the teaching, in this case, may not be in the classroom. Moreover, it is compelled speech, because it requires the university to say something. Yet it trades on an ambiguity between the task of informing students about the law and university regulations, and political indoctrination with respect to particular notions of proper gender relations.[4] The latter would be an intrusion on academic freedom; the former would not.

This issue takes a more extreme form when applied to faculty members. Because the use of anti-discrimination laws to justify various forms of preferential treatment in admissions have repeatedly been curtailed by the courts, universities have asserted an alternative argument: there is an educational value in "diversity" that warrants certain forms of discrimination in favor of particular underrepresented groups. The courts have partially accepted this argument in the case of university admissions, subject to some limitations. In addition to these measures, universities have sought to assure the commitment of its faculty members to the concept of diversity. The need to generate such commitment has taken both positive and punitive forms. In a widely publicized case, a Duke theology professor was disciplined for sending an internal email critical of a "racial equity" training program that the dean was promoting. In an email to the faculty, the dean stated: "It is inappropriate and unprofessional to use mass emails to make disparaging statements—including arguments ad hominem—in order to humiliate or undermine individual colleagues or groups of colleagues with whom we disagree. The use of mass emails to express racism, sexism, and other forms of bigotry is offensive and unacceptable, especially in a Christian institution" (Stancill 2017). The dean and a professor sponsoring the training filed a complaint, which included a charge of sexual harassment on the basis of the theology professor's internal email. In response, the faculty member noted that there was nothing bigoted about his posts and objected that his intellectual freedom had been infringed. Nonetheless, he was disciplined. The sanctions included a ban from faculty meetings and a promise "that he would not receive future funds for research and travel" (Stancill 2017). He subsequently resigned.

This case illustrates some of the problems of the interaction of employment law, contractual assertions of academic freedom, Title IX, and other anti-discrimination policies. The oddity of Title IX–based policies is that they are directed against such things as "racism, sexism, and other forms of bigotry," none of which is mentioned in Title IX or any other anti-discrimination law. Categories like racism and sexism are doctrinal and rooted in controversial theories rather than neutral rules, such as the one against discrimination in the actual statute. If we incorporate doctrinal statements into a policy, however, they are no longer merely doctrines, but instead are the official policies of the employer. In the Duke case, objecting to these policies, or even to the means of promoting them, was construed as a form of sexual harassment, or the creation of a hostile environment. The law offers no protection here: the employer has a right to demand agreement with the policy. If the faculty member's statement had been public (e.g., to a newspaper), this would have been grounds for discipline, and even for the firing of a tenured professor. Moreover, simply as an internal discussion, it would also be grounds for dismissal under normal employment law, because, as we have seen, there is no employment law provision for free speech within the normal activities of employment. A private university, such as Duke, is free, in principle, to demand doctrinal conformity.

The problem of doctrinal conformity in *public* institutions that also cannot, in principle, demand doctrinal conformity, arises in other ways, but it involves the same ambiguity between intellectual doctrines and policies. Ironically, given the long history of issues over oaths, Title IX and anti-discrimination law have generated oaths of their own. These take the form of "diversity statements," which faculty are required either to sign or to submit as part of the job application process (Oregon Association of Scholars 2017; for guidelines, see UC 2015). The statements are designed to compel the applicant to both affirm and prove their commitment to diversity. This form of oath taking has yet to be tested in court, although the requirement of oath taking to demonstrate commitment to diversity is widespread, and the statements are taken seriously. As sociologist Tanya Golash-Boza (2016), in an *Inside Higher Ed* article, advises job applicants:

> Many faculty members truly care about diversity and equity and will read your statement closely. I have been in the room when the diversity statement of every single finalist for a job search was scrutinized. The candidates who submitted strong statements wrote about their experiences teaching first-generation college students, their involvement with LGBTQ student groups, their experiences teaching in inner-city high schools and their awareness of how systemic inequalities affect students' ability to excel. Applicants mentioned their teaching and activism and highlighted their commitment to diversity and equity in higher education.

A typical statement (from a sociologist), which was recommended as a model on the official website of the University of California system, includes this example of evidence of one's commitment: "In my advising capacities, I encouraged my students to ponder the roles they might play in the alleviation of the vast inequities that continue to shape our world" (UCSD n.d.). Are these oaths political tests of the kind rejected in the California loyalty case? It depends. If diversity is a *political* issue, these are political tests. To the extent that doctrinal statements of political beliefs, such as a conviction regarding the evils of inequality, are considered as a basis for employment, there are First Amendment issues, at least in a public institution. If it is a *policy* commitment, it is plausible for an employer to require adherence to the employer's policies. Separating the two presents the same kinds of difficulty as harassment guidelines.

Some of these oaths are simple affirmations that have to be signed off on by the applicant. It is an open question as to whether they are enforceable after employment—that is, whether someone could be said to have violated the oath, or have made it falsely, or have renounced it. Nonetheless, the requirement is designed to have an effect on hiring. The act of assessing a person's commitment to a policy—even if this were an appropriate requirement, consistent with academic freedom—is a matter of largely arbitrary personal judgment, exercised by people who are unconstrained by rules or the possibility of appeal. Moreover, they may have an ideological commitment to the policy and to a personal view of its meaning, as the statement by Golash-Boza (2016) makes clear. When academics adapt their behavior to vague threats of this kind, they are giving up some of their freedom, and other academics are complicit in depriving them of it.

Research Misconduct Proceedings

Research misconduct operates in the same way as other administrative law domains, with the addition of a federal Office of Research Misconduct that issues federal funding bans for institutions involved in the individual cases that reach it. The primary bodies in this regard are internal to universities, which adopt their own research misconduct rules and procedures. The cases that have occurred in sociology include the highly visible University of Texas project, which indicated that children of same sex marriages were harmed by this practice (Regnerus 2012). It resulted in multiple misconduct and ethics charges. Citation of this research in a related court case led to judicial examination of the editorial decision making of the journal in which the study was published. Cases prosecuting research misconduct in the social sciences are quite rare, and also extremely selective. Lenore Weitzman (1987) produced data showing differential economic harm for women as a result of divorce proceedings. These findings influenced legislatures and were warmly supported as an example of effective policy-oriented research. Yet such results, which fit a political agenda but did not mesh with the research's overall consensus, were dubious. As Christian Smith points out, it was never treated as a research misconduct case, and Weitzman's results were never subjected to juridical or quasi-juridical scrutiny, despite such red flags as missing data sets (Smith 2014, 97–101). The risk to academic freedom by the combination of selective prosecution and unclear standards is that the threat of misconduct charges will deter research that undermines dominant political biases. If scholars adapt to vague standards and the likelihood of the threat of politically motivated complaints by self-silencing or by choosing to avoid controversial topics, they forfeit their academic freedom.

The IRB Puzzle

Institutional review boards (IRBs) were mandated as part of the same kinds of administrative law procedures as anti-discrimination and research misconduct rule making, but they work in ways that are especially problematic from the point of view of the First Amendment. They represent a form of prior restraint on speech, rather than a system of sanctions on speech. The issue of clear lines is thus particularly important here, because enforcing sanctions on past actions requires some clarity in the rules *in advance* of the action. This is why courts have repeatedly ruled against universities' punishment of faculty for speech violations. IRBs, however, review research proposals on human subjects before that research is conducted. Moreover, they are, in the usual manner of administrative law requirements imposed on institutions, removed legally from the authorizing legislation and the possibility of judicial review.

The "Belmont Report" (HHS 1979) provided the philosophical basis for the regulatory regime that was established. Medical research was the model. The report focused on such topics as informed consent and harms, as well as the confidentiality of records. Social scientists were not involved in the writing of the report, and the application of these standards to social science research was an accidental outcome. The bulk of research similar to that in the social sciences is psychological and educational research. As with medical research, anonymity and the protection of subjects, particularly through informed consent, has been a primary focus. The effect of applying these standards to academic social science fields has been to restrict social research in ways in which non-academics, such as journalists, were not hampered, even when the risk of harm was minimal. For example, IRBs have been prone to require elaborate statements regarding the purposes of projects, based on the requirement of informed consent.

Much of the discussion of issues over the application of these standards has involved ethnography and oral history, the areas closest to journalism and non-academic writing. The key topics have involved informed consent and anonymity requirements, which are hot button issues for medical records, and thus strenuously enforced by IRBs. These issues have been partially resolved by a change in the rules, redefining "research" so that some kinds of human subjects research, such as oral history, journalism, biography, literary criticism, legal research, and historical scholarship, are no longer regarded as research per se.

The distinction that this redefinition was grounded in, however, produces an additional complication for social research. These activities were excluded because they were not "designed to develop or contribute to generalizable knowledge" (Abbo 2007, 575). Taken literally, many of the classics of social research (such as the Middletown books or the Yankee City series, as well as many classic ethnographies) included material that could be identified with specific incidents and persons and thus violate privacy requirements. The thin protection of not naming the cities in which the research was done speaks to the desire to generalize, but it did little to protect identities. Neither was informed consent, typically associated in medical research with consent forms, possible for public events or the casual conversations between participant and observer on which the researchers depended.

This change is not mandated for university IRBs, which can continue to treat federal regulations as the "floor," and thus do not exempt any researchers. An employee's relation to the IRB is mediated by employment law: the requirement to submit one's research proposals to an IRB is a matter of honoring the rules of the university. IRBs typically do not offer blanket exclusions. Ordinarily, exemptions must be specifically approved by the IRB. Many IRBs, which have become de facto representatives of a university's concerns about other subjects—including liability, bad publicity, and political exposure—have not adopted a permissive attitude to these projects, and some advocates of the IRB process bristle at the thought that the social sciences would not follow the rules imposed on medicine. Evidence on IRB workings is scant, because these boards operate secretly, and researchers tend to conform rather than risk sanctions. The AAUP, however, has collected a large number of horror stories about aggressive IRBs, some of which relate to social science projects (AAUP 2006).

IRBs exercise considerable power. They can tell the applicants what kinds of research they may do, and even rewrite protocols. Proponents of the IRB system treat these actions not as a matter of the application of clear rules, but as a means of balancing the interests of research against other interests. But do IRBs actually affect the kind of research that is done, and the topics studied, or are they merely a paperwork hurdle whose effects are largely random? Ceci, Peters, and Plotkin (1985) conducted a survey that showed IRB members were less likely to approve research that challenged left-wing biases. There is also much evidence of inconsistency. One ethnographic study of IRBs tells the story of a study of landlords in impoverished areas that was rejected at Brandeis for consent reasons but accepted at the University of Wisconsin (Stark 2012, 54). Another case, reported in an AAUP journal, reflected the extensive sense in which the notion of "harm" could be applied outside of medical contexts to block research. A Caucasian PhD student studying ethnicity and career expectations was told that it might be traumatic for Black PhD students to be interviewed by him (Thomson et al., 2006, 96).

The overall effects of the IRB system on actual research choices are more difficult to detect. Within sociology, however, one can observe a few long-term changes that might well be attributed to the increased difficulty of performing human subjects research. Areas that require IRB approval have declined, while those that do not necessitate it have grown. Social psychology, as a field within sociology, has suffered a radical decline in section membership in the IRB era, and some forms of politically sensitive research, notably community power studies, have disappeared entirely. At the same time, areas such as cultural sociology, which can rely on public material and thus not have to face IRB scrutiny, and autoethnography, which does not directly involve subjects other than the author and, hence, not require IRB approval, have flourished.

IRBs present the clearest of all threats to academic freedom. They are explicitly designed to curtail research in the name of other goals and values. Yet it is controversial whether these restrictions represent the kind of abridgement of speech by the First Amendment doctrine forbidding prior restraint (Bledsoe et al. 2007; Charrow 2007). It is apparent, however, that the absence of clear rules and the IRBs' use of their discretionary power to mandate changes in research protocols create an environment to which researchers must adapt, consciously or unconsciously.

Do the Two Forms of Academic Freedom Conflict?

In his history of the German idea of freedom, Leonard Kreiger (1957, 435) mentions the "traditional German notion of freedom as the essential harmony between popular liberty and monarchical authority."

For most of the twentieth century, there was a similarly strong relationship between the two forms of academic freedom: freedom of the individual faculty member, and freedom of the institution from state interference. Threats to a person's academic freedom often came from the state, such as from politicians incensed at something done at a state university, as in the California loyalty oath case. The freedom of a higher education institution was a means of protecting faculty from political interference, and, in turn, faculty members supported the freedom of their university as the basis of their own freedom. The current situation raises new issues that disrupt this commonality of interests. The conflict is especially well articulated in a recently decided Wisconsin Supreme Court case, which pitted a faculty member against Marquette University. Both concepts of freedom were articulated in detail in the rulings, which divided the court. The legal facts of the case, as recorded in the majority opinion, were the following:

> Marquette University suspended a tenured faculty member because of a blog post criticizing an encounter between an instructor and a student. Dr. John McAdams took exception to his suspension, and brought a claim against the University for breach of contract. He asserts that the contract guarantees to him the right to be free of disciplinary repercussions for engaging in activity protected by either the doctrine of academic freedom or the United States Constitution. The University denies Dr. McAdams' right to litigate his breach of contract claim in our courts. Instead, it says, we must defer to its procedure for suspending and dismissing tenured faculty members. It claims we may not question its decision so long as it did not abuse its discretion, infringe any constitutional rights, act in bad faith, or engage in fraud. (*McAdams* 2018, ¶1)

The university was declaring its freedom from state supervision and the legal priority of its own procedures in relation to employment questions. McAdams was defending his constitutional rights and the guarantee of academic freedom explicitly written into his employment contract. The university believed—and asserted—that it could define, through its own procedures, what these guarantees meant and act accordingly.

The university won its initial case. The circuit court adhered to the notion that "public policy compels a constraint on the judiciary with respect to Marquette's academic decision-making and governance," out of a recognition that "professionalism and fitness in the context of a university professor are difficult if not impossible issues for a jury to assess" (*McAdams* 2018, ¶55). The university nevertheless lost on McAdams's appeal to the Wisconsin Supreme Court. The majority opinion was that the university was not free to define the terms that appeared in its employment rules. The court also ruled that Marquette's quasi-judicial procedure, which was the basis for its actions, was merely an informal dispute-resolution process, and that "as a replacement for litigation in our courts, it is structurally flawed" (*McAdams* 2018, ¶2). Thus it rejected the circuit court's finding that McAdams had received due process. It noted as dubious the claim that juries could not assess fitness cases and rejected deference as an unsound practice. These responses recapitulate the standard issues with administrative law generally: lack of due process, lack of access to a jury trial, and quasi-judicial processes where their authority, particularly with respect to a question of the autonomy of the hearing officer, is suspect.

The definition of academic freedom came from the Marquette handbook itself, which was explicitly based on the AAUP definitions of academic freedom. As this is a frequent feature of faculty handbooks, and thus forms part of the contract with faculty members, the above analysis is important. The higher court made the point that the 1940 AAUP statement is out of date and does not reflect current practice, which is that faculty members are largely unconstrained in their extramural comments. The current standard, rather, was one that was narrowly related to the performance of the faculty member's job: "The controlling principle is that a faculty member's expression of opinion as a citizen cannot constitute grounds for dismissal unless it clearly demonstrates the faculty member's unfitness for his or her position" (*McAdams* 2018, ¶67).

As the AAUP pointed out (*McAdams* 2018, ¶68), this was a stringent standard, one which was rarely invoked by universities. Marquette University, as the higher court indicated, did not show that the particular expression by McAdams proved his unfitness, and it invoked considerations that uncoupled the doctrine of academic freedom from any stable reference points. The form of this argument is important, for it goes to the heart of the notion of academic freedom as a right, rather than as just one consideration among many. The university argued that educational institutions assume academic freedom as just one value that must be balanced against "other values core to their mission." Some of those values, it said, include the obligation to "take care not to cause harm, directly or indirectly, to members of the university community"; to "respect the dignity of others and to acknowledge their right to express differing opinions"; to "safeguard the conditions for the community to exist"; to "ensur[e] colleagues feel free to explore undeveloped ideas"; and to carry out "the concept of *cura personalis*," which involves working and caring "for all aspects of the lives of the members of the institution" (*McAdams* 2018, ¶69).

This line of argument would have the effect of eliminating academic freedom as a contractual right and subjecting its exercise to a wide range of other, largely subjective considerations. The minority opinion of the higher court, which may reflect the dominant legal reasoning on these issues, affirmed the superiority of an institution's academic freedom to the academic freedom of an individual. This argument was based on the concept of shared governance: "Within academic freedom lies the concept of shared governance. It includes the right of faculty to participate in the governance of the institution on academic-related matters. Shared governance in colleges and universities has been forged over decades to address the specific issues that arise in the workplace of higher education" (*McAdams* 2018, ¶139).

The relevant faculty right, in short, is to participate in shared governance.[5] Thus, as the dissent claimed: "The majority [opinion] errs in conducting only half of the academic freedom analysis. It fails to recognize, much less analyze, the academic freedom of Marquette as a private, Catholic, Jesuit university. As a result, it dilutes a private educational institution's autonomy to make its own academic decisions in fulfillment of its unique mission" (*McAdams* 2018, ¶140).

The dissent also rejected the idea that courts, rather than faculty operating in shared governance structures, should be able to define the meaning of academic freedom: "Apparently, the majority thinks it is in a better position to address concerns of academic freedom than a group of tenured faculty members who live the doctrine every day" (*McAdams* 2018, ¶141). The dissent also added, significantly, that McAdams's "contract does not give him the full-throated First Amendment rights that would be given a private citizen vis-à-vis the government," despite its affirmation of his academic freedom (*McAdams* 2018, ¶145). Therefore, the institution, in accordance with its autonomy, can regulate McAdams's extramural speech.

Conclusion

As all of these examples show, the present legal system produces an unequal conflict between academic freedom, which has only the most fragile and indirect legal basis, and employment law. The latter is backed by administrative law, which, in turn, is supported by the practice of judicial deference and the absence, in most cases, of statutory law providing for and defining academic freedom. A recent University of Texas lawsuit indicated how low on the legal hierarchy academic freedom is. A lawyer representing the state and the university affirmed the state's view that academic freedom was a "workplace policy," not a First Amendment right (Ellis 2018). This is the language of standard employment law. If a university is allowed to define academic freedom as a workplace policy, then it has little legal significance. Policy is a prerogative of the employer. Employers have been reluctant to act on this prerogative, but they have been less hesitant in applying regulations backed by administrative law, which represent different policy values. In the cases we have discussed, academic freedom is considered to be one policy value among several and, therefore, subject to being balanced against other interests or public purposes.

The effect of this new regime of administrative law, which holds employers responsible for fulfilling a vast array of policy *desiderata*, is to create an equally vast array of new discretionary powers for academic administrators and committees, such as IRBs. The mere existence of these powers marks the end of academic freedom as it was traditionally understood: both as a right, instead of an interest against which other interests are balanced, and as a concept superior to employment policy, rather than subject to it. Without clear demarcations and the legal priority of a right—even if it is only an implied contractual right in employment law, with a defined meaning apart from the interpretation placed on it by universities—it is impossible to defend traditional academic freedom against the ever-encroaching body of administrative law and university procedures.

One may ask, however, whether there is much traditional academic freedom left to defend. The "marketplace of ideas" image referred to in the classic legal defenses of academic freedom depended on the real autonomy of faculty members to pursue inquiry as they saw fit and to occasionally express their opinions in public without penalty. The present regime of science is governed by a grant system that ties a scientist to the judgments of peers through a brutal system of competition for funds. The rest of academia is bound to a competitive system of quantitative reputation assessment, to which our submission is, as Gloria Origgi (2017, 218) has called it, a form of voluntary epistemic servitude that has the same effects. This coincides with, and perhaps produces, a cultural change in the professoriate. The constituency for traditional academic freedom within a university would be the people who were exercising freedom in accordance with the liberal theory of science. This constituency barely exists today. It is noteworthy that of the university cases discussed here, three of them (at Texas, Duke, and Marquette) involved objections to either an ideologically dominant position or to practices enforcing ideological conformity. The suppression of one faculty member was supported by much of the rest of the faculty. Conformity has an active constituency. Indeed, for topics involving diversity, it has an institutionalized presence in the university, many means to enforce it, and enthusiastic support among the faculty. Academic freedom has only the few legal means outlined above. We have come full circle, culturally as well as legally, from the California loyalty oath case.

Acknowledgments
My thanks to Joerg Tiede for useful suggestions. I am responsible for errors.

Notes

1. One complication with this kind of "law" is that for most of its application to universities there is no direct constitutional basis for them in the "enumerated powers" of the US Constitution, which do not include any authority to regulate research or education. The regulations instead are conditions of contractual relations between the federal government and universities or states, relations that result from grant programs.

2. This case involved a letter to the editor criticizing actions of the school board and affirmed Marvin Pickering's First Amendment right as a citizen to speak on public issues.

3. It is worth noting that a loyalty oath requirement was already under attack from the 1930s on by the Communists of the era, and the requirement was defended against their contestation of it by such figures as Michael Polanyi and Sidney Hook.

4. Seminars on "whiteness" directed at employees and students characteristically take the form of indoctrination, by directing them against resistance to the message and by declining to respond to counter-arguments, which are treated as pathologies (Watt 2007).

5. As Henry Reichman points out in his commentary on this case, shared governance was something of a sham. This point is also made in the majority opinion. Marquette's president imposed an unusual and legally problematic demand that went beyond the advice of the faculty committee, namely that McAdams apologize (Reichman 2019, 101). This apology would have the effect of protecting McAdams against a civil lawsuit by the instructor who was criticized by him.

References

AAUP (American Association of University Professors). June 2016. "The History, Uses, and Abuses of Title IX." AAUP, https://www.aaup.org/file/TitleIXreport.pdf.

AAUP (American Association of University Professors). 2006. "Research on Human Subjects: Academic Freedom and the Institutional Review Board." AAUP Reports and Publications, https://www.aaup.org/reports-publications/.

AAUP (American Association of University Professors). 1940. "1940 Statement of Principles on Academic Freedom and Tenure." AAUP Reports and Publications, https://www.aaup.org/reports-publications/.

AAUP (American Association of University Professors). [1915] 2015. "1915 Declaration of Principles on Academic Freedom and Academic Tenure." *Policy Documents and Reports*, 11th edition, 3–12. Baltimore: Johns Hopkins University Press.

Abbo, Elmer D. 2007. "Promoting Free Speech in Clinical Quality Improvement Research." *Northwestern University Law Review* 101(2):575–591.

Ali, Russlyn. "Dear Colleague" [re. Title IX and sex discrimination]. April 4, 2011. US Department of Education, Office for Civil Rights, https://www2.ed.gov/about/offices/list/ocr/letters/colleague-201104.pdf.

Bledsoe, Caroline H., Bruce Sherin, Adam G. Galinsky, Nathalia M Headley, Carol A. Heimer, Erik Keldgaard, James Lindgren, Jon D. Miller, Michael E. Roloff, and David H. Uttal. 2007. "Regulating Creativity: Research and Survival in the IRB Iron Cage." *Northwestern University Law Review* 101(2):593–641.

Ceci, Stephen, Douglas Peters, and Jonathan Plotkin. 1985. "Human Subjects Review, Personal Values, and the Regulation of Social Science Research." *American Psychologist* 40(9):994–1002.

Charrow, Robert. 2007. "Protection of Human Subjects: Is Expansive Regulation Counterproductive?" *Northwestern University Law Review* 101(2):707–721.

Dickerson (Dickerson v. New Banner Inst. Inc.). 1983. 460 U.S. 103. Justia, https://supreme.justia.com.

Ellis, Lindsay. July 24, 2018. "What Is Academic Freedom? Statement That Alarmed Professors at U. of Texas Sets Off Debate." *Chronicle of Higher Education*, https://www.chronicle.com.

Forasté (John Forasté, Plaintiff, v. Brown University and Laura Freid, Defendants). 2003. 290 F.Supp. 2d 234. Justia, https://supreme.justia.com.

Garcetti (Garcetti v. Ceballos). 2006. 547 U.S. 410. Justia, https://supreme.justia.com.

Gardner, David P. 1967. *The California Oath Controversy*. Berkeley: University of California Press.

Golash-Boza, Tanya. June 10, 2016. "The Effective Diversity Statement." *Inside Higher Ed*, https://www.insidehighered.com.

Hamburger, Philip. 2017. *The Administrative Threat*. New York: Encounter Books.

Hamburger, Philip. 2014. *Is Administrative Law Unlawful?* Chicago: University of Chicago Press.

HHS (Health and Human Services). April 18, 1979. "Belmont Report: Ethical Principles and Guidelines for the Protection of Human Subjects of Research." US Department of Health and Human Services, Office for Human Research Protections, https://www.hhs.gov/ohrp/regulations-and-policy/.

Kaplin, William A. and Barbara A. Lee. 2013. *The Law of Higher Education: A Comprehensive Guide to Legal Implications of Administrative Decision Making*, 5th edition, vol. 2. San Francisco: Jossey-Bass.

Keyishian (Keyishian v. Board of Regents of the State Univ. of New York). 1967. 385 U.S. 589. Justia, https://supreme.justia.com.

Lange, Greg. 1999. "University of Washington Is Said on March 24, 1948, to Have More Than 150 Communists or Sympathizers." HistoryLink.org, http://www.historylink.org/File/1483/.

McAdams (McAdams v. Marquette University). 2018. Supreme Court of Wisconsin, case no. 2017AP1240, https://www.wicourts.gov.

McMahon, Paula. December 11, 2017. "Jury Rules Against Fired FAU Prof James Tracy in Free Speech Case." *Sun Sentinel* (Palm Beach, FL), https://www.sun-sentinel.com.

Norman-Eady, Sandra. June 24, 2006. "Analysis and Holding." In "Summary of *Garcetti et al. v. Ceballos* and Impact of Decision on Connecticut Whistleblower Laws." OLR Research Report 2006-R-0399. Connecticut General Assembly, https://www.cga.ct.gov.

North Haven (North Haven B[oar]d of Educ[ation] v. Bell). 1982. 456 U.S. 521, quoting *United States v. Price*, 383 U.S. 787, at 801 (1966). Justia, https://supreme.justia.com.

Oregon Association of Scholars. 2017. "The Imposition of Diversity Statements on Faculty Hiring and Promotion at Oregon Universities." Oregon Association of Scholars, https://www.oregonscholars.org/wp-content/uploads/2017/01/DiversityStatements_Rev16Mar17.pdf.

Origgi, Gloria. 2017. *Reputation: What It Is and Why It Matters*. Translated by Stephen Holmes and Noga Arikha. Princeton, NJ: Princeton University Press.

Pickering (Pickering v. Board of Education). 1968. 391 U.S. 563. Justia, https://supreme.justia.com.

"Prelude to Controversy 1940–1949." 1949. California Loyalty Oath Collection, Bancroft Library, University of California-Berkeley, https://bancroft.berkeley.edu/collections/loyaltyoath/timeline_prelude.html.

Ramadan, Lulu. August 29, 2016. "FAU Fires Professor Who Said Sandy Hook Shooting May Have Been Staged." *Palm Beach Post*, https://www.palmbeachpost.com/news/local/fau-fires-professor-who-said-sandy-hook-shooting-may-have-been-staged/iqECze68gbWAxQ8DwKegRL/.

Regnerus, Mark. 2012. "How Different Are the Adult Children of Parents Who Have Same-Sex Relationships? Findings from the New Family Structures Study." *Social Science Research* 41(4):752–770.

Reichman, Henry. 2019. *The Future of Academic Freedom*. Baltimore: Johns Hopkins University Press.

"Revised Sexual Harassment Guidance." January 19, 2001. US Department of Education, Office of Civil Rights, https://www2.ed.gov/about/offices/list/ocr/docs/shguide.html.

Schrecker, Ellen. 1999. "Political Tests for Professors: Academic Freedom during the McCarthy Years." The University Loyalty Oath: A 50th Anniversary Perspective, http://www.lib.berkeley.edu/uchistory/archives_exhibits/loyaltyoath/symposium/schrecker.html.

Smith, Christian. 2014. *The Sacred Project of American Sociology*. Oxford: Oxford University Press.

Stancill, Jane. May 9, 2017. "Duke Divinity Professor Calls Diversity Training 'a Waste,' Faces Discipline." *News & Observer* (Raleigh, NC), https://www.newsobserver.com.

Stark, Laura. 2012. *Behind Closed Doors: IRBs and the Making of Ethical Research*. Chicago: University of Chicago Press.

Strauss, Peter L. 1989. *An Introduction to Administrative Justice in the United States*. Durham, NC: Carolina Academic Press.

Svrluga, Susan. December 14, 2017. "Professor Who Says Sandy Hook Was a Hoax Sued the University that Fired Him: A Jury Ruled Against Him." *Washington Post*, https://www.washingtonpost.com.

Thomson, Judith Jarvis, Catherine Elgin, David A. Hyman, Philip E. Rubin, and Jonathan Knight. 2006. "Research on Human Subjects: Academic Freedom and the Institutional Review Board." *Academe* 92(5):95–100.

Tiede, Hans-Joerg. 2015. *University Reform: The Founding of the American Association of University Professors*. Baltimore: Johns Hopkins University Press.

UC (University of California). 2015. "Guidelines for Addressing Race and Gender Equity in Academic Programs in Compliance with Proposition 209." University of California, https://diversity.universityofcalifornia.edu/files/documents/prop-209-guidelines-ogc-full.pdf.

UCSD (University of California-San Diego). n.d. Examples of diversity statements. University of California-San Diego, https://facultydiversity.ucsd.edu/_files/Ex-1to3-C2D-Statements.pdf.

US Department of Labor. 1972. "Title IX, Education Amendments of 1972 (Title 20 U.S.C. Sections 1681–1688)." US Department of Labor, Office of the Assistant Secretary for Administration & Management, https://www.dol.gov/agencies/oasam/centers-offices/civil-rights-center/statutes/title-ix/.

Watt, Sherry K. 2007. "Difficult Dialogues, Privilege and Social Justice: Uses of the Privileged Identity Exploration (PIE) Model in Student Affairs Practice." *College Student Affairs Journal* 26(2):114–126.

Weitzman, Lenore. 1987. *The Divorce Revolution: The Unexpected Social and Economic Consequences for Women and Children in America*. New York: Free Press.

CHAPTER 3

Waiting for Their Day in Court

A History of Professors and the Legal Status of Academic Freedom

John R. Thelin

The Courts and the Conceptual Chasm in Defining Academic Freedom

In the United States, faculty consider academic freedom essential to their profession. They see it as worthy of protection under the law. The historical record, however, shows that when academics have "sought their day in court," Supreme Court justices have not given them much attention. Perhaps this will change in the future. For now, the puzzle I wish to unravel is the history of this disconnect. How is it that professors have seen the legal status of their academic freedom as important, whereas the court's justices have viewed it as marginal, if they have considered it all?

Several factors contributed to the void that professors find surprising. First, academic freedom as a professional right may have been overlooked, due simply to judicial overload. After all, each year the US Supreme Court culls through thousands of potential cases, with only a handful being selected for a hearing. Academic freedom evidently has not been sufficiently compelling to make it onto the docket. A second related but distinct explanation is that academic freedom, as a legal term, has received only belated mention, let alone recognition, by the Supreme Court, because the definition used by the justices differed from the meanings and connotations embraced by professors. Finally, federal court cases about academic freedom often were limited to the purview of the First Amendment. So long as academics' grievances were about free speech, they may have had a reasonable chance to be heard in the courts. The Supreme Court, however, usually rejected other Constitutional issues associated with professors' claims about abuses of academic freedom. The cumulative result of these assorted precedents was that faculty who counted on the federal courts to protect academic freedom as a professional right found that their cause was too little, too late.

Although the Supreme Court's strict constructionist view was disappointing to those who think the academic profession warrants distinct, special legal status, the court's logic could not be easily refuted or disregarded. The burden, then, was for professors individually and collectively to construct a compelling case that revisited the issue, either by advancing a new interpretation based on review of the First Amendment, or by looking elsewhere in the Constitution for principles to which academic freedom might be effectively linked. Faculty in the twenty-first century would do well to recognize that the academic enterprise has changed, due to the recent intrusion of corporations such as Novartis and Elsevier, along with pharmaceutical manufacturers, into formal contracts made by and for the administration and trustees. This current generation of large-scale commercial compacts has extended to patents, funding, access to data and findings, publication rights, and other elements that place fundamental constraints on scholars and scholarship. Seeking new legal directives has gained in urgency, based on the detailed research of Sheila Slaughter (2011), whose analyses have persuasively documented an unprecedented set of threats to traditional academic freedom as a result of administrative initiatives to commercialize scholarship, especially at major research universities. Before exploring these potential new initiatives to bring academic freedom up to date, the first step is to delve into the history of how and why the courts and professors ended up being disconnected.

A crucial starting point in this historical reconstruction was that academic freedom did not surface in the Supreme Court until 1951, when Justice William O. Douglas introduced the term into deliberations. This led then to its formal entry as part of his dissenting opinion in the 1952 case of *Adler v. Board of Education* (Bauries 2014). In contrast, academic freedom had gained attention in the national press, in professional associations, on campuses, in faculty groups, and in many other settings since the late nineteenth century. As historian Hans-Joerg Tiede (2015) has shown, defining and then defending academic freedom for professors was central to the emergence of great American universities and the founding of the American Association of University Professors (AAUP). Nonetheless, the campaign to codify academic freedom was contentious and consequential (Tiede 2015). Its historic episodes were numerous and extended over more than a century. Given this heritage and publicity, why, then, was the Supreme Court either slow or reluctant to consider the term "academic freedom" until 1951, more than sixty years after the phrase and topic had become newsworthy?

One answer, according to some legal scholars, was that the Constitution gave no more and no less protection to professors than it would to any citizen (Bauries 2014). Even as recently as August 2018, legal counsel for the University of Texas argued that academic freedom was an institutional right and did not extend to individual professors (Ellis 2018). Omitting academics, as a unique professional group, from court cases also was due in part to differences in organizational perspectives that separated faculty and the courts—specifically, the distinction of *vertical* versus *horizontal* institutions in American higher education. The Supreme Court treated academic freedom as a principle vested in *vertical institutions*—namely, colleges and universities. By extension, that meant the legal custodians were boards of trustees and, perhaps, the president of these academic institutions. The court left out the category of *horizontal institutions*—that is, formal organizations that cut across the landscape of the academic profession (Thelin 2010). Central to this horizontal category were academic groups, ranging from the AAUP to the American Historical Association, the American Mathematical Society, the American Sociological Association, and numerous other organizations created by and for scholars in their respective academic fields.

This restriction was consequential, because many clashes over academic freedom were not confined to universities acting as guardians of this concept against external threats associated with populist movements, tirades by a conservative newspaper editor, or political campaigns by a governor or a state legislature intent on purging a higher education institution of what they considered radical professors. Reasonable historical evidence suggests a bittersweet irony: college or university officials often denied academic freedom to their own faculty. For over a century, scholarship on these episodes, which took place starting around 1890 and accelerated into the 1930s, was formidable. It included studies published in the 1950s and 1960s by highly regarded historians in their reconstruction of the landmark events dealing with economist Richard Ely and the Board of Trustees at the University of Wisconsin between 1890 and 1910 (Hofstadter and Metzger 1955; Hofstadter and Smith 1961; Rudolph 1962; Veysey 1965). One fascinating case in the 1890s was that of Benjamin Andrews at Brown University—who was both a professor of political economy and president of the university. He was a scholarly expert on trade policies and currency who spoke out in the public forum, including in opposition to the gold standard. After having served as president of Brown for a decade, in 1898 he resigned this position, due to criticisms of his scholarly articles and speeches by the Board of Trustees. Comparable cases surfaced in the early 1900s. At Columbia University, nationally known scholars—such as psychologist J. McKeen Cattell and, later, historian Charles Beard—stood their ground to defend professors' academic freedom against the university's famous and autocratic president, Nicholas Murray Butler (Rudolph 1962).

The history of professors and their disputes over academic freedom a century ago was lively, because it included such controversial scholars as Thorstein Veblen. Veblen, the son of Norwegian immigrants who had settled in Minnesota, earned a PhD in anthropology—a relatively young discipline at the time. His dubious claim to fame was that over the course of his career, he ended up being both hired and fired by some of the greatest universities in the United States, including Stanford and the University of Chicago. No doubt Veblen's writings, such as *The Higher Learning in America*, were both controversial and perceptive in their analyses. *Higher Learning*, for example, dealt with the culture and structure of university boards, seeing them as indelibly linked to corporations (Veblen [1915] 2015). Advancing such terms as "captains of erudition" to describe business executives who were wealthy donors to higher education institutions generated both heat and light, which made him an obvious target of disgruntled board members. If Veblen had been fired for such writings, it would have made sense to invoke the protections we think of as associated with a professor's academic freedom. Veblen, however, complicated his professional standing as a university employee. At Stanford, he once began a semester by deliberately mumbling and shuffling disorganized lecture notes, leading him to urge students to drop his class and transfer to other courses, so he would be spared the burdens of teaching. According to campus lore, he made his own personal life interesting and, in so doing, was accused of adultery and affairs with spouses of colleagues, including, in one case, the wife of a university president. It was not clear whether violations of academic regulations or his alleged personal conduct were the basis for his dismissal. Whether one or the other of these acts was the impetus, it was unlikely that either would make its way to the Supreme Court as a landmark case in academic freedom (Veysey 1965, 422–25).

In the heroic cases between 1890 and 1930, one finds that they radiated from the newly created academic organizations—that is, the horizontal institutions. The contentious episodes dealt with a generation of new scholars who had completed PhDs either in the United States or at European universities. At institutions that were charter members of the Association of American Universities (AAU)—now the American Association of University Professors—the high-profile and high-stakes cases tended to involve scholarly debates on issues of public policy, economics, social policy, government, and political economy. Individual cases in this era led to collective responses. Foremost were initiatives by national scholarly associations, which became a major source of pronouncements on advanced scholarship. Illustrative of this collective action was the publication in 1915 of the AAU's "Declaration of Principles." It distinguished *Lehrfreheit* (i.e., a professor's right to pursue knowledge and truth—and then write and speak about it as scholarship) from *Lehrnfreheit* (i.e., a student's right to learn by seeking out teachers, courses, and universities). The association's position papers noted emphatically that their concern was with the rights of faculty, leaving the students' distinctive concerns to other appropriate groups.

Ellen Schrecker's (1986) book, *No Ivory Tower*, presented a detailed study of how universities fared in the McCarthy era, following World War II. Drawing on hundreds of oral histories, along with archival data, she came up with original findings about the interaction of three pivotal groups between 1946 and 1953: outside critics of the university, university presidents and their boards, and university professors. She concluded that in important cases—such as the imposition of loyalty oaths on faculty at the University of California and the University of Washington—state university presidents capitulated to external popular groups and Far Right newspaper editors. These presidents applied constraints on their own faculty way beyond what the external critics ever dreamed to achieve. *Lehrfreheit* for professors in state colleges and universities in America was fragile. In contrast to state university presidents, the presidents of some prestigious private institutions, notably Nathan Pusey at Harvard and Robert Maynard Hutchens at the University of Chicago, took the lead in protecting academic freedom for both their own institutions and members of their faculty (Schrecker 1986; Heins 2013; 2018).

When one shifts from academic freedom to the highly related but still distinct issue of free speech, one finds some important, perhaps surprising, nuances. According to legal scholar Scott Bauries (2014), the First Amendment of the US Constitution does *not* give special protection of free speech to professors. This is contrary to the expectation that there would be numerous court cases in which faculty petitioned for (and were granted) freedom of speech based on their official position as tenured college professors. Bauries argued that the Constitution gave no more and no less protection to professors than it would to any citizen.

Furthermore, if one looked at professors as institutional employees, the divide was along public and private lines. Faculty at state colleges and universities were categorized as "public employees"—and their rights and restraints on free speech rest with those of civil service staff, police, fire marshals, bailiffs, coroners, clerks, and other positions one finds in a local, state, or federal bureaucracy. Academics employed at private, or independent, colleges had no special protections or privileges conferred by the First Amendment and were subject to their employing institution's internal regulations. What was surprising to professors was that they were not even the plaintiffs in landmark cases. For example, the 1952 *Adler* case dealt with public school teachers, not college and university professors, further undermining any claims that the academic profession was special. Reviewing the historical record and court case precedents, it seems ineffective and unwise today to rely exclusively, or even primarily, on the dubious, illusory relationship between freedom of speech and academic freedom as the foundation for faculty protections.

The safeguards afforded by tenure also tended to be exaggerated, usually with the effect of depicting professors as irresponsible and without accountability. A popular belief was that tenure provided "lifetime job security," a characterization that was patently inaccurate. According to most professional associations, including the AAUP, tenure offered protection against a vindictive dean, president, or trustee who tried to fire a professor for some act or statement deemed inappropriate. In fact, firing a faculty member often was comparable to firing any professional employed in civil service or a bureaucracy. It was not necessarily a matter of tenure being a universal and automatic protection. Rather, it was that administrators and supervisors were required to follow regulations, have documentation, and then go through appeals committees, quite apart from being upset by a professor's scholarship or speeches. Deans and department chairs often took a path of least resistance, because terminating a faculty member was too much work, due to administrative regulations, not tenure policies. Being tenured often had little to do with the decision to purge "deadwood" or dissidents on the faculty.

The 1957 case of *Sweezy v. New Hampshire* was hailed as a triumph for the protection of academic freedom in a university. For example, Derek Bok (1980), the president of Harvard, started his article in *The Public Interest* with the reminder that the *Sweezy* case established "four essential freedoms of a university": the freedom to determine for itself (1) who may teach, (2) what may be taught, (3) how it should be taught, and (4) who it may admit as students. The legacy of this case was that the courts were ascertaining the right of the *university* to do so. This neither referred nor extended to individual professors, or even to associations of professors as decision makers. The court decision was a substantial gain in academic freedom for the institution, not for the faculty—either as individuals or as a group. Once again, this seemed peculiar to professors, since they ascribed to a customary belief in the primacy of the faculty. A good example of this was their invoking an instance from 1948, when Dwight D. Eisenhower was inaugurated as president of Columbia University. According to the lore, "At one meeting, it is said, he prefaced his remarks with the phrase, 'Now, you employees of Columbia University . . .' A senior member of the faculty rose and stiffly reprimanded the General: 'Mr. President,' he said, 'We ARE Columbia University'" (Friedrichs 1967). The harsh news for professors, however, was the message from the Supreme Court that, by law, the trustees and the president, not the professors, were the university.

Sociologists Christopher Jencks and David Riesman wrote about an "academic revolution," charting the rise to power and influence of the faculty in American colleges and universities. Looking back over more than a half century of skirmishes and contests over academic freedom, "professors may have lost the battles, but they won the war" (Jencks and Riesman 1968). This meant that over several decades, the prestige of universities—and of faculty as experts—had risen. There was a shortage of PhDs to fill vacant faculty slots. This meant that in the marketplace and in hiring negotiations, professors could demand (and receive) offers of tenure (or at least tenure-track appointments), along with rising salaries and other perks. Dorothy Finnegan's (1993) research on academic labor markets indicated that around 1964, someone who received a PhD from an established, respected university typically received four to five tenure-track faculty job offers. These favorable market conditions diverted attention from concerns for faculty rights and legal protections. When faculty hiring tapered by 1970, however, questions about academic freedom resurfaced.

One question was that of clearly locating academic freedom and identifying to whom it pertained. Historian Richard Hofstadter of Columbia University gained widespread attention for his book, *Anti-Intellectualism in American Life*. One of his chapters dealt with the rise of professors as experts (Hofstadter 1963, 197–323). The complication was that although it often referred to a professor at a university, this was not the exclusive setting in which academics spoke or wrote. Faculty members may have had a variety of forums quite apart from the university and the classroom, made possible by appointments at a proliferation of research centers and institutes. The residual question was whether academic freedom followed scholars in these new, varied settings.

Recent Historical Research

The important implication for both the study and maintenance of academic freedom is that history matters. This takes on two forms: first, the past events themselves are consequential, and second, the subsequent analyses of those issues and events by historians continually bring those issues into contemporary policy discussions. We are heirs to an impressive body of events and assessments of them. Furthermore, historical scholarship on academic freedom is robust today (Loss 2012; Gelber 2016). A good example is the forum on academic freedom hosted by the History of Education Society, with papers published in the August 2018 issue of their journal, *History of Education Quarterly* (Cain 2018; Heins 2018; Tiede 2018; Williamson-Lott 2018). These recent studies revisited the classic cases of a century ago and resurrected seminal episodes that provide an important reminder: staking out academic freedom for faculty usually shared the stage with parallel negotiations over campus governance.

Even though professors as a special group pushed hard to protect scholarship from being grounds for arbitrary firing, often these same academic leaders devoted a great deal of attention to negotiating with presidents and boards of trustees over institutional provisions for including professors and their faculty senates as partners in campus decision making. This commitment was, in large measure, a gesture of cooperation with the Carnegie Foundation for the Advancement of Teaching (CFAT), whose priority was to promote standards and standardization in the operation of universities, including faculty hiring and promotion (Thelin 2017a). CFAT's search for order within academic institutions, however, did not necessarily mean advocacy for protecting professors' academic freedom (Lagemann 1983).

The downside for faculty who ratified the structures of shared governance was that in recent decades, university legal counsels and presidents have tended to compress the range of institutional activities where faculty bodies have a voice, let alone a vote. For example, all sides usually accepted initiatives for new academic programs and courses as a faculty prerogative. Yet even this compact was compromised when professors had the exclusive right to approve or deny a new academic degree program. It was limited because, at the same time, administrative regulations included the clause that decisions over funding and appropriations for newly approved programs were excluded from faculty control.

Meanwhile, most university regulations effectively limited faculty involvement in such matters as intercollegiate athletics, investment policies, and oversight of university foundations. For example, each college or university belonging to the National Collegiate Athletic Association was required to have an official faculty athletic representative (FAR). The catch was that the FAR was handpicked by the university president, rather than elected by the academic senate. In sum, faculty had a formal role in shared governance, but it was not at all an equal or central seat at the table.

Incorporation of these findings by a current generation of historians of higher education has rekindled professors' interest in resuming initiatives, and even battles, over the maintenance of academic freedom in the twenty-first century. The major point to keep in mind is that prospects for establishing genuine academic freedom are weak, if not implausible, without a connection to the horizontal institutions representing academic disciplines and their scholarly associations. The accounts and analyses provided by scholars in the discipline of history, along with the other social sciences, is essential—not expendable or marginal—in bringing academic freedom to an integral place in American society, in its institutions, and, ultimately, in the law.

New Questions about the Varieties of Academic Freedom

A legacy of the historical study of pioneering cases involving professors was that often the host university was the nemesis of academic freedom. This was reinforced by the Supreme Court's decisions to treat a higher education institution as the repository and protector of academic freedom. Beyond the clashes between professors and universities, scholarship dealing with recent events has opened new, interesting areas where historical research has continued to illuminate the nuances of academic freedom in modern colleges and universities.

One important strand of scholarship and strategy that has flourished in recent years was the proposition that academic freedom ought to be understood as part of the "common good" (Reichman 2016). The essence of this rationale was that legal protections of academic freedom for faculty were not merely a protection of professors as an academic guild. Rather, this protection had a broad and high purpose and, as such, was imperative for fulfilling national priorities and principles. According to this logic, informed discussion of issues, events, and ideas in a democratic society required a foundation of expert, legitimate scholars whose works ultimately are a public good that benefits the nation and its institutions. Yet this new emphasis on the common good has faced counter-arguments and disagreements from some influential, respected scholars. This latter response was welcomed in that it illustrated genuine, healthy debate within scholarly ranks. At the same time, it signaled that even professors were collectively unlikely to reach agreement on how to cast academic freedom to external audiences, ranging from the Supreme Court to the American public.

One unresolved dilemma was how to protect academics' inquiries while simultaneously guarding against dubious arguments offered by professors themselves, especially when such articles and addresses gained coverage in the media and public forums. Significant scholarship often became part of national policy debates, creating challenges for academic freedom standards. Consider the case of William Shockley, a professor of engineering at Stanford, who was awarded a Nobel Prize in 1956 for his original contributions in physics. His research changed in the late 1960s, when he wrote papers and gave talks about relationships of race and intelligence, topics about which he was not an informed expert. To make matters worse, he adopted a posture of polemics and strident advocacy, including claims about racial inferiority. How, then, did the academic profession monitor its own members, including its highly honored scholars? The danger with such extreme cases by highly visible scholars such as Nobel laureate Shockley was that the marketplace of ideas was susceptible to becoming a marketplace of ideologies.

Another line of argument to provide new protections for academic freedom was that it was an essential feature of organized, collective scholarship. Without recognition of and protection by the courts, genuine academic freedom remained at risk. Legal scholar Michael Olivas's (2013) book, *Suing Alma Mater*, provided a refreshing look at higher education and the courts by bringing attention to the growing role of what he called "purposive organizations." These referred to formal groups whose advocacy of beliefs and points of view entered into college and university forums, including classroom discussions. They spanned the political and religious spectrum. One situation illustrative of the tension was a biology class in which a professor was lecturing on evolution. A student asserted that the instructor should have presented the perspective of creationism and that, furthermore, since the lecture on evolution as a theory conflicted with personal religious beliefs, that student should be exempted from accepting this as fact and, hence, should have been exempted from writing about evolution on an examination. Such claims introduced an extreme relativism into academic discussions that jeopardized scholarly expertise. Further, an examination of such topics indicated that debates within a discipline customarily included a wide, varied range of perspectives and arguments that were subjected to peer review.

Another variation on these clashes was that of trigger warnings, in which instructors were expected to send advance alerts to students about course materials whose themes and content might be painful or controversial. Since college and university officials fear litigation from disgruntled students, the campus most likely will continue to be fertile ground for these kinds of complaints that raise continual questions about academic freedom. One sign of push-back by professors who opposed succumbing to the internal pressures of students' stifling of uncomfortable and unpopular scholarly themes and arguments was the group known the Foundation for Individual Rights in Education (FIRE). In September 2015, FIRE launched a national campaign "asking colleges and universities to adopt the free speech policy statement drafted by the University of Chicago's Committee on Freedom of Expression." The statement guaranteed "all members of the University community the broadest possible latitude to speak, write, listen, challenge, and learn" and made it clear that "it is not the proper role of the University to attempt to shield individuals from ideas and opinions they find unwelcome, disagreeable, or even deeply offensive" (Lukianoff 2015).

These initiatives did not exhaust sources that provided faculty with certain measures of academic freedom. A crucial category was the code officially adopted within each college and university—found in documents known as general regulations (GRs) and the administrative regulations (ARs). If, for example, a board of trustees approved adherence to the AAUP's guidelines on tenure and promotion and drafted commensurate language into the GRs and ARs, this was an important commitment for both the board and the administration, as well as for hired faculty. It provided a script approved by the university's legal counsel. If a board of trustees and a president did not follow the AAUP guidelines, or the ARs and GRs, or some other approved protocol or regulation, a faculty member had grounds for an internal appeal. If that did not provide relief, it left room for that person to file suit against the college or university. The merit of the grievance hinged on selected criteria that had to be clearly stated. A grievance resting on allegations of gender discrimination, for example, was different from one in which the plaintiff professor focused on the institutional review process's failure to document decisions about lack of scholarship or other criteria, or failure to adhere to institutional procedures (Thelin 2017b). For proponents of scholarship without fear of censorship or retribution as the heart of academic freedom, there have been some promising developments. For example, one source for optimism came in 2008 from Robert Post, the dean of Yale Law School, in his talk at Northwestern University's law school as part of the Julius Rosenthal Lecture Series. Post later refined and expanded his argument for his book, *Democracy, Expertise, and Academic Freedom*, dealing with a First Amendment jurisprudence for the modern state (Post 2012; see also McLemee 2012). Central to Post's commentary was that academe is distinctive in a need for safeguarding freedom of speech, because professors and their scholarly associations and journals deal largely with the "production of expert knowledge" and the "reproduction of expertise," both of which ought to be protected by academic freedom. The logic is that one cannot simply ignore the codification, synthesis, reconsideration, and discovery of arguments within scholarly disciplines, as well as their protocols of peer review, in understanding free speech and its treatment in the First Amendment. Post's public scholarship and ideas on the topic continued by his helping to draft crucial documents for the AAUP. An important example is the statement "In Defense of Knowledge and Higher Education," prepared by a subcommittee of the AAUP's Committee A on Academic Freedom and Tenure (AAUP 2019).

A central thread of Post's (2012) argument is that, on matters of scholarly analysis and inquiry, not all opinions are of equal weight. One may be free to pontificate on a topic, ranging from anthropology to zoology, but at some point, this must be reconciled with the rigorous, established theories and interpretations that constitute *informed* discussion.

According to this line of analysis, statements by a professor affiliated with a bona fide academic group or discipline gained, by association, a measure of special consideration. They carried more weight than, for example, popular opinion or conventional wisdom. Therefore, academic disciplines such as political science, biology, chemistry, economics, sociology, and history fulfilled this litmus test and, as such, warranted respect as a collective, institutionalized entity of established expert knowledge that would be acknowledged and perhaps even utilized by the US Supreme Court as its justices reviewed data on their own court decisions (Thelin 2017b, 100). A decade after Post's original presentation, however, there has been no clear sign that his argument has carried the day and gained legal status.

New Problems for Faculty and Academic Freedom

One limit on academic freedom was its close linkage with professors who had been granted tenure. Organizations such as the AAUP periodically have reported that the percentage of faculty within a university who are tenured or on a tenure track is relatively small—and shrinking. For example, on October 31, 2018, the senior program officer of the AAUP released a report on "The Scary Stats on Contingency in Higher Education." Although noting differences among categories of institutions, the general profile was that "at all US institutions combined, the percentages of instructional positions that is off the tenure track amounted to 73 percent in 2016, the latest year for which data are available" (Bailey 2018).

This signaled that presidents, deans, and boards of trustees had defused tenure as a protection of academic freedom not by testing it or confronting it head on. Rather, academic freedom has been muted by a strategy of avoidance and exclusion. If a tenured professor retired, there was no assurance that the replacement would be a tenured or tenure-track appointment. To use the argot of boxing, boards and administrators "cut the ring" as tenured faculty ranks were reduced over time. Historian Kim Tolley's (2018) recent anthology consists of essays by scholars who analyze the emergence of what she calls "professors in the gig economy." Adjuncts, lecturers, and clinical professors who have time-limit contracts forfeited the long-term protections of academic freedom provided by tenure. When the AAUP advocated for inclusion of contingency faculty in the voting rights of an academic senate, it also recommended: "There should be no invidious distinctions between those who teach and/or conduct research in higher education, regardless of whether they hold full-time or part-time appointments or whether their appointments are tenured, tenure-track, or contingent. All faculty members should have access to the same due-process protections and procedures" (AAUP 2018, n14).

The initiative was well intentioned, but there was no certainty that administrators and boards would approve it. If adopted, it might be a Pyrrhic victory, because any faculty member who did not have tenure remained predictable, easy prey if an administrator did not renew that contract. Hence it was unclear if this initiative advanced academic freedom in research and scholarship. One unfortunate prospect was that faculty of all ranks achieved an equity of sorts, but it was reduced for all.

A potential dysfunction accompanied extending membership in a campus's academic senate to an expanded constituency of non-tenure-track faculty—that is, lecturers and adjuncts. First, within a research university, it tended to give an academic medical center disproportionate suffrage. Academic units such as colleges of medicine and dentistry included large numbers of clinical faculty who typically were employed in full-time private practice elsewhere. It was not likely that they had much interest or involvement in publication and promotion. As a group, they tended to be supportive of and deferential to the dean of the college of medicine or the vice president of the medical center. Did it make good sense for the self-determination of the academic profession that a dentist with a prosperous full-time private practice who sometimes assisted with supervising clinical training could be elected as an academic senator and have as much voice and vote in shared governance as did, for example, a tenured full professor of sociology?

The American Legacy of Distrust for Faculty Governance and Academic Freedom

These developments show how an issue comes full circle. As noted earlier, court cases that affirmed academic freedom usually did so by confirming the institution and its president and board of trustees as the overseers and protectors. Yet these were the same officials who often curbed academic freedom. If one goes back in time, prior to the landmark episodes involving professors and universities between 1890 and 1920, there are unexpected clues about this legacy. Conventional wisdom held that colleges in the American colonies transplanted the charters, bylaws, and structures of the Universities of Oxford and Cambridge. This was accurate, with one important exception. Faculty at Oxford and Cambridge oversaw institutional governance, with little provision for administrators within the endowed residential colleges that endure today as the crucial units of living and learning at both Oxford and Cambridge.

This lesson was not lost on the founders of Harvard, the College of William and Mary, and Yale. These American colleges could not have been more different in provisions for governance from England's two degree-granting universities. Whereas masters and dons in the various colleges of Oxford and Cambridge had endured and even ignored kings, queens, and bishops for centuries, American college faculty faced daily scrutiny by a stern governing board and its appointed administrators. A president reported to the board, not to a peer committee of faculty. Signs of faculty governance included in the original charters and bylaws were misleading, as their language sometimes gave an illusion of formal statutes for faculty governance in American higher education and, by extension, given the sanctity of charters and contracts, to American jurisprudence. The 1693 charter of the College of William and Mary in Virginia was supplemented with bylaws in 1727 that delineated official provision for a perpetual "College Senate." On close inspection, one finds that this was not a provision for faculty governance, since the bylaws defined its membership as being drawn exclusively from the board of visitors and college governors, not from the faculty. The legacy from the colonial period was that of power vested in an external board, combined with their appointment of a strong college president. This has continued to shape and define colleges and universities throughout the twentieth century and still does so today (Thelin 2011, 11–12).

A New Deal for Professors and Academic Freedom in the Twenty-First Century

Given this situation, what might be some promising, pragmatic approaches to increase the likelihood that a college or university would respect faculty rights associated with academic freedom and tenure? Most strategies relied on the AAUP as the crucial external body that could either persuade or force a board of trustees and a president into compliance with academic freedom, as spelled out in the AAUP guidelines to which that institution was a signatory. A weakness of this approach was the presumption by professors and the AAUP (in both its local and national bodies) that a university's administration would be wary of risking AAUP censure in cases that violated academic freedom. This was doubtful, because AAUP censure carried few binding institutional penalties. The chair of the university's trustees and the president often merely shrugged off the threat of AAUP censure.

Since there was little precedent to show that the AAUP alone could prevail in the federal courts to gain legal status for professors' academic freedom, it may be time for the AAUP to consider aligning with another horizontal institution that has the potential to impose a substantive penalty on a defiant college or university. To elaborate on the commentary presented at the start of this chapter, a *horizontal institution* is an organization or agency that cuts across the higher education landscape to provide services and resources or, perhaps, impose regulations and conditions on *vertical institutions*. In this taxonomy, colleges and universities are vertical institutions that carry out the essential missions of teaching, learning, research, and the conferral of academic degrees. Horizontal institutions include foundations, federal agencies (e.g., the National Institutes of Health or the National Science Foundation), along with lobbying groups, trade associations, institutional consortia, myriad state offices and auxiliary support groups, and professional scholarly associations (Thelin 2010).

An organization that fulfilled this criterion of a crucial vertical institution that has oversight power over colleges and universities is a *regional accrediting agency*. Such bodies include the Southern Association of Colleges and Schools (SACS), the Western Association of Schools and Colleges (WASC), the Middle States Commission on Higher Education, the New England Commission on Schools and Colleges, and their counterparts in other multistate domains. They are voluntary associations to which an institution applies for membership via its board of trustees. It is important to note that joining a regional accreditation agency is voluntary, although this becomes contractually binding for those colleges and universities that opt to become members. One reason for this distinctive power is that after World War II, the US Congress looked to regional accrediting associations to be a proxy for federal review of academic institutions, as a condition of institutional eligibility for the receipt of scholarship monies from students enrolling under the sponsorship of the GI bill. In sum, a university that is a member of SACS, WACS, or their counterparts elsewhere agrees to comply with the elaborate standards of accreditation review.

The regional accrediting associations typically rely on a ten-year cycle of self-study, in which a member institution documents and explains its conduct in two distinct but ultimately related areas: the standards and internal consistency of its educational programs, and its adherence to appropriate financial conduct. Egregious misconduct in one or both categories can lead to a college or university being placed on probation. In extreme cases, violations can cause an institution to forfeit its status as an *accredited institution*.

This is a serious matter, because without regional accreditation, a college or university runs the risk of its degrees not gaining recognition by professional licensure boards, employers, graduate schools, foundations, and other funding agencies. In addition, the US Congress and federal research agencies have continued the policy set in place in the late 1940s of requiring or accepting regional accreditation as a requisite for eligibility on the federal level. This meant it could be a necessary condition for a university's receipt of federal research grants across all fields and specialties within that institution. In other words, a president and trustees cannot summarily ignore their regional accrediting agency in the way that one might disregard the AAUP or some other association of faculty members.

Regional accreditation standards typically provided some safeguards against arbitrary administrative actions within, say, a college that were imposed on academic departments and faculty. For university officials to legitimately eliminate an academic program or terminate a professor, they must adhere to protocols of review, including documentation of financial exigency. Above all, if a higher education institution were to lose its accreditation, it would face the burden of appeal, including going to court. No board of trustees wants to be in jeopardy of conferring degrees with the stigma of being debased academic currency.

Looking over the historical record, loss of accreditation by an established college or university has been rare. But the implicit prospect of doing so gives the ongoing accreditation reports understated influence within a campus's administration and its faculty. As with any powerful tool, it should be used carefully, relying primarily on its presence, rather than its implementation, as its source of influence on institutional behavior, including administrative respect for academic freedom. For professors, individually and collectively, the attractiveness of cooperation with a regional accrediting agency as a vertical institution is that it reduces the isolation of the faculty and provides a potential partner, in addition to the AAUP. Furthermore, if loss of accreditation due to an institution's violation of academic freedom led to a lawsuit, then professors would have their day in court as spectators, or perhaps as amicus curiae, leaving the burden of proof and the legal expenses to the trustees (as defendants) versus the regional accrediting agency (as the plaintiff). Such partnerships and collaborations are not easy to arrange, but in an era of high-stakes challenges for professors and their groups, it warrants consideration. All too often, many faculty members see their participation in the once-a-decade institutional self-study and campus visit as perfunctory, reduced to tasks of compiling and reporting performance data in a frantic rush to prepare for the on-site visit by the accreditation team.

This new proposal, in contrast, has the potential to enhance the role of professors as stakeholders in and stewards of policies and organizational conduct. Foremost is that although the visitation team only comes once every ten years, regional accreditation officers have implemented provisions that require an institution's president and administrators to devote professional expertise and shared governance to continual, persistent data collection and planning throughout the entire decade. This change in the formal planning process could be energizing, in that it enhances the faculty's role in the preparation of the accrediting report and, hence, makes them better informed and more engaged in the presentation and external review of their institution on a continuing annual basis. Collective, ongoing participation in the regional accreditation process could fall, at least in part, under the charge of a campus's academic senate, both in monitoring institutional effort and in establishing and staffing standing committees that work on the various components and reports. This would be a fitting compact because, after all, with academic freedom comes academic responsibility, which one hopes leads to increased self-determination.

Pursuance of this plan, however, faces prospects and problems. One heartening sign was the AAUP and the Council for Higher Education Accreditation (CHEA)'s joint statement on "Accreditation and Academic Freedom." That statement posed several questions to the accrediting agencies (AAUP and CHEA 2012):

- To what extent are accrediting organizations alert to the importance of academic freedom?
- To what extent do their standards give adequate guidance on the subject and capture the significance of institutional decision making and the faculty's role in that process?
- To what extent are these standards realized in application, by periodic inspection and, particularly, on occasions when major controversies erupt?

Unfortunately, efforts by the AAUP to follow up with regional agencies to gauge their efforts have not yet been fulfilled. Moreover, it is not clear that promoting the statement has been a high priority for CHEA.

Another important development is that the AAUP has become an increasingly complex organization. For example, it includes an option offering members services in which the AAUP acts as a union—a designation that can allow it to work with other unions, such as the American Federation of Teachers. This aspect of the organization coexists with its more traditional, historic role as a professional association. Although this new identity lacks universal appeal for all members and their institutions. On balance, the AAUP's gestures toward increased interaction and cooperation with other horizontal organizations provide some promise for institutional accreditation to be a locus for new measures to protect and promote academic freedom for faculty. Rather than a job completed and well done, these remain works in progress.

References

AAUP (American Association of University Professors). 2019. "In Defense of Knowledge and Higher Education." AAUP Reports & Publications, https://www.aaup.org/reports-publications.

AAUP (American Association of University Professors). 2018. "Recommended Institutional Regulations on Academic Freedom and Tenure." AAUP Reports & Publications, https://www.aaup.org/reports-publications/.

AAUP and CHEA (American Association of University Professors and Council for Higher Education Accreditation). November 1, 2012. "Accreditation and Academic Freedom." CHEA Advisory Statements, https://www.chea.org.

Bailey, Gwendolyn. October 31, 2018. "The Scary Stats on Contingency in Higher Education." Washington, DC: American Association of University Professors.

Bauries, Scott R. 2014. "Individual Academic Freedom: An Ordinary Concern of the First Amendment." *Mississippi Law Journal* 83(4):677–743.

Bok, Derek. 1980. "The Federal Government and Higher Education." *Public Interest* 58: 80–101.

Cain, Timothy Reese. 2018. "'Friendly Public Sentiment' and the Threats to Academic Freedom." *History of Education Quarterly* 53(3):428–434.

Ellis, Lindsay. August 3, 2018. "Academic Freedom Statement Alarms U. of Texas Professors and Sets Off Debate on Campus." *Chronicle of Higher Education*, A27.

Finnegan, Dorothy E. 1993. "Segmentation in the Academic Labor Market: Hiring Cohorts in Comprehensive Universities." *Journal of Higher Education* 64:621–656.

Friedrichs, Christopher. 1967. "Ike at Columbia: A Lonely Man in Low Library." *Columbia Daily Spectator* 76:5.

Gelber, Scott M. 2016. *Courtrooms and Classrooms: A Legal History of College Access, 1860- 1960*. Baltimore: Johns Hopkins University Press.

Heins, Marjorie. 2018. "A Pall of Orthodoxy over the Classroom: Lessons from the Great *Keyishian* Case." *History of Education Quarterly* 53(3):423–427.

Heins, Marjorie. 2013. *Priests of Our Democracy: The Supreme Court, Academic Freedom, and the Anti-Communist Purge*. New York: New York University Press.

Hofstadter, Richard. 1963. "The Rise of the Expert." In *Anti-Intellectualism in American Life*, 197–232. New York: Alfred Knopf.

Hofstadter, Richard and Walter P. Metzger. 1955. *The Development of Academic Freedom in the United States*. New York: John Wiley.

Hofstadter, Richard and Wilson Smith (eds.). 1961. "Academic Freedom in the University." In *American Higher Education: A Documentary History*, vol. 2, 849–891. Chicago: University of Chicago Press.

Jencks, Christopher and David Riesman. 1968. "The Academic Revolution in Perspective." In *The Academic Revolution*, 1–27. Garden City, NY: Doubleday.

Lagemann, Ellen Condliffe. 1983. *Private Power for the Public Good: A History of the Carnegie Foundation for the Advancement of Teaching*. Middletown, CT: Wesleyan University Press.

Loss, Christopher. 2012. *Between Citizens and the Sate: The Politics of American Higher Education in the 20th Century*. Princeton, NJ: Princeton University Press.

Lukianoff, Greg. September 28, 2015. "FIRE Launches Campaign in Support of University of Chicago Free Speech Statement." Foundation for Individual Rights in Education, https://www.thefire.org.

McLemee, Scott. January 18, 2012. "Ideas of Academic Freedom [review of Robert C. Post's *Democracy, Expertise, Academic Freedom*]." *Inside Higher Ed*, https://www.insidehighered.com.

Olivas, Michael A. 2013. *Suing Alma Mater: Higher Education and the Courts*. Baltimore: Johns Hopkins University Press.

Post, Robert. 2012. *Democracy, Expertise, and Academic Freedom: A First Amendment Jurisprudence for the Modern State*. New Haven, CT: Yale University Press.

Reichman, Henry. 2016. "Academic Freedom and the Common Good: A Review Essay." *AAUP Journal of Academic Freedom* 7, https://www.aaup.org/reports-publications/.

Rudolph, Frederick. 1962. "Academic Man." In *The American College and University: A History*, 394–416. New York: Random House.

Schrecker, Ellen W. 1986. *No Ivory Tower: McCarthyism and the Universities*. Oxford: Oxford University Press.

Slaughter, Sheila. 2011. "Academic Freedom, Professional Autonomy, and the State." In Joseph C. Hermanowicz (ed.), *The American Academic Profession: Transformation in Contemporary Higher Education*, 241–273. Baltimore: Johns Hopkins University Press.

Thelin, John R. 2017a. "Progressivism and the Professionalization of Professors." *Journal of the Gilded Age and Progressive Era* 16(1):103–104.

Thelin, John R. 2017b. "Faculty and the Academic Profession." In *American Higher Education: Issues and Institutions*, 95–121. New York: Routledge.

Thelin, John R. 2011. "Colleges in the Colonial Era." In *A History of American Higher Education*, 1–40. Baltimore: Johns Hopkins University Press.

Thelin, John R. 2010. "Horizontal History and Higher Education." In Marybeth Gasman (ed.), *The History of U.S. Higher Education: Methods for Understanding the Past*, 71–83. London: Routledge.

Tiede, Hans-Joerg. 2018. "The Front Rank: On Tenure and the Role of the Faculty in the Defense of Academic Freedom." *History of Education Quarterly* 53(3):441–447.

Tiede, Hans-Joerg. 2015. *University Reform: The Founding of the American Association of University Professors*. Baltimore: Johns Hopkins University Press.

Tolley, Kim (ed.). 2018. *Professors in the Gig Economy: Unionizing Adjunct Faculty in America*. Baltimore: Johns Hopkins University Press.

Veblen, Thorstein. [1915] 2015. *The Higher Learning in America: A Memorandum on the Conduct of Universities by Business Men*, annotated edition. Baltimore: Johns Hopkins University Press.

Veysey, Laurence R. 1965. *The Emergence of the American University*. Chicago: University of Chicago Press.

Williamson-Lott, Joy Ann. 2018. "Protecting Academic Freedom: Using the Past to Chart a Path to the Future." *History of Education Quarterly* 53(3):420–422.

CHAPTER 4

Extramural Speech, Academic Freedom, and the AAUP

An Historical Account

Hans-Joerg Tiede

Introduction

Since its founding in 1915, the American Association of University Professors (AAUP) has, under the umbrella of academic freedom, included the speech of faculty members in their role as citizens—speech that may be unrelated to their scholarly expertise.[1] This position, however, has long been considered controversial. It has frequently been challenged, including, famously, by the late eminent constitutional scholar and former AAUP president William Van Alstyne (1972), and such challenges continue to this day. At a time when posts by faculty members on Facebook and Twitter about topics ranging from politics to gender to race relations regularly bring about campaigns of targeted harassment against them and their institutions, those who would challenge the notion that these expressions are protected by academic freedom point to the fact that they are unrelated to teaching or research. Why should speech that is not linked to these core professorial functions be protected by academic freedom? Another question relates to the extent to which a faculty member's speech as a citizen is protected under principles of academic freedom. Under what circumstances may institutions discipline faculty members for transgressing limitations—which the AAUP recognizes—to this freedom?

The American conception of academic freedom has a long and storied history that predates, by many decades, its judicial recognition under the First Amendment and has developed largely outside of the legal realm. Arguably, by the time the US Supreme Court recognized academic freedom as a "special concern of the First Amendment," this concept was fully formed. That is not to say that court decisions acknowledging either the principle of academic freedom or the AAUP standards that define it are unimportant, but merely that the prevailing perception of academic freedom in the United States, which was developed and advanced by the AAUP, is not based on such court decisions. That construct, which has its main historical origins in the 1890s, defines academic freedom as one that is extended to members of the professoriate—consisting of freedom of research, freedom in the classroom, and freedom of extramural utterances—and is subject to certain limitations, such as the obligations imposed by professional ethics (Metzger 1961).

Historian Walter Metzger (1967, 70) has called the inclusion of freedom of extramural utterance as a third constitutive element "the distinctively American contribution to the theory of academic freedom." The explicit recognition of this freedom, in its full form, originated in the AAUP's foundational document, the 1915 "Declaration of Principles on Academic Freedom and Academic Tenure" (AAUP 2015a). Its subsequent inclusion in the "Statement of Principles on Academic Freedom and Tenure" (AAUP 1940), jointly formulated by the AAUP and the Association of American Colleges (now the Association of American Colleges and Universities), was the result of negotiations and compromises between the two associations. One central subject concerned the limits of academic freedom, and a famous case on that issue in the 1960s caused the AAUP to examine the meaning of the 1940 compromise. Both that compromise and its subsequent clarification—formulated in the 1960s and subsequently further revised by the AAUP's

Standing Committee A on Academic Freedom and Tenure (AAUP 2018)—continue to serve to this day as the association's most authoritative policy pronouncements on the freedom of extramural speech and its limits.[2]

This chapter traces the historical developments summarized above. It focuses on three aspects of extramural speech: its definition, the justification for its protection under the principle of academic freedom, and the conditions under which it can give rise to institutional sanctions. Its main argument, which contradicts other accounts, is that the AAUP's understanding of extramural speech has changed very little throughout its history.

The Magna Carta of the Profession

Since its inception, the AAUP has defined, advanced, and protected academic freedom, primarily through legislative and judicial activities. The association's legislative actions have taken the form of policy documents and reports, and its judicial ones have taken the form of investigations of violations of individual faculty members' academic freedom and tenure. During the last century, these activities helped bring about a wider understanding and acceptance of academic freedom in US higher education.

The 1915 "Declaration of Principles on Academic Freedom and Academic Tenure" is the greatest accomplishment of the AAUP's first year (AAUP 2015a), and it still provides the primary foundation for the American conception of academic freedom. At the AAUP's second annual meeting, which adopted the declaration, a delegate called it "the Magna Carta of the profession." The primary authors of the 1915 "Declaration" were Columbia University economics professor Edwin Seligman, the chair of the AAUP's Committee on Academic Freedom and Tenure, and Johns Hopkins University philosophy professor Arthur Lovejoy, the association's main founder and first secretary. The inclusion of freedom of extramural speech and the extension of that freedom to speech unrelated to scholarly expertise are among the most important of the contributions the "Declaration" made to the American theory of academic freedom (AAUP 2015a).[3]

When the modern understanding of academic freedom began to take shape in the 1890s, extramural (i.e., outside the walls) speech was understood only as the freedom of faculty members to speak off campus on matters that were *within* their areas of scholarly expertise—a position in sharp contrast to some modern conceptions of extramural speech that seek to restrict it to speech that pertains to matters generally *outside* of faculty members' areas of scholarly expertise. The academic freedom *causes célèbres* of the Gilded Age—such as the cases of Benjamin Andrews at Brown University and Edward Ross at Stanford—had involved extramural utterances by social scientists whose speech was related to their scholarly expertise (for Andrews it was the gold standard, and for Ross, immigration). Cases such as these provided the basis for the concept of extramural speech at the time of the AAUP's founding. Whether academic freedom should be extended to areas outside of a faculty member's disciplinary expertise was, however, subject to debate (Tiede 2015, 22–44).

The question of the boundaries of extramural speech was thus still unsettled when a predecessor statement to the 1915 "Declaration" asked, "If the biologist should give a public address on some economic question or if the physicist should take part in a political campaign, ought interference with this to be considered as an infringement of academic freedom?" To this question, the authors of the 1915 "Declaration," many of whom had served on the committee that authored the earlier statement, responded, "It is not, in this committee's opinion, desirable that scholars should be debarred from giving expression to their judgments upon controversial questions, or that their freedom of speech, outside the university, should be limited to questions falling within their own specialties." And so, they concluded, "academic freedom in this sense comprises three elements: freedom of inquiry and research; freedom of teaching within the university or college; and freedom of extra-mural utterance and action" (Joint Committee 1915, 319; Tiede 2015, 59–74).

Lovejoy, who is credited with persuading his skeptical colleagues on the committee to enlarge the conception of extramural speech, in 1916 offered a rationale for this enlargement in a spirited exchange with AAUP president and Northwestern law school dean John Wigmore that took place in the pages of *The Nation*. Lovejoy observed that restricting freedom of extramural utterance to matters related to a faculty member's expertise would "make it possible for trustees who wished to eliminate from an institution an economist of whose economic views they disapproved to dismiss [that economist] because of an allegation of disagreement between their views and his own on political science or on the theory of evolution." He summed up his position as follows: "In order effectually to protect the investigator within his special province, you must protect him outside of it also" (Lovejoy 1916).

The "Declaration" itself offered three rationales for having championed extramural speech as protected under principles of academic freedom (AAUP 2015a, 4, 10–11). These range from the pragmatic ("All five of the cases which have recently been investigated by committees of this Association have involved, at least as one factor, the right of university teachers to express their opinions freely outside the university or to engage in political activities in their capacity as citizens") to the individual ("it is neither possible nor desirable to deprive a college professor of the political rights vouchsafed to every citizen") and the institutional ("in matters of opinion, and of the utterance of opinion, [governing] boards cannot intervene without destroying, to the extent of their intervention, the essential nature of a university").

The committee also reflected on limitations to the freedom of extramural utterance and observed, "It is obvious that academic teachers are under a peculiar obligation to avoid hasty or unverified or exaggerated statements, and to refrain from intemperate or sensational modes of expression." It hastened to add that disciplinary actions in response to professorial departures from these and other restrictions "cannot with safety be taken by bodies not composed of members of the academic profession" (AAUP 2015a, 10). The 1915 "Declaration" thus established the basis for our contemporary understanding of freedom of extramural utterance, its scope, and its limits, and it provided a mechanism for enforcing these limits.

The Scope of Extramural Speech

Before continuing to the next important historical milestone, it may be useful to consider recent developments in the definition of extramural speech. While the term "extramural" was intended to be understood literally in the 1915 "Declaration," the definition would undergo some changes, and by the time of the 1940 "Statement of Principles" (to be discussed next), the AAUP and Association of American Colleges defined it as a faculty member's speech "as a citizen." Although the two definitions seemingly differ, they share one important aspect: neither employs the *subject matter* of the speech to define it as extramural, an approach that has been challenged by some contemporary theorists of academic freedom.

In a recent book on the professional conception of academic freedom, much of which is informed by the AAUP's policies, Matthew Finkin and Robert Post (2009, 127) define freedom of extramural utterance as "speech made by faculty in their capacity as citizens, speech that is typically about matters of public concern and that is unrelated to either scholarly expertise or institutional affiliation." Although they cite AAUP policy statements throughout, this definition does not coincide with the AAUP's understanding of extramural speech, which can be documented by considering AAUP reports of investigations involving dismissals of faculty members because of their extramural utterances.

In the 1958 case of Professor Bud Hutchinson at Alabama Polytechnic Institute (now Auburn University) and, much more recently, the 2011 case of Professor Ivor Van Heerden at Louisiana State University, the AAUP's investigating committees found that faculty members' speech was protected as extramural utterance, even though it was related to scholarly expertise. In the Hutchinson case, the committee classified a letter on school desegregation that Hutchinson had sent to the student paper as extramural speech, but it found that, because Hutchinson was a social scientist, his letter also fell under the aegis of teaching. Similarly, the investigating committee classified Van Heerden's public statements about levies built by the US Army Corps of Engineers as extramural, while finding it difficult to identify "the boundary between freedom of research and publication and freedom of extramural speech," since he was a coastal geologist and hurricane researcher. These cases illustrate that classifying speech as extramural can be challenging when it is related to scholarly expertise, but what is important to note is that the AAUP has consistently held that an utterance cannot be denied extramural status merely because it is related to one's disciplinary expertise (Oberst and Easton 1958; AAUP Committee A 2011).

The second restriction mentioned by Finkin and Post (2009) is that extramural utterances are "typically about matters of public concern" (which, of course, does not explicitly preclude their not being about such concerns). The US Supreme Court's identification of a limited First Amendment protection for expressions by public employees on matters of public interest in *Pickering* (1968) has repeatedly raised questions about the relationship between such speech and the AAUP's conception of extramural speech. That potential relationship was explicitly addressed in the association's 1970 investigation of the case of Professor Marshall Jones at the University of Florida. There, its administration took the position that Jones's speech on the issue of civil rights could neither be classified as extramural nor regarded as addressing a matter of public interest. The investigating committee disagreed with both claims but further asserted that the AAUP's conception of extramural speech "is not limited in scope to statements on matters of public interest" (AAUP Committee A 1970).

The historical development of the definition of extramural utterance within the AAUP and its application to specific instances of faculty speech in investigative reports make clear that the AAUP's understanding of extramural speech includes not only expressions related to a faculty member's scholarly expertise, but also expressions unrelated to "matters of public interest or concern." Moreover, no AAUP investigative report, as far as I am aware, has deemed any utterances of a faculty member speaking outside his or her capacity as a faculty member as "not extramural." As Walter Metzger (1988, 1275) observed, "By dividing this Gaul into three main parts, the [1915 "Declaration"] provided in effect that academic freedom applied to a certain class of persons, no matter how they chose to express themselves, rather than to certain types of expression found in the repertory of that class." Thus the AAUP's conception of extramural speech apparently simply amounts to speech not made in one's capacity as a faculty member—that is, what remains when freedom of research and of teaching are subtracted.

The 1940 "Statement of Principles"

While the 1915 "Declaration" was a unilateral effort, soon after its adoption, the AAUP's leaders began to pursue opportunities to formulate principles of academic freedom jointly with associations of administrators. These initial efforts resulted in the 1925 "Conference Statement on Academic Freedom and Tenure," which involved the American Council on Education (ACE), the Association of American Colleges (AAC), and several other associations. The primary participants in the development of the 1925 "Conference Statement," however, were the AAUP and the AAC, and negotiations over a statement on academic freedom between only these two associations began in 1934 and continued, off and on, until the end of 1940. These negotiations had two primary areas of focus: (1) establishing a new tenure system, in which tenure was independent of rank and was universally acquired after a probationary period of fixed length; and (2) providing admonitions on how faculty members should conduct themselves when speaking extramurally, or, as that statement referred to it, "as a citizen" (Metzger 1990; Tiede 2015, 212–13).

In the mid-1930s, because of the political and economic circumstances of the Great Depression, both tenure and extramural speech had risen to the top of the list of issues that concerned both the AAUP and the AAC. The Depression had severely affected the academic job market. Opportunities for promotion, which was the only way faculty members could obtain tenure under the prevailing system, became highly limited, stranding a large percentage of the professoriate in insecure term appointments. Moreover, US higher education experienced a Red Scare in 1935 that University of Buffalo chancellor Samuel Capen put into broader historical context—which still seem strikingly relevant today (Tiede 2018)—in the following remarks:

> [Universities] are always on the firing line, because they take all human experience as their province and recognize no limitation of their right to inquire and to discover, to discuss and to analyze. They are on the firing line and from time to time they are under heavy fire. That always happens when public passions are aroused, when considerable bodies of people are obsessed by fears, when social change is in process and is being actively promoted by one part of the population and stubbornly resisted by another.
>
> This is one of those times. Social change is going on and fear is rife in nearly all the democratic countries . . . Hardly a week goes by that the public prints do not report some attack on the intellectual activities of universities made somewhere in the United States. These institutions are charged with harboring dangerous radicals, with teaching socialism or pacifism or atheism or communism or all of them together . . . They are threatened with repressive legislation, or with boycott by one group or another of the population. Or some group of the population insists on the dismissal of teachers whose opinions on controversial public questions are different from the opinions to which the group itself subscribes. (Capen 1935, 597)

Capen was among the presidents who served on the AAC commission that negotiated the 1940 statement. Both he and Brown University president Henry Wriston, who chaired the commission, were strong advocates for academic freedom both within the negotiations and in national debates at the time. But while Capen and Wriston sought to protect faculty members from outside demands for their dismissal, other members of the AAC's commission were more intent on protecting their institutions and establishing grounds for disciplining faculty members.

The AAUP-AAC negotiations yielded a "Statement of Principles, 1938" concerning academic freedom and tenure that asserted the following:

> 3. The college or university teacher is a citizen, a member of a learned profession, and an officer of an educational institution. When he speaks or writes as a citizen, he should be free from institutional censorship or discipline, but his special position in the community imposes special obligations. As a man of learning and an educational officer, he should remember that the public may judge his profession and his institution by his utterances. Hence he should at all times be accurate, should exercise appropriate restraint, should show respect for the opinions of others, and should make every effort to indicate that he is not an institutional spokesman. The judgment of what constitutes fulfillment of these obligations should rest with the individual. ("Statement of Principles" 1939, 27)

The final sentence of this paragraph would become a lightning rod, attracting criticism that undermined the viability of the statement as a whole. That sentence, which was to be abandoned eventually, would have made the standards of faculty responsibility in cases involving extramural utterances unenforceable by institutional sanctions. Even though the inclusion of the final sentence was championed by a majority of the AAC commission, including Capen and Wriston, a vocal minority was strongly against it. Earlham College president William C. Dennis, in particular, objected to its inclusion during the negotiations and sought to convince the annual meeting of the AAC to oppose it with him. As Dennis observed at the meeting ("Remarks" 1939, 185): "The Statement has successfully marched up the hill and down again. It has formulated rights and expressly withheld remedies. It has declared duties and expressly negatived the idea of penalties. It has defied universal experience and violated elementary justice by making the teacher the judge in his own case . . . The Statement says that a teacher even though he is speaking as a citizen, should speak like a scholar and a gentleman. And then . . . it says there is nothing that can be done about it if he doesn't!"

Following Dennis's lead, the AAC's membership refused to accept the final sentence and voted to refer the entire 1938 statement back to its commission. This was a tremendous setback, as the AAUP had already approved it. The AAC commission subsequently deleted the sentence, and the AAC's annual meeting approved the revised statement in 1940. The revision also deleted language that fixed the length of the probationary period, which had been another area of disagreement at the meeting. Both changes jeopardized the future of the statement as a joint agreement (Wriston 1940).

The AAC and AAUP delegations met again in late 1940 to try to iron out their differences. Prior to the meeting, Ralph Himstead, the AAUP's general secretary, identified in a meeting of the AAUP's governing council what he saw as the AAUP's priorities: "I don't think that the deletion of [the final] sentence will make a whole lot of difference in the long run. The thing that is important is the length of the probationary period, without which the rest of this is just so much pious language" (AAUP records 1940a). The final negotiations resulted in a compromise under which the concluding sentence on extramural speech remained deleted, a probationary period of fixed length returned to the statement, and three "interpretations" were affixed to it, the last of which read:

> If the administration of a college or university feels that a teacher has not observed the admonitions of paragraph 3 of the section on Academic Freedom and believes that the extramural utterances of the teacher have been such as to raise grave doubts concerning the teacher's fitness for his or her position, it may proceed to file charges under paragraph 4 of the section on Academic Tenure. In pressing such charges, the administration should remember that teachers are citizens and should be accorded the freedom of citizens. In such cases the administration must assume full responsibility, and the American Association of University Professors and the Association of American Colleges are free to make an investigation. (AAUP Committee A 1943, 80)

It is worth noting that this interpretation makes the admonitions of paragraph 3 of the 1940 statement subject to enforcement *only* when the extramural utterances "have been such as to raise grave doubts concerning the teacher's fitness for his or her position." The wording of the interpretation dates back to the 1925 "Conference Statement" (cited in AAUP Committee A 1943, 76), which had specified the following: "If the extra-mural utterances of a teacher should be such as to raise grave doubts concerning his fitness for his position, the question should in all cases be submitted to an appropriate committee of the faculty of which he is a member."[4]

Thus the insistence on *professional fitness* as the criterion for determining when an institution can impose sanctions on a faculty member for extramural utterances has been an element of AAUP policy since 1925. It is only fair to note, however, that although the interpretation was, in fact, unambiguous as to this condition, the document, as subsequently approved by both parties as the 1940 statement, was perhaps less clear in this regard than it could have been, because the admonitions regarding extramural speech and their enforceability were not included in the body of that statement. Instead, the interpretations were printed as notes following the text. Thus readers not fully informed of the history of the statement's development could not be faulted for concluding that a mere failure to adhere to the admonitions might be sanctionable. To this day, administrations cite the admonitions when disciplining faculty members for their extramural utterances. In fact, immediately after agreeing to the compromise during the final negotiations, President Dennis had to be reminded by a fellow member of the AAC commission that in order to dismiss a faculty member because of an extramural utterance, the utterance would have to be "not merely foolish," but would have to render the faculty member "useless" (AAUP records 1940b).

The Applicability of the Admonitions

In the decades following the adoption of the 1940 statement, several investigations involved charges against faculty members for having violated one or more of the admonitions, including the 1949 investigation at Evansville College and the above-cited one at Alabama Polytechnic Institute. In each case, however, the investigating committee found that no violation of the admonitions had occurred and, therefore, did not assess whether the purported violation was related to the faculty member's fitness.

In the Evansville College situation, which involved the dismissal of Professor George Parker for campaigning for presidential candidate Henry Wallace, the investigative report commented on the administration's claim that Parker had failed "to exercise appropriate restraint," because "he did not so far restrain himself as to avoid all public participation in the Wallace campaign." As the investigating committee found: "To condemn such participation as a violation of the 'appropriate restraint' clause of the 1940 *Statement of Principles* is to wrest the plain meaning of that admonition, which occurs in a context of the teacher's proper behavior 'when he speaks or writes as a citizen'—a phrase which implies the expectation that he will, or at least may, speak or write as a citizen. The evidence indicates that . . . Professor Parker did exercise appropriate restraint and that his dismissal cannot be justified on the ground that his public utterances violated this or any other admonition of the 1940 *Statement of Principles*" (AAUP Committee A 1949).

Similarly, in the Alabama Polytechnic report, the committee addressed at length charges that Professor Hutchinson had violated "the canons of appropriate restraint and proper respect for the opinions of others." In particular, the trustees objected to the following sentence of Hutchinson's letter: "But if assignment and re-zoning are necessary to carry out the task of educating the children of New York, all the children, black or white, rich or poor, then assignment and re-zoning must be supported by all who sincerely believe in education and social justice." In response to the trustees' statement that this sentence was "more emotional than intellectual, more exhortation than communication of knowledge and research," the investigating committee wrote:

> But academic freedom does not exist to protect only dry detailing of facts, and professors must have leeway to speak with vigor and

conviction . . . To be sure, the question of what restraint is "appropriate" cannot be settled in a vacuum. Discussion of the issue of school segregation is charged with even more serious perils of attack on universities in the South than was the issue of national security elsewhere between 1950 and 1955 . . . It must be recognized that academic freedom cannot be measured or limited by vague threats to the welfare of an institution or a community which may or may not result from what a professor says or does. If a professor must hold his tongue lest he cause an alumnus to withhold a gift, a legislator to vote against an appropriation, a student not to register, or a citizen's feelings to be ruffled, he will be free to talk only to himself. (Oberst and Easton 1958, 167)

"The Sort of Case That Tries Men's Souls": The Koch Case

AAUP general secretary Himstead's 1940 prediction that the excision of the final sentence from the paragraph on extramural speech would not "make a whole lot of difference in the long run" turned out to be mistaken. A 1960 case at the University of Illinois provoked sharp controversy within the association about the meaning of that paragraph. It drew national attention, and disagreement about the case within Committee A placed it on the committee's agenda for the better part of two years.

The Koch case has an iconic status in the historiography of academic freedom, not only because of its details, but also because of its oft-cited status as a supposed turning point in the development of the AAUP's views on extramural utterances. In an addendum to the investigating committee's report, Committee A asserted that the 1940 statement permits institutions to discipline faculty members for extramural utterances that violate standards of academic responsibility—by which it meant the admonitions contained in that statement. The committee then issued a policy document on extramural utterances the following year that some have construed as retreating from this very assertion. There are good reasons to doubt this interpretation, not least because Committee A itself claimed that it was not doing anything other than restating the association's long-standing position, dating back to the 1925 "Conference Statement."

In 1960, the student newspaper at the University of Illinois printed a letter by Leo Koch, an assistant professor of botany, which caused an uproar on campus and throughout the state and led to Koch's dismissal. Koch's letter, which decried sexual double standards and endorsed premarital sex between college students, concluded with the following two paragraphs:

> With modern contraceptives and medical advice readily available at the nearest drugstore, or at least a family physician, there is no valid reason why sexual intercourse should not be condoned among those sufficiently mature to engage in it without social consequences and without violating their own codes of morality and ethics.
>
> A mutually satisfactory sexual experience would eliminate the need for many hours of frustrating petting and lead to much happier and longer lasting marriages among our younger men and women. (AAUP Committee A 1963, 26)

University of Illinois president David D. Henry condemned Koch's letter, calling his views "offensive and repugnant," as well as "contrary to commonly accepted standards of morality." He added that "their public espousal may be interpreted as encouragement of immoral behavior." President Henry decided to suspend Koch immediately and announced the termination of his appointment at the end of the academic year, on the grounds that the letter had violated standards of academic responsibility (AAUP Committee A 1963, 28–29).

Following the president's announcement, Koch sought a hearing before the faculty senate's committee on academic freedom. The committee asserted Koch's right to make statements that were "contrary to commonly accepted standards of morality," but, finding the manner in which he had expressed himself to have violated standards of academic responsibility, it recommended that he be reprimanded. This hearing was followed by another before the university's governing board, which overturned the faculty committee's recommendation and upheld the president's decision to dismiss Koch (AAUP Committee A 1963, 31).

Committee A's lengthy deliberations on the case concerned the position taken by the investigating committee, chaired by Yale law professor Thomas Emerson. In the report it submitted for Committee A's consideration, the investigating committee took issue with the AAUP-AAC interpretation of the 1940 statement and argued that the admonitions on extramural speech in the statement were ambiguous. It was not clear, according to the investigating committee's reading, whether these adjurations were merely hortatory or "a standard for the application of discipline," including reprimands. The investigating committee also held that the AAUP-AAC's interpretation of the admonitions was internally inconsistent if it were read to allow for the application of discipline, and that it therefore could only be reasonably construed to have left their ambiguity "unresolved." The investigating committee concluded that the interpretation's reference to the "freedom of citizens" meant "university discipline cannot be applied where legal sanctions would not be," a principle they declared to be "the sound one and the only one consistent with the attainment of academic freedom" (AAUP Committee A 1963, 38).

Because of the position taken by the investigative committee, Committee A, in deliberating on the report, concerned itself less with the question of the specific conditions under which faculty responsibility in cases involving extramural utterances was enforceable by institutional sanctions, including reprimands, and more with whether faculty members could *ever* be disciplined for extramural utterances under the 1940 statement and its interpretation. This distinction is crucial for understanding subsequent developments, as Committee A would come to be faulted for neglecting to stress the former over the latter in its response to the Koch case.

Following year-long deliberations, Committee A concluded, on the basis of the history of the adoption of the 1940 statement, that an institution *could* enforce faculty responsibility in cases involving extramural utterances. Since it did not concur with the Emerson committee's full investigative report, Committee A published the report in two parts. The first consisted of those findings of the investigating committee with which Committee A agreed. The second contained the investigating committee's findings on the matter of "academic responsibility," presented as a statement of the investigating committee only. Committee A then attached its rebuttal of the latter. Because Committee A had not been unanimous in disagreeing with the Emerson committee's report, its rebuttal was followed by a dissent written by Oberlin College English professor Warren Taylor and a concurring opinion by Indiana University law professor Ralph Fuchs. Columbia University history professor Walter Metzger requested to be recorded as "not voting" (AAUP Committee A 1963, 41).

In a later article about the Koch case, Metzger explained why he could see both sides of the argument but felt unable to come down on one side or the other:

> On the one hand, I could see good reasons for not conceding to administrators the right to police a teacher's public words . . . When a university punishes professors for certain utterances, it . . . entraps itself in the paradox of being ever more compromised the more it struggles against being compromised . . . But the arguments I could muster against the Emerson position were of equal power. In [Emerson's] AAUP report . . . he proposed a kind of exclusionary rule: an administration, or a faculty, may never use the public expressions of a professor against him, no matter how they reflect on his mentality or character. I could not agree that such evidence was inadmissible in a dismissal trial. (Metzger 1965, 30)

Metzger went on to propose a different rationale for including extramural speech under the umbrella of academic freedom. He suggested that the purpose for its inclusion was to "open a door" rather than to "create an exemption": "To hold that professors retained the rights of citizens . . . was to say that the norms of neutrality and obedience, which were binding on the professor as pedagogue and bureaucrat, did not apply to the professor as a public man; but it did not say that the professor as a public man was bound by nothing but his own sense of propriety (Metzger 1965, 30)."[5]

In its rebuttal to the report of the investigating committee, Committee A observed:

> The Administration of the University of Illinois did not err in proceeding on the assumption that a violation of academic responsibility on the part of a faculty member fell within the disciplinary powers of the institution. Committee A also concludes that the University of Illinois Senate Committee on Academic Freedom had jurisdiction in this case.
>
> Whether one agrees with the Illinois Senate Committee that Professor Koch violated proper standards of academic responsibility, and therefore should have been reprimanded, or with the *ad hoc* committee that there was no violation of academic responsibility, it is clear to Committee A that the sanction of discharge was outrageously severe and completely unwarranted.
>
> Committee A does not conceive it to be its function to decide independently whether the *ad hoc* committee or the Illinois Senate Committee is correct in its assessment of Professor Koch's action. Reasonable minds dedicated to intellectual freedom could—and do—differ on this issue. The important point is not that there are differences of opinion concerning the question [of] whether Professor Koch's action warranted imposition of the sanction of reprimand or whether his action did not justify imposition of any sanction whatsoever. The crucial fact is the unanimous agreement of the Illinois Senate Committee, the *ad hoc* committee, and Committee A that Professor Koch should not have been discharged. (Committee A 1963, 41)

Committee A justified its disagreement with the Emerson committee's contention that "the notion of academic responsibility, when the faculty member is speaking as a citizen, is intended to be an admonition rather than a standard for the application of discipline" by citing the language of the 1925 "Conference Statement" on professional fitness and by referring to the AAUP-AAC's interpretation. Recognizing that "institutions may abuse the power to discipline faculty members for established breaches of academic responsibility," Committee A nevertheless insisted: "The possibility that power may be abused is not a proper ground for denying its existence. The remedy is, instead, insistence on proper procedural safeguards, a highly significant role for the faculty in the exercise of the power, and a vigilant oversight by this Association. Oversight by the Association in this sensitive area will, of course, include examination and review of faculty as well as administrative action" (AAUP Committee A 1963, 41).

Nonetheless, Committee A made what, in retrospect, appears to have been a blunder. When it concluded that administrations have "the power to discipline faculty members for established breaches of academic responsibility," it failed to reiterate that exercising this power required the administration to demonstrate the professional unfitness of the faculty member, although it had cited this long-standing AAUP position earlier. Again, this conclusion, like the interpretation of the 1940 statement itself, was expressed less clearly than it could have been. As a result, Warren Taylor considered it to constitute the establishment of a new, separate standard for the imposition of discipline, unrelated to professional fitness, which led him to take strong exception to the majority opinion. He concluded his dissent by pointing to "the victims of 'standards of discipline' in the expression of opinion from Socrates and Jesus and Joan of Arc to the victims of the Alien and Sedition Laws of 1798, the Espionage Act of 1917, and the Sedition Act of 1918 on to the victims of totalitarian coercion of opinion during this century." He then added: "There is no need now to seek or to create a new standard to silence teachers. To fire a teacher for his utterances the administrator cannot rely on such an ambiguous test as that of 'academic responsibility.' The opinions of a teacher as citizen are not enough to justify termination. The administrator will have to establish proof that beyond the utterance lies unfitness to teach: professional incompetence, dereliction of duty" (AAUP Committee A 1963, 42–43).

Strangely, however, during the three meetings in which Committee A discussed the Emerson committee's report, Taylor never raised this specific objection and, in the last meeting prior to the report's publication, simply expressed agreement with the Emerson committee in that a faculty member may never be dismissed because of an extramural utterance. It appears, then, that Taylor formulated his specific objection after the final Committee A meeting, in which the Koch case was discussed, and asked for it to be attached to Committee A's rebuttal. In any event, it is not difficult to conceive how, by perusing his dissent, together with the statement by Committee A on the matter the following year, a disinterested observer might conclude that the committee had changed its position and had come to agree with Taylor (AAUP records n.d.)—except that, in my opinion, this is not what occurred.

Following the 1963 publication of its report on the Koch case, Committee A's rebuttal of the Emerson committee's report provoked opposition within the association, some of which was expressed in letters to the editor of the *AAUP Bulletin.* Speaking at the 1963 annual meeting, Committee A chair and University of Wisconsin political science professor David Fellman (1963, 127) acknowledged the strong responses the case had elicited on all sides of the issue: "I am resigned to the fact that, as in most hard cases, we cannot hope to please everyone, and that any position will run into opposition. If I may paraphrase Tom Paine, this is the sort of case that tries men's souls." At that meeting, the University of Illinois's AAUP chapter presented a resolution asking the association to amend the 1940 statement, "so that enforcement of the standard of academic responsibility stated therein would constitute a solely self-governing function of the academic profession." The delegates referred the resolution to Committee A for further consideration.

At its next meeting, Committee A did discuss the resolution of the Illinois chapter but decided that it could not accede to the chapter's request, citing the association's inability to unilaterally amend the jointly approved 1940 statement. In his report to the 1964 annual meeting, Fellman offered a lengthy rationale for the committee's decision. He acknowledged that the 1940 statement had called attention to special obligations of faculty members, but he cautioned that "the Association ha[d] never established these obligations as standards of academic responsibility which, when proved to be violated, permit an administration to take action against a teacher without further academic procedures." He then added:

> Unethical conduct of the kind implied by violation of obligations is not punishable without further judgment; such conduct, if it is to be assessed, may of course become a basis for charges in established procedures designed to try issues of termination for cause. As Committee A emphasized in the Koch case, in all cases involving such charges, the hearing must be conducted by an appropriate faculty committee, preferably an elected committee free of administration domination or control. *It was also stressed that the administration, in considering whether or not to prefer charges, and the faculty committee, in deliberating on the evidence, should bear in mind that only demonstrated lack of professional fitness for the position can constitute grounds for dismissal.* Accordingly, an expression of opinion can be taken into account only insofar as it relates to the faculty member's fitness for his position. Furthermore, in precisely such cases the conclusions and recommendations of the faculty hearing committee should be decisive, and should not be set aside or rejected by the governing board except for special and very weighty considerations. It follows that in the absence of serious evidence of unfitness, the administration should not prefer charges. (Fellman 1964, 129–30, emphasis added)

Although Fellman did not engage with Taylor's dissent directly, his report made it clear that Committee A's stance in the report on the Koch case was the long-standing position of the AAUP. The 1964 Fellman report served as the basis for the "Statement on Extramural Utterances" that Committee A subsequently adopted (AAUP 2015b). Fellman also reported that Committee A favored attempting to renegotiate the 1940 statement "along the lines indicated by the Illinois resolution," and that the association's governing council had authorized the conduct of negotiations to that end (Fellman 1964, 129–30). These negotiations would subsequently lead to a set of interpretive comments to the 1940 statement that, as I will recount below, failed to modify the statement's position on extramural speech—or on any other of its positions, for that matter.

The "Committee A Statement on Extramural Utterances" and the 1970 Interpretive Comments

Although Committee A had already spent an immense amount of time discussing the Koch case, after the 1964 annual meeting, its members decided to issue a version of Fellman's report as the committee's statement on the topic of extramural utterances. In order to stress that this statement was merely a clarification—rather than a unilateral modification—of existing association policy, the committee chose not to submit the statement to the AAUP's governing council for approval.

The headnote of the "Committee A Statement on Extramural Utterances" explained its purpose: "to clarify those sections of the 1940 *Statement of Principles on Academic Freedom and Tenure* relating to the faculty member's exercise of his freedom of speech as a citizen." The Committee A statement then identified a "controlling principle":

> A faculty member's expression of opinion as a citizen cannot constitute grounds for dismissal unless it clearly demonstrates the faculty member's unfitness to serve. Extramural utterances rarely bear upon the faculty member's fitness for continuing service. Moreover, a final decision should take into account the faculty member's entire record as a teacher and scholar. In the absence of weighty evidence of unfitness, the administration should not prefer charges; and if it is not clearly proved in the hearing that the faculty member is unfit to continue, the faculty committee should make a finding in favor of the faculty member concerned. (AAUP 2015b)

What was the response to Committee A's promulgation of its statement on extramural utterances? In a word, disappointment. None other than a university president, J. W. Maucker of the University of Northern Iowa, took aim at the statement in 1968 and opined, upon being bestowed the AAUP's Alexander Meiklejohn Award for contributions to academic freedom:

> "Unfitness" is a slippery word. This is exactly what John Q. Public says: "Professor X is unfit because he advocates an immoral and dangerous

> doctrine and he has done so in harsh or intemperate or scathing or disgusting language. This is no way for a professor to act. How can his students respect him? Consequently you must, by your own doctrine, discipline him." The 1964 AAUP statement goes on to say, "Extramural utterances rarely bear upon the faculty member's fitness for his position." But the allegation that it doesn't happen very often provides little help in a specific case. The crucial question remains: By what criteria are we to identify that rare extramural utterance which the AAUP statement indicates may properly be used to demonstrate a faculty member's unfitness for his position? ("Tenth Alexander Meiklejohn Award" 1968, 254)

The previous year, an article in the *AAUP Bulletin* called Committee A's invocation of rarity to limit the applicability of its own provision a disingenuous tactic "to evade the consequences" of insisting on the special obligations of the profession (Schier 1967, 26). Even the AAUP's own self-study committee, on the event of the association's fiftieth anniversary in 1965, concluded, as Fellman had in 1964, that "a rediscussion of the 1940 *Statement* should be undertaken," and that "it would be highly desirable if [the admonitions on extramural speech] could be clarified and restated in a mutually acceptable manner" (Fellman et al. 1965, 148), which clearly meant that the self-study committee considered the statement on extramural utterances not to have accomplished that task.

A restatement of the admonitions, however, never came to pass. While a full history of the 1970 interpretive comments on the 1940 statement cannot be attempted here, it appears that the AAUP entered into negotiations with the AAC in hopes of significantly revising several thorny provisions of the 1940 statement. Those hopes were not to be fulfilled. Instead of rewriting the admonitions along the lines of the Illinois chapter's resolution, as Fellman had proposed at the 1964 annual meeting, negotiations with the AAC regarding extramural speech resulted only in the insertion of the "Committee A Statement on Extramural Utterances" into a footnote, as one of the 1970 interpretive comments. If the Committee A statement had not modified the 1940 statement materially, then clearly its incorporation into latter did not, either. Similar interpretive comments were inserted in other places. Whether *any* of the interpretive comments resulted in material changes to the 1940 statement is a matter of debate. That they were approved only by the AAUP, and not by the AAC, led a subcommittee of Committee A (on the topic of the applicability of the 1940 statement to religious institutions) to subsequently conclude that they should not be regarded as having constituted a change in association policy (Kadish 1970, 167–68; AAUP 1988).

This failure to modify the AAUP's long-standing position on extramural speech was acknowledged in two prominent early assessments. The authors of these assessments viewed the statement on extramural utterances as Committee A's having reverted from the position it had taken in its report on the Koch case to the original, literal position of the 1940 statement, a position Committee A had, in their view, failed to acknowledge in the Koch report. Thus the AAUP's report on the dismissal of Angela Davis from UCLA described the statement on extramural utterances as having "substantially moved [from the position in the Koch case's report] to the position we believe implicit in the 1940 'Interpretation'" (AAUP Committee A 1971, 396). William Van Alstyne (1972, 155) characterized it as a "strict construction" of the 1940 statement. These two assessments seemingly agreed with Taylor's dissent concerning the position taken by Committee A in the report on the Koch case, however.

It is therefore somewhat inexplicable how later interpreters have come to see the statement on extramural utterances and its subsequent incorporation into the 1940 statement via one of the 1970 interpretive comments. Finkin and Post (2009, 146) described the incorporation as having "vindicated" the investigating committee's report on the Koch case. That claim is demonstrably incorrect, as the statement on extramural utterances plainly does *not* take the position of the Emerson committee. In fact, it acknowledges that extramural utterances *can* be grounds for dismissal. Even more emphatically, John Wilson (2015, 12) claimed that the interpretive comments "often transform all previous interpretations of the words or effectively nullify them altogether," citing as an example of the latter the case of extramural speech. I have argued here that, in the case of extramural speech, nothing could be further from the truth.[6]

Conclusion

In this account of the development of the AAUP's position on extramural speech, I have argued that it has been marked by constancy—a constancy that remains to this day. The association's definitive policy statement on extramural speech continues to be the 1964 Committee A statement, which has not been superseded by any other policies.

Attacks on faculty members for their extramural speech have also been constant, as the AAUP's investigative reports attest. In closing, it seems appropriate to quote from a report of an investigation conducted at the same time that Committee A was discussing the Koch case. Illustrative of Chancellor Capen's (1935, 597) observation that universities are on the firing line "when public passions are aroused," the AAUP addressed the issue of academic freedom in Mississippi during the time of desegregation. On the freedom of extramural speech, that report observed:

> There was an almost total unanimity among faculty members, administrators, and state officials in the opinion that freedom of public utterance in Mississippi is severely hampered. The limitation is not, to any great extent, a matter of law or of official policy; it is primarily a matter of fear. The consequences of publicly expressing unpopular opinions on segregation are, or at any rate are universally thought to be, extremely dire . . . Most are deterred . . . by the reluctance that any sensitive person feels about incurring the displeasure or the wrath of his neighbors in the community. This reluctance is encouraged by the fact that in Mississippi, more than in most places, the neighbors' displeasure or wrath may take the form of abusive telephone calls, ostracism or bullying of children at school and in other community activities, police harassment, damage to property, and physical violence ranging up to and including murder. Several people observed to committee members that, in effect, a man has about as much freedom as he has guts. But not

many faculty members want to risk being shot at in the night. (Adams et al. 1965, 347–48)

Notes

1. The opinions expressed in this chapter are the author's.

2. Some AAUP policy documents cite a fourth constitutive element, speech on matters of institutional governance; other policy documents, including the "Statement on Government of Colleges and Universities" (AAUP 2015a), regard speech on governance as a special case of freedom of extramural speech.

3. For its history, see Tiede (2015, 114–30).

4. Arthur Lovejoy, who served on the drafting committee, as, incidentally, did Samuel Capen, is most likely responsible for the inclusion of this particular provision in the 1925 conference statement, which was based on an earlier AAC report that did not include it.

5. Walter Metzger's historical explanation of the original purpose for including extramural speech under the umbrella of academic freedom is intriguing but has, regrettably, received little attention in subsequent discussions of the concept.

6. It should be noted that Thomas Emerson, in a jointly authored paper published the same year as the Koch case's report (AAUP Committee A 1963), took a less absolute position than he had taken in that report (Emerson and Haber 1963).

References

AAUP (American Association of University Professors). 2018. "Recommended Institutional Regulations on Academic Freedom and Tenure." AAUP Reports and Publications, https://www.aaup.org/reports-publications/.

AAUP (American Association of University Professors). 2015a. "1915 Declaration of Principles on Academic Freedom and Academic Tenure." In *Policy Documents and Reports*, 11th edition, 3–12. Baltimore: Johns Hopkins University Press.

AAUP (American Association of University Professors). 2015b. "Committee A Statement on Extramural Utterances." In *Policy Documents and Reports*, 11th edition, 31. Baltimore: Johns Hopkins University Press.

AAUP (American Association of University Professors). 2015c. "Statement on Government of Colleges and Universities." In *Policy Documents and Reports*, 11th edition, 117–122. Baltimore: Johns Hopkins University Press.

AAUP (American Association of University Professors). 1988. "The 'Limitations' Clause in the 1940 Statement of Principles," *Academe* 74(5):52–59.

AAUP (American Association of University Professors). 1940. "Statement of Principles on Academic Freedom and Tenure." AAUP Reports and Publications, https://www.aaup.org/reports-publications/.

AAUP (American Association of University Professors) records. 1940a. "Transcript of the April 12–13, 1940, Council Meeting." Special Collections Research Center, George Washington University.

AAUP (American Association of University Professors) records, 1940b. "Transcript of the November 8, 1940, AAUP-AAC Conference." Special Collections Research Center, George Washington University.

AAUP (American Association of University Professors) records. n.d. Transcripts of the Committee A meetings. Special Collections Research Center, George Washington University.

AAUP (American Association of University Professors) Committee A. 2011. "Academic Freedom and Tenure: Louisiana State University, Baton Rouge." *Bulletin of the American Association of University Professors* 97:21–50.

AAUP (American Association of University Professors) Committee A. 1971."Academic Freedom and Tenure: University of California at Los Angeles." *AAUP Bulletin* 57:382–420.

AAUP (American Association of University Professors) Committee A. 1970. "Academic Freedom and Tenure: University of Florida." *AAUP Bulletin* 56:405–422.

AAUP (American Association of University Professors) Committee A. 1963. "Academic Freedom and Tenure: University of Illinois." *AAUP Bulletin* 49:25–43.

AAUP (American Association of University Professors) Committee A. 1949. "Academic Freedom and Tenure: Evansville College." *Bulletin of the American Association of University Professors* 35:74–111.

AAUP (American Association of University Professors) Committee A. 1943. "Academic Freedom and Tenure." *Bulletin of the American Association of University Professors* 29:75–81.

Adams, Richard P., Frances C. Brown, Gladys Kammerer, and Forrest W. Lacey. 1965. "Academic Freedom in Mississippi: A Report of a Special Committee." *AAUP Bulletin* 51:341–356.

Capen, Samuel P. 1935. "The Obligation of the University to American Democracy." *Bulletin of the American Association of University Professors* 21:596–601.

Emerson, Thomas I. and David Haber. 1963. "Academic Freedom of the Faculty Member as Citizen." *Law and Contemporary Problems* 28:525–572.

Fellman, David. 1964. "Report of Committee A, 1963–1964." *AAUP Bulletin* 50:125–135.

Fellman, David. 1963. "Report of Committee A, 1962–1963." *AAUP Bulletin* 49:125–135.

Fellman, David, William P. Fidler, Glenn R. Morrow, and James M. Darlington. 1965. "Report of the Self-Survey Committee of the AAUP." *AAUP Bulletin* 51:99–209.

Finkin, Matthew W. and Robert C. Post. 2009. *For the Common Good*. New Haven, CT: Yale University Press.

Joint Committee on Academic Freedom and Academic Tenure. 1915. "Preliminary Report of the Joint Committee on Academic Freedom and Academic Tenure." *American Economic Review* 5:316–323.

Kadish, Sanford H. 1970. "Report of Committee A, 1969–1970." *AAUP Bulletin* 56:153–168.

Lovejoy, Arthur. December 14, 1916. "Academic Freedom." *Nation* 103:561.

Metzger, Walter. 1990. "The 1940 Statement of Principles on Academic Freedom and Tenure." *Law and Contemporary Problems* 53:3–77.

Metzger, Walter. 1988. "Profession and Constitution: Two Definitions of Academic Freedom in America." *Texas Law Review* 66:1265–1322.

Metzger, Walter. 1967. "Essay II." In Samuel Gorovitz (ed.), *Freedom and Order in the University*, 59–78. Cleveland: Press of Western Reserve University.

Metzger, Walter. 1965. "Academic Freedom: An Analysis of a Recent Case." In Owen Knorr (ed.), *Order and Freedom on the Campus: The Rights and Responsibilities of Faculty and Students*, 22–30. Boulder, CO: Western Interstate Commission for Higher Education.

Metzger, Walter. 1961. *Academic Freedom in the Age of the University*. New York: Columbia University Press.

Oberst, Paul and Lloyd D. Easton, 1958. "Alabama Polytechnic Institute." *AAUP Bulletin* 44:158–169.

Pickering (*Pickering v. Board of Education*). 1968. 391 U.S. 563, Justia, https://supreme.justia.com.

"Remarks of Dr. William C. Dennis of Earlham." 1939. *Bulletin of the Association of American Colleges* 25:181–191.

Schier, Richard F. 1967. "Academic Freedom and Political Action." *AAUP Bulletin* 53:22–26.

"Statement of Principles, 1938." 1939. *Bulletin of the American Association of University Professors* 25:26–31.

"The Tenth Alexander Meiklejohn Award." 1968. *AAUP Bulletin* 54:251–255.

Tiede, Hans-Joerg. 2018. "The Front Rank: On Tenure and the Role of the Faculty in the Defense of Academic Freedom." *History of Education Quarterly* 58:441–447.

Tiede, Hans-Joerg. 2015. *University Reform: The Founding of the American Association of University Professors*. Baltimore: Johns Hopkins University Press.

Van Alstyne, William. 1972. "The Specific Theory of Academic Freedom and the General Issue of Civil Liberty." *Annals of the American Academy of Political and Social Science* 404:140–156.

Wilson, John K. 2015. "Academic Freedom and Extramural Utterances: The Leo Koch and Steven Salaita Cases at the University of Illinois." *AAUP Journal of Academic Freedom* 6.

Wriston, Henry. 1940. "Report of the Commission on Academic Freedom and Academic Tenure." *Bulletin of the Association of American Colleges* 26:99–107.

CHAPTER 5

Attacks on Tweets

Academic Freedom, Social Media, and the Corporate University

Gaye Tuchman

When scholars founded the American Association of University Professors (AAUP) in 1915, they announced their personal and organizational allegiance to the notion of academic freedom, defined as "freedom of inquiry and research; freedom of teaching within the university or college; and freedom of extramural utterance and action" (quoted in Wilson 2016, 44). The AAUP considered academic freedom a defense against attacks on what others deemed unacceptable political expression (Scott 2017). That potentially problematic term necessarily asks, Unacceptable and political according to whom?

This chapter examines three cases in which administrators claimed that a professor had used social media to exceed the limits of their rights under the aegis of academic freedom. Top administrators publicly lambasted and punished each of them. I will argue that these cases are examples of a general administrative practice in the corporate university: *preventing professors from tarnishing the university's brand*. This practice is itself part of the corporate university's accountability regime—"a politics of surveillance, control, and market management disguising itself as the value neutral and scientific administration of individuals and organizations" (Tuchman 2009, 12; 2016).

The cases involve (1) Steven Salaita, whom the chancellor of the University of Illinois "de-hired" from a tenured position as associate professor of American Indian studies in 2014, nine months after Salaita had received and accepted a provisional job offer; (2) Johnny E. Williams, then a tenured professor of sociology whom the president of Trinity College summarily placed on paid leave in 2017; and (3) Saida Grundy, whose job the president of Boston University threatened in May 2015 while Grundy was still completing her doctoral work at the University of Michigan, before she had even arrived at her first job as an assistant professor of sociology. Their so-called objectionable statements were published on either Twitter or Facebook and resulted in death threats, as well as menacing racist, sexist, and obscene posts, e-mails, phone calls, and letters.

Of the numerous academics who have been ferociously criticized, these three were chosen because each case originated on social media and resulted in an extended national controversy, and because each person expressed opinions within their area of academic expertise and published at least one article about their experiences (Salaita 2015; Grundy 2017; Williams 2018). Accordingly, these particular cases facilitate my ability to ask about the intersection of two areas specified in the AAUP's 1915 and 1940 statements of principles: "freedom of research and inquiry" and "freedom of extramural utterance."

The three cases also share other relevant characteristics. Each post concerned a political or social controversy. Salaita wrote about the relationship among Gaza, Israel, Zionism, and anti-Semitism. Grundy's and Williams's posts concerned white racism. None of these professors is white. Grundy and Williams are black. The child of immigrants, Salaita identifies as Palestinian and Jordanian. Scholars have suggested that racism played a role in each case (e.g., Finley et al. 2018). Racist threats were directed at all three.

In each instance, the employer was found to have violated the professor's academic freedom. Using public information and limited personal conversations, I argue that the three cases illustrate the tendency for corporate universities to place their economic interests before academic principles, and that the media encourages this practice. I tie each case to a query pertinent to academic freedom. First, I discuss two questions associated with the Salaita case. How is academic due process related to academic freedom? And does academic freedom apply to posts on the social media? In conjunction with the Williams case, I ask how academic freedom applies to obscenity and critical, unpopular viewpoints. Finally, I use the Grundy posts and the writings of all three professors to ask, How does the structure of academia, including increasing corporatization expressed through accountability regimes and decreasing faculty governance, affect academic freedom?

Of course, there are exceptions to generalizations that I draw. Paradoxically, during a period when scholarship is increasingly suffused with the hegemonic influence of neoliberalism (Busch 2014), universities and social media continue to offer some possibility of dissent. As Rothberg (2015) put it, both higher education institutions and the social media "are sites that remain partially open, that remain spaces from which alternative interpretations and counter-narratives can emerge." The remarks of President Patricia McGuire of Trinity Washington University, when accepting the AAUP's 2010 Meiklejohn Award, typify the possibilities present at even the highest level of university bureaucracy. She noted that threats to academic freedom include the "self-censorship" associated with what many incorrectly view as a president's main task—to raise money—and also emphasized the "devolution of higher education's purpose from the discovery of knowledge and cultivation of intellect to the mundane task of job training" (McGuire 2010).

Recent Changes in the Media and Higher Education

Both social media and corporatized higher education are relatively recent phenomena. Legacy media, such as newspapers, television, and radio, remain important. Citizens using them may react to news content by contacting legislators to tell them to cut funding to a university embroiled in controversy. Social media, however, have become increasingly powerful, although not all of the activities they support are common knowledge. More people learn about the news from social media than from more-traditional media. Social movements use them to gather strength and coordinate activities, as Black Lives Matter has done (Daniels 2009; Ince et al. 2017). Political groups employ them to incite conflict. They trawl Facebook and Twitter to identify, criticize, and harass people they think may be vulnerable, including academics. As they attack scholars, they create and feed controversies about accepted social science and encourage the rejection of established facts. Some mount death threats. Abby Ferber (2018), describing both her experiences and those of others (Cuevas 2018), entitled her presidential address for Sociologists for Women and Society, "Are You Willing to Die for This Work? Public Targeted Online Harassment in Higher Education." Like racism, obscenity is common. Here is part of a text sent to Johnny E. Williams through Facebook's message service: "You wouldn't have toilet paper to wipe your worthless black ass if it was not for white people. Your [*sic*] so fucking stupid running your fucking mouth in a white society. What did you expect?" Other messages attacked his family. One even crudely referred to his wife's genitalia.

The current version of corporatized higher education is also a relatively recent historical development. To be sure, Thorstein Veblen ([1918] 2015) appeared to refer to corporatization more than a century ago, when he wrote about "captains of industry" and "captains of erudition." Contemporary scholars, however, only started to formulate theories and gather data about both corporate universities and social media in the past few decades.

By corporatization, I mean the increasing dominance of academic capitalism, defined as "the way . . . universities [and colleges] were responding to neoliberal tendencies to treat higher education policy as a subset of economic policy . . . Academic capitalism deals with market and market-like behaviors on the part of administrators and faculty" (Slaughter and Leslie 2001, 154). They then continue: "Market-like behaviors refer to institutional and faculty competition for monies [that] involve competition for funds from external resource providers, including . . . endowment funds . . . Market behaviors refer to for-profit activity on the part of institutions, such as patenting and subsequent royalty and licensing agreements." Put differently, higher education has been thoroughly and competitively monetized (McMillan Cottom and Tuchman 2015; see also McMillan Cottom 2017). Whether public or private, the structure of the contemporary nonprofit university is different in kind than the universities about which Veblen wrote.

Clearly in 1915, as today, the donors to universities and colleges demanded a say in how administrators shaped institutions of higher education, including who was hired and which disciplines were favored. For instance, in 1900, several years after the death of her husband with whom she cofounded Stanford University, Jane Elizabeth Lathrop Stanford engineered the forced resignation of distinguished economist Edward Ross because of his political views (Metzger 1955, 438). She complained that Ross's political associations with socialist elements "bring tears to the eyes" (quoted in Scott 2018, 43; see also Metzger 1955, 438). One of the men who investigated the Ross case for the American Economic Association helped found the AAUP and became the first chair of its Committee on Academic Freedom and Tenure (Tiede 2014). Another famous example is economist Scott Nearing, whom the trustees of the University of Pennsylvania dismissed from the Wharton School of Business because alumni objected to him, despite praise from his department, department head, and dean (Scott 2018, 43).

Recent examples of controversy, however, involve more than either political disagreement or the demand for recognition of their elite status that had been implicit in the Stanfords' and Cornelius Vanderbilt's establishment of their namesake universities.[1] As typified by the activity of the Koch brothers and their foundations, contemporary donations to higher education are different *in kind*. They are part of an attempt to accrue influence in order to introduce and then implement specific types of social change. For instance, Jane Mayer (2016) sees the Koch brothers' extensive involvement with universities as part of their strategy to establish structural social change by promoting libertarian ideas. Quoting a top Koch strategist, *SourceWatch* summarizes, "Universities are the first step in the Koch network's 'Structure of Social

Change,' a process of influencing politics and culture" ("Koch Universities" n.d.; see also Levinthal 2015; Paul 2015). Because they believe that the control of ideas enables control of society, the Koch brothers and their foundations donate extensively to both public and private universities. The *New York Times* reported that they gave millions of dollars to George Mason University with strings attached; they even demanded a say in what others viewed as academic decisions (Green and Saul 2018). *SourceWatch* asserts that to promote their politics, the Koch brothers' foundation also significantly involved itself with the University of Florida and the College of Charleston. It lists well over 150 public and private institutions to which they or their foundations have donated as little as $5,000 or as much as $1,300,000 ("Koch Universities" 2019). As Slaughter and Leslie (2001) might put it, competition for foundation monies, such as donations from the Koch entities, are characteristic of academic capitalism.[2]

There are other key differences between the universities that Veblen described and today's nonprofit higher education institutions. Veblen ([1918] 2015) wrote about the involvement of "captains of erudition" in the bureaucratization of organizations. Contemporary bureaucratic universities have far exceeded his descriptions. As the number of administrators multiply, their reproductive rate puts rabbits to shame. As for professors, they are required to raise funds. In some fields, they are to underwrite their own salaries through fellowships or, preferably, grants replete with provisions for overhead. Colleges and universities expect today's professors-turned-administrators to behave as managers of for-profit corporations (Tuchman 2009). They are to follow such seemingly harmless rules as recognizing authority by never criticizing their superiors in public and always keeping to their own domain (the bureaucratic equivalent of "mind your own business"). Boards of trustees and institutional administrators employ such techniques and, as do their corporate counterparts, assiduously promote their own brand. They also expect professors to protect the institution's brand (Tuchman 2009). High-placed administrators at the University of Illinois, Trinity College, and Boston University seem to have believed that

Steven Salaita, Johnny Williams, and Saida Grundy had tarnished the reputation of their respective institutions. Administrators held them accountable.

The Posts

Sometimes politics and academic research become so intertwined that it is difficult to distinguish academic research *about* political topics from controversial political topics that scholars have studied. Environmental transformation, especially climate change, is an apt example of this seemingly inextricable entanglement. Whether research has informed politics or political concerns have prompted research, however, is irrelevant to a consideration of academic freedom. So, too, is the publication site of a scholar's comments, although, when considering their colleagues for hiring, tenure, or promotion, academics customarily weigh the "quality" of the location (usually the book or journal) where their colleagues' work is disseminated.

The "new" social media are not conventional locations for scholarly publication. To say the least, one would not expect a professor to list social media on his or her curriculum vitae. Nonetheless, the nationally debated Facebook and Twitter posts of Salaita, Williams, and Grundy involved academic research that is entangled with political disputes. Steven Salaita's posts are a case in point.

Salaita's controversial tweets occurred in the summer of 2014, during Israel's Gaza offensive. His de-hiring raises several issues. Can a university rescind a job offer, and, if so, under what conditions? Do such social media as Twitter constitute extramural utterances? Is intemperate language protected speech?

To understand the hullabaloo surrounding Salaita's tweets, one must understand something of his academic background and the character of his posts. Salaita had earned his doctorate in Native American studies, with an emphasis on literature, at the University of Oklahoma. His dissertation concerned what he termed "indigenous peoples": to wit, Native Americans and Palestinians.[3] His tweets concerned Palestinians. All told, when the University of Illinois hired him, Salaita had published six books, mostly about Arabs and Israel. One of these was based on his dissertation, and another concerned anti-Arab sentiment in the United States. The latter had won an award from the Gustavus Myers Center for the Study of Bigotry and Human Rights. (Founded in 1984 and centered in Boston, it closed for lack of funds in 2009.) Robert Warrior, both the chair of the University of Illinois's program in America Indian studies and a member of Salaita's former dissertation committee, observed to a reporter from *Indian Country*: "What became compelling about this work is the analysis of the experiences of American Indian people and the Palestinian people, which is at the heart of his work" (Rothberg 2015).

Salaita's controversial posts are mainly about colonialism, Zionism, and anti-Semitism. Some are relatively mild. For example: "The logic of 'antisemitsm' [*sic*] deployed by Zionists, if applied in principle, would make pretty much everybody not a sociopath 'antisemitic.'" Another is about colonialism: "This is not a conflict between #Israel and 'Hamas.' It's a struggle by an indigenous people against a colonial power" #Gaza #Free Palestine. A third combines those themes: "If it is 'antisemitic' to deplore colonization, land theft, and child murder, then what choice does any person of conscience have?" #Gaza. Others are nasty personal insults: "At this point, if Netanyahu [Israel's prime minister] appeared on TV with a necklace made from the teeth of Palestinian children, would anybody be surprised?" #Gaza. Yet others condemned the United States' treatment of Native Americans and African Americans: "#Israel's bombardment of #Gaza provides a necessary impetus to reflect [on] the genocides that accompanied the formation of the United States." All of these posts appeared many months after the University of Illinois had sent Salaita a conditional letter of employment.

Can a university rescind a job offer? And how is job rescission related to academic freedom? The AAUP first promulgated rules about hiring and firing in the 1915 document where it defined academic freedom. These rules were components of academic due process, part of professors' right and responsibility to exercise self-governance, so they can teach and search for truth. As Joughin (1963) put it, academic freedom is the "master" of academic due process. These rules were consequential for the University of Illinois, as Salaita's "provisionally" contracted employer.

Academic due process underlines the fact that a university is an employer, but it does not play by the same rules as a small business, a white-collar firm, or a factory. If the human resources department of a unionized factory were to hire a skilled laborer and then fire him the day before he had been told to report for work, the appropriate union would raise a commotion that potentially carried financial implications. There would also be repercussions at a small business or a white-collar firm. Personnel disputes are much more consequential for institutions of higher education, since adverse publicity often has a negative impact on both donors and potential students. In the case of public colleges and universities, all disputes with a political tinge may also have an adverse effect on the state legislature, which has historically provided a portion of the budgets of public institutions of higher education. Publicized controversies tarnish the brand. Donors are more likely to give monies to a university after its football or basketball team has won a championship (e.g., Smith and Willingham 2015; Putterman 2019). Conversely, they are less likely to do so after public scandals or unfavorable publicity, whether disseminated on social or legacy media (Blair 2017).

Bad publicity may also discourage potential students from applying and enrolling. (Many institutions of higher education have special departments to assess, prevent, and control risks.) Applications matter, as higher education institutions have increasingly become starved for funds. State governments have cut back on their financial support of higher education. In several states, public funding now constitutes less than 10 percent of the flagship university's budget. Some public university administrations fear that if significant political players complain to legislators about professors' or students' activities, the state will decrease its financial support. Private universities fear having to cut into their hefty endowments. Some small, specialized liberal arts colleges, such as women's colleges, religious colleges, and historically black colleges and universities, are finding that their financial situation is untenable, in part because they cannot attract enough students to pay tuition set high enough to balance the college's budget (Hartocollis 2016; see also Schifrin 2013).[4]

Among the factors that might rescue a disparaged school is the current academic labor market that, in most fields, currently favors employers. In some disciplines there are so few tenure-line positions that the search for a stable, well-paying job frequently qualifies as a disaster. At one time, most higher education faculty were tenured or on a tenure track; today many experience precarity. (I have heard adjunct faculty who speed between their part-time jobs called "freeway flyers.")

By custom and (sometimes) contract, every aspect of hiring, tenure, and promotion has its season.[5] Advertisements for jobs appear in late summer or mid-fall (unless an institution must wait for its budget to be finalized, as has become increasingly common). With administrative approval, interviews usually occur between late November and March. (Departments try to schedule interviews as early as the appropriate administrator will permit, so as to have the pick of the applicant pool and minimize competitive offers from other institutions with comparable jobs.) It is unethical for applicants who have accepted an offer to change their minds and quit, in order to accept what they believe is a better position.

Because the phases of academic hiring are so seasonal, the rescission of an appointment has terrible consequences for those seeking faculty positions. Consider the timing associated with Salaita's rescinded job, as summarized in the AAUP Committee A's report (2015). Notification of the job opening in the University of Illinois's Native American studies program went out early, and 80 candidates applied. (This is a fair number for a rare specialty.) Six of them were interviewed. After his visit, Salaita was the unanimous choice. On September 23, 2013, the university's promotion and tenure committee approved the tenured appointment, which then moved up the administrative ladder. Chancellor Phyllis Wise approved it three days later. A provisional letter of appointment was sent on October 3, and Salaita accepted on October 9, requesting that the start date be moved from January 2014 to August 2014. He then resigned from his position as a tenured associate professor at Virginia Technical University. In late spring, he and his wife put a deposit on a condominium in Champaign-Urbana.

Before acting, Chancellor Wise appears to have anticipated censure and decided her action would be worth any risk (Rothberg 2015).[6] Around July 21, Wise began receiving emails from donors protesting the appointment of Professor Salaita. One complainant reminded Wise that, "having been a multiple 6 figure donor to Illinois over the years, I know our support is ending." A graduate wrote, "We will now cease our contributions to the university and will let our fellow alumni know why we are doing so" (Des Garennes 2014). Wise consulted lawyers, members of the board of trustees, and select faculty members, none of whom were associated with the American Indian studies program or had been involved in the hiring process. Despite Salaita's stellar recommendations and the customary academic practices, Wise acceded to donors' demands. Salaita had tainted the brand and had to be held accountable. On August 1, two weeks before the start of the semester, Wise informed Salaita that she would not forward his appointment for a vote by the trustees, as she was rescinding his job offer.

Officially, the AAUP identified the University of Illinois's action as a "summary dismissal." Because it had not held the appropriate hearings before notifying Salaita that it was withdrawing its provisional offer, the university had violated academic due process. AAUP Committee A (2015) associated this failure with a transgression of academic freedom. For this and related missteps, the AAUP chastised the University of Illinois.

When Chancellor Wise explained her decision, she criticized the tenor of Professor Salaita's tweets: "What we cannot and will not tolerate . . . are personal and disrespectful words or actions that demean or abuse either viewpoints or those who express them" (Scott 2015). She felt that they lacked mannerliness and implied that Salaita might be intemperate in the classroom. Chancellor Wise apparently believed criticizing specific viewpoints was an anathema—that is, Salaita had apparently proved himself unqualified to teach by critiquing those who defended both Israel's treatment of Palestinians and its conflict in Gaza. More bluntly, she had called Salaita's ideas "uncivil."[7]

It is relevant that in 2014, criticism of Israel was relatively uncommon. According to Michelle Alexander (2019), disparagement of Israel's policies and actions toward Palestinians today are as unacceptable as were demonstrations against the Vietnam War in 1967. After invoking Martin Luther King's objections to the Vietnam War and comparing Israel's treatment of Palestinians in the occupied territory to South African apartheid, she observed: "Many civil rights activists and organizations have remained silent . . . not because they lack concern or sympathy for the Palestinian people, but because they fear loss of funding from foundations, and false charges of anti-Semitism."

Is a tweet an extramural utterance? The hiring cycle in higher education exemplifies how organizational factors are associated with academic due process and faculty governance. Social media have a different relationship to academic freedom. By my argument, a tweet, in as much as it refers to a scholar's search for truth, warrants academic freedom, especially if the post's content falls within that person's area of expertise. If it does not belong in that sphere of knowledge, freedom of speech may only arguably apply.[8]

Because social media are involved in both research and teaching, the AAUP had launched a study of the relationship between them and academic freedom before the Salaita case had occurred. Instructors assign materials on social media to their classes; they use them in lectures; academics, scholarly associations, journals, and universities (among others) post on social media. As the AAUP's report on "Academic Freedom and Electronic Communication" summarized, "Social-media sites blur the distinction between private and public communications in new ways." Nonetheless, "teachers are entitled to full freedom in research and in [its] publication," and those rights apply "with no less force to the use of electronic media for the conduct of research and the dissemination of findings and results than to the use of more traditional media" (AAUP 2014, 17, 19).

Even though Salaita was recognized as an expert on Arabs, other indigenous peoples, and the relationship between Israel and Palestine, some complainants objected on the grounds that his tweets were political, not scholarly. Such criticism might apply to much of social science research, especially work about inequality, gender, race, and ethnicity. Ultimately, the definition of "political" may be as difficult to compose as the definition of "truth." To cope with these many complexities, the AAUP expressed an institutional, rather than an epistemological response to this definitional quandary. It said politics involves running for office and explained, "While a public employee may reasonably be barred, for instance, from using a university website to run for public office or raise funds for a campaign, [academic] policies that discourage or prohibit, either explicitly or through imprecise or ill-defined language, faculty members, staff members, and students from expressing political preferences clearly violate fundamental principles of academic freedom and free expression" (AAUP 2014, 25). When Chancellor Wise criticized Professor Salaita, this administrator expressed an explicit concern. "Their" professor had been uncivil. As we have seen, Wise believed Salaita's purported lack of respectfulness meant that he would engage in unacceptable behavior in the classroom.

Johnny E. Williams's posts decried racism and appeared on Facebook. Some people publish on both Facebook and Twitter, as each platform facilitates different kinds of expression. Natalie Zemon Davis characterized tweets in a letter to Chancellor Wise: "Tweets have to be read both in their context—as an ongoing conversation, a set of calls and responses—and as a genre, a form of spontaneous expression limited to 140 characters: a short quick burst of feeling, not a reasoned argument . . . They are quick comments on something, in praise or anger" (quoted in Scott 2015). Facebook posts can encompass thousands of words. For instance, magazines and newspapers, such as the *Atlantic*, the *Washington Post*, and the *Guardian*, place stories there. So do such outlets as the *National Review*, *Breitbart News Daily*, and the *Las Vegas Review-Journal*.

The length of the stories posted on these media serves a purpose. Tressie McMillan Cottom (pers. comm.) has observed that people use Twitter to establish their brand, and Facebook to deepen it. Both platforms employ hashtags. Often people who post use a hashtag to indicate how they think or feel about the topic of their commentaries, though hashtags can also avoid any reference to ideas or emotions.

Williams was attacked for both the content of his posts and their shared hashtag, "LetThemFuckingDie." Trinity College president Joanne Berger-Sweeney found the hashtag "reprehensible" (Megan 2017). Others—including *Campus Reform*, the right-wing bulletin that had surveyed Facebook to locate Williams's post and then publicized it—insisted the posts were racist attacks on white people (Gockowski 2017). Williams argued that he had used the obscene word to emphasize his point and that it was the title of an article in *Medium* that he had shared on Facebook the previous week (see Son of Baldwin 2017). "That piece argues that 'indifference' to their well-being is the only thing that 'terrifies' bigots and so people of color should 'Let Them Fucking Die' if they are ever in peril" (Flaherty 2017).

Does academic freedom safeguard what President Berger-Sweeney had called a "reprehensible" hashtag? The AAUP protects what some may view as intemperate speech. As AAUP Committee A (1992) has noted: "Some may seek to defend a distinction between the regulation of the content of speech and the regulation of the manner (or style) of speech. We find this distinction untenable in practice because offensive style or opprobrious phrases may in fact have been chosen for their expressive power."

In their opposition to systemic racism, Williams's tweets, articles, and books are often both vivid and powerful. He believes, as he stated when he posted the article from *Medium*, that it is "past time for the racially oppressed to do what people who believe themselves to be 'white' will not do, put end to the vectors of their destructive mythology of whiteness and their white supremacy system" (Flaherty 2017). Williams's concern with institutionalized racism is so pervasive that sometimes even his posted criticisms of specific people can be read as generalizations about the social system. Perhaps because his structural analyses are not rooted in ideas espoused by a coterie of whites, some people placed the two controversial tweets in a context different from the one he used. Conservative websites read Williams's tweets as a reference to the shooting of Representative Steve Scalise the previous week, because the *Medium* article had included a link to a piece in *Fusion* that concerned the attack on the Republicans during their practice for the annual Congressional baseball game (Gockowski 2017; see also Flaherty 2017; Son of Baldwin 2017). Williams wrote that he had been reacting specifically to "the not-guilty verdict for the police officer who murdered Philando Castile in Minneapolis and the subsequent Seattle police killing of Charleena Lyles . . . after she called the police to report an attempted burglary at her home." He said, "Such *consistent, systemic, extrajudicial* killing of black people in the US has enraged me for as long as I can remember" (Williams 2018, 39, emphasis added).

Saida Grundy's controversial tweets also criticized white people. One of them asks, "Why is white america [*sic*] so reluctant to identify white college males as a problem population?" According to *Inside Higher Ed* (Jaschik 2015), after a multitweet conversation about the uniqueness of European slavery, Grundy allegedly wrote, "In other words, deal with your white sh*t [*sic*] white people. Slavery is a *YALL* thing." Unfortunately, there is a distinct difference between research findings and dominant American beliefs.[9] Frequently, when people form opinions, they treat facts as though they are irrelevant. Thus, although considerable social science research discusses the problematic behavior of white male college students, popular culture is more likely to celebrate, say, drunken fraternity parties rather than condemn them (although the news media currently decry such practices as fraternity hazing when a pledge dies). In movies depicting fraternity life, fraternities are almost always exclusively white, or at best contain a token person of color.

The three professors discussed above argued that racism is inherent in the American social structure, including its institutions and complex organizations. Many sociologists agree. Today the relevant sociological question is not, Are Americans racist? It is, How can we explain the perseverance of class, race, and gender inequalities within organizations? In addition, it is important to ask, How do these processes operate in academe and how are they related to academic freedom?

Academic Freedom in the Corporate University

What makes the attack on academic freedom in the corporate university different from how Jane Stanford demanded the dismissal of Edward Ross? She was acting during the last years of the age of the robber barons, when captains of industry presupposed their right to dominate all sorts of institutions. Today, the dominant ideology—the values that most people are said to avow—officially condemns millionaires and billionaires who would use their money to impose their will on such important institutions as politics, the media, and higher education. The values associated with corporate capitalism, however, have taken hold within academe, where they claim to offer a path to economic stability during a time when inequality among both people and institutions has become ever more pervasive. Branding is particularly important to academic freedom in the corporate university. It helps to reinforce the inequality regimes that are implicit in the accusations involving academic freedom that I have reviewed. It is wedded to a demand for accountability.

Such regimes are universal. As Joan Acker (2006, 443) notes, "All organizations have inequality regimes, defined loosely as interrelated practices, processes, actions, and meanings that result in and maintain class, racial, and gender inequalities within particular organizations." Inequality itself, she adds, refers to "systematic disparities in power and control over goals, resources, and outcomes," including "how to organize work . . . These [inequality] regimes are linked to inequality in the surrounding society, its politics, history, and culture," but the manner in which these links operate varies from one organization to another.

Salaita, Williams, and Grundy have suggested how such links may work in academe. Each case illustrates, in its own way, the phenomenon of the reproduction of power. Salaita refers to professors who believe they have the right to speak for the oppressed but do not acknowledge their "default power to reproduce inequality." He avers, "They do not need to acknowledge that power to reinforce the structure that sustains it." Salaita then adds: "Such professors like to think they uphold the decency of the profession. In reality, they merely fortify the authority in which they're so comfortably ensconced" (Salaita 2015, 45). Williams distinguishes between the treatment of critics and courtiers: "Academicians are told that tenure and academic freedom protect us whenever we speak out and pursue political or provocative research. But more often than not, this autonomy is not afforded faculty who are of the wrong political persuasion, race, or religion" (Williams 2018, 38). Grundy cares about the marginalization of careers: "Colleges and universities . . . push black scholars . . . into the professional margins and [so] directly [affect] tenure cases, career advancement, resources, productivity, and networks" (Grundy 2017, 1865). For instance, if appointed to numerous committees or asked to advise numerous students of color who seek them out, black professors with jobs that require publications for tenure may be placed at a disadvantage, compared with whites.

Branding, another method that reproduces inequality in the corporate university, is also implicated in issues of academic freedom. Branding is so basic to contemporary higher education that it may be viewed as a hallmark. The most common example is sports. Logically, if one important element of an academic organization, such as sports, emphasizes branding, other components do also. As Samantha King and Sheila Slaughter (2004) report, even though few athletic departments turn a profit, the sports components of universities are replete with the hallmarks and practices of modern capitalism.

The theories with which sociologists describe the links among inequalities, organizations, and social structure are complex, as is the language they use (see Ray 2019). But the theories all predict that if a university's athletics department is actively branding teams, endeavors such as teaching and research will be subject to branding, too. For instance, some higher education institutions hang banners lauding their outstanding faculty from poles on the city's streets near their campus (Tuchman 2009). Academic and athletic branding also cooperate with one another. Commercial advertisements aired during the breaks of a televised college football or basketball game brag about the quality of the teaching and research at the given institutions.

Branding through research activity extends its reach into academic freedom in various ways. A professor at "Wannabe University" recalled a mandated training session about research.[10] There was no subtlety in either its emphasis on branding or its suggestion that protecting their institution is a preeminent professorial responsibility. To stress how much every faculty member is responsible for the reputation of their employer, the organizers gave each of the participating researchers a handheld mirror, embossed with the words "Individual Responsibility" and "Institutional Reputation." It conveyed the duty of each researcher *not* to harm the university's public presentation—its brand. The professors would be held accountable. According to an informant, it was not clear whether the trainers were implying that safeguarding the institution's brand was *more* important than conducting (preferably funded) research that would be placed in a recognized (preferably eminent) publication, but his example underscores the feeling of Salaita's, Williams's, and Grundy's administrators that each of these professors *could harm* a brand.

When facing problems that may tarnish their brand, administrators may even choose to lie, in order to present the best possible image. For instance, the *Hartford Courant* (Megan 2017) reported that Johnny E. Williams, whom Trinity College cleared of posting inappropriate tweets, apologized to the college's administrators. Supposedly the newspaper's source was the college administration, since Williams maintains (pers. comm.) that he did not do so. In this instance, as in others, it is difficult to say who is lying. Williams seems to be a forthright fellow; I have never met President Berger-Sweeney, but the respected *Hartford Courant* reporter Colin McEnroe has praised her honesty.

Still, I have heard other administrators tell some very creative stories. In one instance, a former dean was publicly vilified for having allegedly taken inadequate action to investigate a charge that a professor had been involved inappropriately with students.[11] The former dean sued. With court authorization to examine university files, his legal team located significant documents that confirmed what the former dean had told the investigators (whom the administrators had hired). The university gave the former dean a monetary settlement and granted him full rights of disclosure, so he could discuss the case publicly. The former dean, however, simply moved to another state. The university itself kept silent, presumably to protect its brand, though in a letter, the university's provost and an associate provost apologized for the incident. Intent on demonstrating that both past and current top administrators had acted "to protect students," the university shielded itself from accusations of wrongdoing. It lied. It did not, however, defend itself with the institutional devotion customarily used in episodes of sports scandals.

Appearances—reflections in the mirror—are always paramount, but the behavior of many university presidents and trustees seems to indicate that academic freedom is nowhere as important as sports. Sports are not just a big business that personifies branding (King and Slaughter 2004); all components of a university supposedly care about sports, especially winning (i.e., revenue-producing) basketball and football teams.[12] When a major scandal erupted because athletes at the University of North Carolina, Chapel Hill had been enrolled in phony courses that granted credits (although no work was done by those students), administrators did everything they could to bury the stories and find a seemingly insignificant person to blame (see Smith and Willingham 2015). (By an "insignificant person," I mean someone who supposedly could neither help nor hinder administrators in the future.) Sports scandals at other universities, such as the 2015–2018 investigations at the University of Louisville (Sokolove 2018), have come and gone. Some scandals linger longer than others. Stories about Pennsylvania State University, where a member of the coaching staff sexually molested minors, remain in the collective memory. Although administrators do not always succeed in their attempts, in such cases they do their best to emerge unscathed. They also do not want the institution to lose financial support. Trustees and university administrators care more about social media, donations, and their brand than about academic freedom. So do the many fans serving in the state legislature.

I have argued that accusations of faculty members having violated their academic freedom are expressions of how the corporate university is embedded in today's social structure. They are a specialized case of a more general practice—protecting the brand—that is, in itself, part and parcel of accountability regimes. Attacks on professors' rights spread through social media, and they have become all too common as the corporate university fights for the survival of nonprofit higher education in an age of increasing corporate power, inequality, and economic struggle.

Notes

1. According to the official version on each university's webpage, the Stanfords founded a university "to promote the public welfare by exercising an influence in behalf of humanity and civilization," as well as to memorialize their son. Cornelius Vanderbilt's donation to start a southern university was meant to "contribute to strengthening the ties which should exist between all sections of our common country."

2. Ferber (2018, 301) notes that the activities of the "alt-right and other sectors of the right-wing across the spectrum, from mainstream to extreme, are intended to silence faculty and censor the curriculum."

3. After the fact, Cary Nelson, then a professor of literature at the University of Illinois and a former president of the AAUP, criticized Salaita by claiming that Palestinians are not an indigenous people (Nelson 2015; but see also Warrior 2015). Publishing criticism of the academic work of someone another department has just hired, as Nelson did, is generally considered a violation of academic norms. For instance, a physicist would not be deemed qualified to judge the quality of a cytologist's research, and a scholar of indigenous peoples would not be seen as an expert on modern poetry.

4. A demographic transformation, predicted in the 1980s, has decreased the supply of white, male high school graduates who want to go to college. This group had been nonprofit higher education's preferred clientele. (A majority of college students are now women.) Because student tuition has become a vital source of public universities' general budgets, they now compete to enroll students from other states. To establish a flow of potential applications, higher education institutions also send representatives to other countries, such as China, because international students pay out-of-state tuition. Administrators celebrate when a struggling rivulet of such applications begins to bubble and express anxiety when national governmental policies decrease them.

5. The rhythm of scheduling has different consequences for adjunct professors. Often hired just before or at the beginning of a semester and frequently teaching more than one course, sometimes each in a separate location, adjuncts are often too harried by preparing classes and commuting from job to job to apply for full-time appointments. Academic job postings require a slew of paperwork that takes a substantial amount of time to prepare, complete, and submit. These include a curriculum vitae, several examples of one's published scholarship, a statement of one's teaching philosophy, and a statement of one's research program. Adjuncts cannot skimp on their (unpaid) teaching preparation to compose these documents, because their re-employment to teach depends, to a substantial degree, on favorable student reports. Further, their heavy teaching loads typically preclude publication activity, which works directly against career mobility.

6. Before Salaita had interviewed at the University of Illinois, he had published a controversial article in *Salon* that displeased some administrators at his previous employer, Virginia Technical University. Either Wise did not know about this piece, or she found Salaita's previous general publications irrelevant until she received complaints from donors.

7. There is a growing literature on incivility and academic freedom. Examples of articles on incivility and the Salaita case include those by Cloud (2015), Scott (2015), and Moshman and Edler (2015).

8. On the distinction between academic freedom and freedom of speech, see Scott (2017) and Joseph Hermanowicz's introduction to this volume.

9. Latour (2018, 23) gives a marvelous definition of fact: "No attested knowledge can remain on its own, as we know very well. Facts remain robust only when they are supported by a common culture, by institutions that can be trusted, by a more or less decent public life, by more or less reliable media."

10. This example does not appear in Tuchman (2009).

11. That case illustrates how far a university will go to protect its past and current top administrators and, thus, safeguard its brand. It involved a professor said to have become inappropriately involved with undergraduates. The university hired a law firm to investigate and its widely publicized report falsely criticized a former dean for taking insufficient action. For reasons that are irrelevant here, the former dean gave the interviewer key records concerning the accused professor, including a notification sent some years before to the university's president, provost, and head of the campus police. The interviewer claimed never to have seen these records. Some months later, the state's media, providing extensive coverage with prominent placement, summarized the law firm's report that praised the current administration and strongly criticized the former dean, claiming that he had not acted promptly when he learned of the professor's behavior. When the former dean sued, his lawyers located the letter that was sent to the former president, advising him about the professor's improprieties, as well as a participant's notes about a meeting where five administrators had discussed whom to blame for the university's previous lack of action.

12. Departments of athletics may also do their best to hide the racism and sexism too often inherent in their enterprise. An athletic director once told me that he would not discuss internal findings about racism with his coaches. One of his colleagues worried that if parents caught wind of the university teams' failings, they would not want their children to attend that institution.

References

AAUP (American Association of University Professors). 2014. "Academic Freedom and Electronic Communications." *Bulletin of the American Association of University Professors* 100(July–August):16–34.

AAUP (American Association of University Professors) Committee A. 2015. "Academic Freedom and Tenure: The University of Illinois at Urbana-Champaign." AAUP Reports & Publications, https://www.aaup.org/reports-publications/.

AAUP (American Association of University Professors) Committee A. 1992. "On Freedom of Expression and Campus Speech Codes." AAUP Reports & Publications, https://www.aaup.org/reports-publications/.

Acker, Joan. 2006. "Inequality Regimes: Gender, Class, and Race in Organizations." *Gender and Society* 20:441–464.

Alexander, Michelle. July 19, 2019. "Time to Break the Silence on Palestine." *New York Times*, www.nytimes.com.

Blair, Russell. August 1, 2017. "Trinity Loses Donations, Students after Facebook Posts." *Hartford Courant*, https://www.courant.com/.

Busch, Lawrence. 2014. *Knowledge for Sale: The Neoliberal Takeover of Higher Education*. Cambridge, MA: MIT Press.

Cloud, Dana. 2015. "'Civility' as a Threat to Academic Freedom." *First Amendment Studies* 49(1):13–17.

Cuevas, Joshua A. 2018. "A New Reality? The Far Right's Use of Cyberharassment against Academics; A Firsthand Account by a Targeted Faculty Member." *Academe* 104(1):24–28.

Daniels, Jessie. 2009. *Cyber Racism: White Supremacy Online and the New Attack on Civil Rights*. Lanham, MD: Rowman & Littlefield.

Des Garennes, Christine. September 2, 2014. "Salaita Prompted Donors' Fury." [*Urbana*] *News Gazette*, https://www.news-gazette.com/.

Ferber, Abby L. 2018. "Are You Willing to Die for This Work? Public Online Harassment in Higher Education; Presidential Address." *Gender and Society* 32(3):301–320.

Finley, Stephen C., Biko M. Gray, and Lori Latrice Martin. 2018. "'Affirming Our Values': African American Scholars, White Virtual Mobs, and the Complicity of White University Administrators." *AAUP Journal of Academic Freedom* 9, https://www.aaup.org/reports-publications/.

Flaherty, Colleen. June 27, 2017. "Trinity Clears Threatened Professor." *Inside Higher Ed*, https://www.insidehighered.com.

Gockowski, Anthony. June 20, 2017. "Prof Calls Whites 'Inhuman Assholes,' Says 'Let Them Die.' " *Campus Reform*, https://www.campusreform.org.

Green, Erica L. and Stephanie Saul. May 5, 2018. "What Charles Koch and Other Donors to George Mason University Got for Their Money." *New York Times*, https://www.nytimes.com/.

Grundy, Saida. 2017. "A History of White Violence Tells Us Attacks on Black Academics Are Not Ending (I Know Because It Happened to Me)." *Ethnic and Racial Studies* 40(11):1864–1871.

Hartocollis, Anemona. April 29, 2016. "At Small Colleges, Harsh Lessons About Cash Flow." *New York Times*, https://www.nytimes.com/.

Ince, Jelani, Fabrio Rojas, and Clayton A. Davis. 2017. "The Social Media Response to Black Lives Matter: How Twitter Users Interact with Black Lives Matter through Hashtag Use." *Ethnic and Racial Studies* 40(11):1814–1830.

Jaschik, Scott. May 13, 2015. "Regret Over Tweets on Race." *Inside Higher Ed*, https://www.insidehighered.com.

Joughin, Louis. 1963. "Academic Due Process." *Law and Contemporary Problems* 28: 573–601.

King, Samantha and Sheila Slaughter. 2004. "Sports 'R' Us: Contracts, Trademarks and Logos." In Gary Rhoades and Sheila Slaughter (eds.), *Capitalism and the New Economy*, 256–278. Baltimore: Johns Hopkins University Press.

"Koch Universities." n.d. *SourceWatch*, https://www.sourcewatch.org.

Latour, Bruno. 2018. *Down to Earth: Politics in the New Climactic Regime*. Cambridge: Polity Press.

Levinthal, Dave. October 30, 2015. "Spreading the Free-Market Gospel." *Atlantic*, https://www.theatlantic.com.

Mayer, Jane. 2016. *Dark Money: The Hidden History of the Billionaires Behind the Radical Right*. New York: Doubleday.

McGuire, Patricia. 2010. "Acceptance Remarks for AAUP Meiklejohn Award." June 2010. https://www.aaup.org/NR/rdonlyres/5E4DA45C-8C0A-40FB-AEF6-8D85C4614795/0/MeiklejohnAward.pdf.

McMillan Cottom, Tressie. 2017. *Lower Ed: The Troubling Rise of For-Profit Colleges in the New Economy*. New York: New Press.

McMillan Cottom, Tressie and Gaye Tuchman. 2015. "The Rationalization of Higher Education." In Robert Scott, Marliss C. Buchman, and Stephen M. Kosslyn (eds.), *Emerging Trends in the Social and Behavioral Sciences*. Hoboken, NJ: John Wiley & Sons.

Megan, Kathleen. June 27, 2017. "Trinity Professor Flees Campus after Threats Over Facebook Comments, Issues Public Apology." *Hartford Courant*, https://www.courant.com/.

Metzger, Walter. 1955. "The Age of the University." In Richard Hofstadter and Walter Metzger, *The Development of Academic Freedom in the United States*, 277–506. New York: Columbia University Press.

Moshman, David and Frank Edler. 2015. "Civility and Academic Freedom after Salaita." *AAUP Journal of Academic Freedom* 6, https://www.aaup.org/reports-publications/.

Nelson, Cary. 2015. "Steven Salaita's Scholarly Record and the Problem of His Appointment." *AAUP Journal of Academic Freedom* 6, https://www.aaup.org/reports-publications/.

Paul, Rand. April 16, 2015. "Charles Koch & David Koch." *Time*, https://time.com.

Putterman, Alex. February 5, 2019. "UConn Applications Have Risen When Huskies Basketball Teams Perform Well." *Hartford Courant*, https://www.courant.com/.

Ray, Victor. 2019. "A Theory of Racialized Organizations." *American Sociological Review* 84(1):26–53.

Rothberg, Michael. July 31, 2015. "The Salaita Case, One Year Later." *Inside Higher Ed*, https://www.insidehighered.com.

Salaita, Steven. 2015. *Uncivil Rights: Palestine and the Limits of Academic Freedom*. Chicago: Hallmark Books.

Schifrin, Matt. June 24, 2013. "Is Your College Going Broke? The Most and Least Financially Fit Schools in America." *Forbes*, https://www.forbes.com.

Scott, Joan W. 2018. *Knowledge, Power, and Academic Freedom*. New York: Columbia University Press.

Scott, Joan W. 2017. "On Free Speech and Academic Freedom." *AAUP Journal of Academic Freedom* 8, https://www.aaup.org/reports-publications/.

Scott, Joan W. April 15, 2015. "The New Thought Police." *Nation* 300(18):12–17.

Slaughter, Sheila and Larry Leslie. 2001. "Expanding and Elaborating the Concept of Academic Capitalism." *Organization* 8(2):154–161.

Smith, Jay M. and Mary Willingham. 2015. *Cheated: The UNC scandal, the Education of Athletes, and the Future of Big-Time College Sports*. Lincoln: University of Nebraska Press.

Sokolove, Michael. 2018. *The Last Temptation of Rick Pitino: A Story of Corruption, Scandal, and the Big Business of College Basketball*. New York: Penguin Press.

Son of Baldwin. June 16, 2017. http://kalamu.com/neogriot/2017/06/21/pov-let-them-fucking-die/.

Tiede, Hans-Joerg. April 24, 2014. "The Ross Case." *Academe Blog*, https://academeblog.org.

Tuchman, Gaye. 2016. "Accountability Regimes in Flagship Universities: How Strategic Planning Encourages Academic Capitalism." In Sheila Slaughter and Barrett J. Taylor (eds.), *Stratification, Privatization and Workforce Development*, 193–211. New York: Springer.

Tuchman, Gaye 2009. *Wannabe U: Inside the Corporate University*. Chicago: University of Chicago Press.

Veblen, Thorstein. [1918] 2015. *The Higher Learning in America*, annotated edition. Baltimore: Johns Hopkins University Press.

Warrior, Robert. 2015. "Response to Cary Nelson." *AAUP Journal of Academic Freedom* 6, https://www.aaup.org/reports-publications/.

Williams, Johnny Eric. 2018. "The Academic Freedom Double Standard: Freedom for Courtiers, Suppression for Critical Scholars." *AAUP Journal of Academic Freedom* 9, https://www.aaup.org/reports-publications/.

Wilson, John K. 2016. "The AAUP's 1915 *Definition of Principles*: Conservative and Radical, Visionary and Myopic." *AAUP Journal of Academic Freedom* 7, https://www.aaup.org/reports-publications/.

PART III

THE UNIVERSITY AND ITS INTERNAL WORLD

CHAPTER 6

Academic Freedom in a Contingent Academy

Gary Rhoades

Academic freedom, as promulgated and protected by the American Association of University Professors (AAUP), is contingent. It is contingent on the formal terms of employment that define due process and security for academic employees. It is also contingent on the willingness of individuals and groups to exercise it—like a muscle, it atrophies if not used. Moreover, academic freedom is contingent on organized groups of academic employees working to advance and defend it. All of these conditions are influenced by the sociopolitical and economic contexts in which higher education institutions exist, and by the structures of power they perpetuate within and beyond the academy.

This chapter examines the question, In a contingent academy, what are the problems and prospects of academic freedom? It is explored here by examining the contractual work conditions of adjunct faculty, graduate assistant employees, and postdocs. The status of academic freedom is compromised in an institution of higher education in which the employment conditions of its academic employees are increasingly affected by this contingency. It has been compromised by the insecurity that leaves such employees with limited due process protections and, thus, subject to the will, wishes, and caprice of supervisors.

This problematic situation is compounded by two external situations. The first consists of the increased market orientation of colleges and universities. "Academic capitalism" can undermine quality in the pursuit of and service to the "customer" (Slaughter and Rhoades 2004). Further, it can threaten—through censorship by authorities and peers, as well as self-censorship—the freedom of academic employees to engage in work that is critical of established social, economic, and political structures of power. The second consists of the increasingly hostile situation of ongoing "culture wars" (Hunter 1991). These, too, play out in higher education institutions, affecting academics' willingness to address targeted topics and positions.

Given these situations, academic freedom is dependent on the collective ability of college and university employees to establish (and enforce) employment structures and policies to protect such freedom. The first two decades of the twenty-first century have seen substantial advocacy and organizing efforts by segments of the academic workforce with the least due process protections—adjunct faculty, graduate assistant employees, and postdocs. This chapter casts some light on academic freedom issues that have emerged for these three groups and their collective responses to them.

Background and Literature

This chapter is situated in the evolving understandings of academic freedom coming from the AAUP. Over time, the association has variously defined academic freedom as it pertains to faculty, graduate student assistants, and postdocs. The chapter draws on literature and cases about these three types of academic employees to address problems of and prospects for academic freedom.

Academic Freedom and Adjunct Faculty

The academic freedom of adjunct (part-time) faculty is subsumed under that of faculty generally, though, over the decades, there have been statements specific to faculty in part- and full-time contingent positions. For example, a 1980 report on "The Status of Part-Time Faculty" states, "Moreover, increasing numbers of part-time faculty members are being appointed in an attempt to avoid any institutional commitment to tenure; the presence of large numbers of faculty serving 'at will' can have a chilling effect on general conditions of academic freedom at the institution as well as on academic quality" (AAUP Committee A 1980). A subsequent 2003 statement, "Contingent Appointments and the Academic Profession," notes that "currently, neither peer review nor academic due process operates adequately to secure academic freedom for most contingent faculty" (AAUP 2015, 175).

The AAUP has sought to light paths to tenure-stream positions and tenure-like due process rights for contingent faculty. Interestingly, one of the early cases that led to the association's formation was that of Scott Nearing in 1915, an assistant professor at the University of Pennsylvania whose writings on child labor and on World War I offended some alumni and board members. The newly formed organization conducted an investigation and found that although Nearing was on a one-to-three-year contract, its formal nonrenewal constituted a dismissal that violated his academic freedom. This framing was expressed in the headline of an article in the *New York Times*, "Professors Assail Nearing Dismissal: Academic Freedom Violated by University of Pennsylvania, Committee Finds" (1916), which covered the association's release of its report. In the words of the AAUP investigating committee, "If a continuance in office which he might otherwise expect to enjoy is refused a teacher because of objections to his opinions, or his public expressions of opinion, it makes little practical difference, so far as the inquiry to academic freedom is concerned, whether the result is called 'non-reappointment,' or 'removal,' or 'dismissal'" (Robins et al. 1916, 11).

Much the same reasoning is found in the association's "Recommended Institutional Regulation #13" on "Part-Time Faculty Appointments" (AAUP 2015, 86), which shifts the burden of proof to the institution in cases of non-reappointment for academic freedom violations. This regulation also details additional protections of due process leading up to reappointment beyond a seventh year, which carries some features of tenure.

The AAUP's classic 1940 "Statement of Principles on Academic Freedom and Tenure" (AAUP 2015, 13–20) provides for freedom of teaching, research, and extramural speech, "free from institutional censorship or discipline."[1] In language that some have regarded as selling short faculty's constitutional rights (see Slaughter 1980), the phrasing indicated that, "as scholars and educational officers, they should remember that the public may judge their profession and their institution by their utterances. Hence, they should at all times be accurate, should exercise appropriate restraint, should show respect for the opinions of others, and should make every effort to indicate that they are not speaking for the institution" (AAUP 2015, 14).

Subsequently, in response to a key US Supreme Court case and ensuing lower court rulings, AAUP Committee A issued a report that offered guidance for including protections on speech about institutional matters, although that was already embedded in the association's conception of shared governance. The pattern of court cases, however, led Committee A to conduct deliberations on *Garcetti v. Ceballos* and prompted the association to launch a national campaign encouraging faculty senates and unions to embed new language in the academic freedom clauses of their handbooks on collective bargaining agreements (O'Neil et al. 2009). This made particular sense, given that, in preceding decades, a major issue that led to AAUP investigations consisted of cases in which professors had been critical of administrators (Slaughter 1988).

Academic Freedom and Graduate Employees

From the standpoint of the AAUP, graduate assistants are both students and employees. In 2009, the association revised its statement on "Recommended Institutional Regulation on Academic Freedom and Tenure," with reference to what, in regulation #13, had been termed "graduate student academic staff" (AAUP 2006). An additional regulation (#14), relabeled "graduate student employees," included new, stronger language that provided considerably greater due process rights, evident in four additional bullet points (doubling the number in the previous policy). On behalf of academic freedom, this regulation added a burden of proof on the administration in cases of non-reappointment, indicating that "it is incumbent on those who made the decision to come forward with evidence in support of that decision." Further still, in cases of dismissal, the new regulation (#14.c) indicated that "dismissal will not be used to restrain graduate student employees in their exercise of academic freedom or constitutional rights," and that in an adjudicative hearing, "the administration will have the burden of showing adequate cause for dismissal" (AAUP 2015).

Academic Freedom and Postdocs

The AAUP does not have a separate statement regarding postdoctoral employees and academic freedom. As with contingent faculty, these academic employees are subsumed within other promulgations of academic freedom. Postdoctoral employees are spoken about most directly in the association's 2003 statement on "Contingent Appointments and the Academic Profession": "The concept of 'contingent faculty' includes postdoctoral fellows who are employed off the tenure track for periods of time beyond what could reasonably be considered the extension and completion of their professional training" (AAUP 2015, 171).

Postdocs, however, are significantly distinct from other contingent faculty by virtue of their direct dependence on the individual principal investigators who employ them. Perhaps for that reason, much of the national policy discussion about them centers on their *independence* in being able to pursue their own work (National Research Council 2005). In a 2014 National Academy of Sciences report, there is no reference to "academic freedom," yet there are repeated statements about the "research independence needed to pursue his or her career path" (NAS 2014, 3).

Academic Freedom and Sociopolitical Economic Contexts

Context matters in considering the problems and prospects of academic freedom. Arguably the most dramatic historical situation that politically and socially compromised academic freedom was the McCarthy period, during which the people associated with defending academic freedom were almost entirely silent, and where self-censorship was widespread (Schrecker 1986; Lewis 1988). A case could also be made that the culture wars of the last several decades have compromised academic freedom (Baez and Slaughter 2001; Turk 2014; Dougherty et al. 2017), which has been confounded by centuries of a white patriarchy that controls higher education.

The mid-1970s onward witnessed the ascension of a political-economic academic capitalism (Slaughter and Rhoades 2004) that has presented its own challenges to academic freedom. Part of this rise has involved the growth of managerial capacity and segments of contingent academic employees with "deep job insecurity and an almost total lack of due process, which fundamentally compromises academic freedom. Adjunct activists commonly assert that contingent faculty members are one student complaint away from non-renewal. Similarly, postdocs are 'one unhappy principal investigator away from non-renewal'" (Rhoades 2014a, 122). Institutions have upped their demands for productivity. Junior faculty pursuing tenure are increasingly evaluated by their capacity to leverage institutional revenue. This interest has arguably come to out-compete any concern for their creative exercise of academic freedom (Rhoades 2009). For those aspiring to the tenure track, such as postdocs, who are the core of research production in universities (Cantwell and Taylor 2015), their lives are increasingly defined by an overriding vulnerability (Camacho and Rhoades 2015).

Although academic employees have grown more unionized, partly in response to these sociopolitical/economic trends (Rhoades 1998), the AAUP, as a defender of academic freedom, was a relative latecomer to union activity, having been riven by internal divisions about collective bargaining (Hutcheson 2000). Over time, it has become clear that union organizing has yielded benefits in higher education institutions' formal terms of employment, including strengthened academic freedom for graduate employees (Rogers et al. 2013) and adjunct faculty (Tolley and Edwards 2018).

The Data

Given the link between formal terms of employment and academic freedom, the following discussion examines whether and how academic freedom is defined in collective bargaining agreements (CBAs) for three categories of academic employees: adjunct faculty, graduate employees, and postdocs. For all three groups, I utilized the Higher Education Contract Analysis System (HECAS), a national database compiled by the National Education Association. This database includes contracts negotiated by a variety of unions. For faculty contracts, it includes 82 percent of all contracts nationally, identified in the *Directory of the National Center for the Study of Collective Bargaining in Higher Education and the Professions* (Berry and Savarese 2012). The present chapter focuses on adjunct faculty in part-time-only (PTO) bargaining units, because these employees' academic freedom is most at risk. HECAS has sixty-two such contracts—sixteen in four-year institutions and forty-six in two-year institutions (Rhoades 2017).

HECAS also includes a substantial proportion (77 percent) of graduate employee contracts nationwide (thirty-two at the time of this analysis). The HECAS database was supplemented by online downloading of any missing contracts. Finally, the number of postdoc contracts is so small (five) that it was straightforward to go to the websites of the bargaining units/institutions to view them.

The contracts were analyzed for content regarding four items. The first consisted of the *incidence* of academic freedom language. The second involved the *meaning and scope* of academic freedom, as expressed in the language of the contract, and how this compares with the prevailing AAUP articulation (which includes teaching, research, and extramural speech), as well as the more recent concern about speech on institutional matters. The third dealt with language *strength*. This meant considering the placement and specificity of language. For example, a passing reference in a preamble suggests less strength than a separate article or a statement in a section on personnel matters (e.g., regarding discipline). Similarly, mitigating or countervailing language in a subsequent section arguably weakens protections.

Finally, the fourth item consisted of language about *non-discrimination clauses*. For graduate and postdoc employees, there can be protections of academic freedom in other provisions of CBAs. The principal place in a unionized setting is in non-discrimination clauses. Such articles establish that institutions cannot discriminate against individuals because of "union membership or activity," or for "political membership or activity." This protects those in unions who are critical of institutional policies and practices. Similarly, non-discrimination language about political affiliation and political activity can provide some safeguards against retaliation for "controversial" extramural speech.

Adjunct Faculty

Here I consider the four elements of central interest in contract construction, insofar as contracts pertain to academic freedom. I look, by turn, at the amount of academic freedom–related language in the contracts, its meaning and scope, and then language strength, followed by non-discrimination elements pertaining to union and political activity, where they arise. Further, given the under-examination of these matters in community colleges, where so many adjunct faculty work, this section compares academic freedom language in four- and two-year settings.

The incidence of academic freedom clauses in the contracts of PTO units is relatively high. Among four-year institutions, fourteen (87.5 percent) of the PTO contracts in HECAS had such language, slightly higher than the 83 percent found by Tolley and Edwards (2018) in the thirty-five contracts they examined at four-year institutions (at least ten of which included combined full- and part-time faculty units).

Among two-year institutions, thirty-seven (80 percent) of the PTO contracts had academic freedom language.

If the incidence of language was generally high, how comprehensive was its scope and meaning? In four-year-institution contracts, just over half (eight) of the academic freedom articles covered teaching, research, and extramural speech. In three cases, the language addressed teaching and research; in one case, just teaching; and in one other case, teaching and extramural speech. (In two additional cases, there was a one-sentence mention of academic freedom.) None of the contracts addressed speech about institutional matters.

In two-year institutions, two-thirds of the contracts covered teaching, research, and extramural speech. In four cases, the language addressed teaching and research; in three cases, teaching and extramural speech; and in two cases, just teaching. (In four other cases, academic freedom was mentioned in a sentence.) As with four-year institutions, none of the language addressed speech about institutional matters.

The strength of the contracts was revealed in the specificity of their language and whether there were caveats and countervailing phrasing. At one end of a spectrum, a handful of contracts (six) simply mentioned the concept, or, as in the case of American University's contract, mentioned it and then countered it with subsequent language: "Unless limited by the principles and obligations of academic freedom, nothing in this Agreement shall prevent Management from modifying the title, description, or content of a course that an employee has been assigned to teach. Employees will be notified of changes in course title or course content of the courses they have been assigned."

Such language points to the distinctive position of adjunct faculty in the courses they teach—that is, their assignment to preexisting courses, the content of which is already established, usually by the department in which they teach. A stronger phrasing of the rights of adjunct faculty on this theme can be found in Roosevelt University's contract: "An adjunct faculty member shall have full freedom to conduct classes consistent with the course description or outline and established academic policies or standards." Similarly, Emerson University's contract indicates, "Part-time faculty are entitled to academic freedom in the classroom to teach effectively their subject, consistent with the academic requirements of the College." Yet the departmental constraints are clear, as in the following phrasing by the City Colleges of Chicago: "Subject to departmental and College policies and procedures, part-time faculty members shall be free to present instructional materials, including, where practicable and with the permission of the Department Chair, textbooks, which are pertinent to the subject and level taught in their courses." Morton College's contract has almost the same language.

An example of a provision that strengthens the academic freedom claims of adjunct faculty in their teaching is from George Washington University:

> If there is a standard course syllabus, a Faculty member who is teaching a course for the first time at the University shall receive from the Dean/Department Chair/Program Director, or designee, within a reasonable time before the beginning of his or her teaching assignment, a copy of the standard course syllabus to be used in the course. If there is no standard course syllabus, or if the Faculty member believes that the standard course syllabus should be modified, then the Faculty member shall develop a new syllabus in consultation with the Dean/Department Chair/Program Director, or designee, based on the following: the syllabus for the course when it was recently taught, the most recent Department-approved course description and/or outline, and/or a Department-approved statement of the course's purposes and objectives. In all cases, the Dean/Department Chair/Program Director shall retain the right to review and approve any new or modified syllabus.

Such phrasing gives some agency to the faculty member, although it still accords final approval to the department.

The most typical academic freedom clauses were invocations of the classic 1940 AAUP statement (AAUP 2015, 13–20). Provisions either cited, drew on the statement verbatim, or paraphrased it to give adjunct faculty academic freedom in teaching, research, and extramural speech. In many cases that included the provisos embedded in the 1940 statement. For instance, in wording from Mt. Hood Community College: "This special position of the employee in the community imposes responsibility. The public may judge the profession and the College by the employee's utterances. Hence, an employee should make every effort to be accurate at all times, exercise appropriate restraint, show respect for the opinions of others and indicate that he/she is not a spokesperson for the College."

A few contracts speak directly to academic freedom in relation to personnel matters, such as discipline. Such clauses go beyond the standard phrasing of bargaining unit members that are "protected against institutional discipline or restraint," comparable to the 1940 "Statement of Principles" (AAUP 2015, 13–20). For example, Columbia College Chicago notes: "Because of the commitment of the College to academic freedom, no faculty member's appointment will be terminated for any belief, opinion, expression, or conduct, however unconventional or controversial, that is protected by the principles of academic freedom as defined in Article V, Section 1. Further, any explicit or implicit threat of termination or discipline for the purpose of constraining a faculty member in the exercise of his or her rights under such principles of academic freedom is contrary to the policies of the College.

Similarly, in spelling out a grievance and adjudication process, Triton College's contract reads, "In disposing of a complaint, the Board shall not violate the academic freedom section of this agreement." Another example along these lines is the PTO contract of the Vermont State Colleges, which mentions non-reappointment decisions, a major issue addressed in the AAUP policy and of substantial importance to adjunct faculty, who are subject to renewal decisions every semester, year, or few years: "A faculty member may receive a notice of non-reappointment from the College indicating he or she will no longer be considered for future assignments. A faculty member who receives such notice may file a grievance claiming that such action has violated the Anti-Discrimination Article or Academic Freedom Article." This type of language adds some layer of protection to academic freedom.

Graduate Employees

A second employee category in the contingent academy consists of graduate teaching and research assistants. To what extent is academic freedom built into their CBAs? What is the incidence of academic freedom–related language in the contracts? What are the meanings and scope of academic freedom that are covered? What is the strength of the language?

Only fifteen of the thirty-two CBAs related to graduate employees make any reference to the term "academic freedom" (including three with clauses that do not use the phrase but invoke the idea). All but two of the contracts with academic freedom language have it in a separate article. Two of the contracts (City University of New York and Rutgers University) are instances in which graduate employees are a part of larger faculty bargaining units. As for meaning and scope, most of the academic freedom language addresses teaching and research in the graduate employee contracts. Seven of the contracts address the freedom of graduate employees as citizens in extramural speech, and four discuss speech about institutional matters.

The strength of their academic freedom language was analyzed in terms of its specificity and whether there were mitigating or countervailing clauses in the contract. Once again, there is a spectrum. At one end, with very limited phrasing, is a one-sentence statement in the "Management Rights" section of the University of Illinois at Chicago's Graduate Employee Union contract: "The University and the Union agree that academic freedom is one of the values essential to higher education." Yet the following sentence offers countervailing language: "It is further agreed, except as abridged by the specific terms of this Agreement, that the University retains sole and exclusive control: to make all academic judgments [about courses, content, methods of instruction] . . . to determine all academic policies . . . to make academic evaluations." The contract for the Association of Graduate Employees at the University of Illinois, Springfield has the same sentence in its "Management Rights" clause. It, too, offers countervailing language, not just about management having control over the curriculum, but also that "the University retains sole and exclusive control [of] . . . (e) the nature and the form of assignments required including examinations and other work."

Three contracts invoke the idea of academic freedom without utilizing this term. For example, a "Professional Conditions" article in the contract of New York University's Graduate Student Organizing Committee reads, "Consistent with program guidelines, Graduate Employees shall have reasonable latitude, where appropriate, to exercise their professional judgment within their area of expertise in deciding how best to accomplish their assignments within the scope of the directions given by the individual supervisor as well as fiscal and time constraints." Similarly, Michigan State University's contract has one sentence in an "Employee Rights" article: "Employees shall have the right to take reasoned exception to information and views offered in courses in which they are employed to make suggestions for improvement." Wayne State University's contract bears similar language: "Employees shall have the right to make suggestions for improvements and to offer alternative views in courses in which they are employed."

At the other end of the spectrum is language found in two contracts in Florida (Graduate Assistants United at both Florida State University and the University of South Florida), as well as in the contract of the Professional Staff Congress of the City University of New York (CUNY), a faculty/professional staff union which includes graduate employees. The fact that these articles address speech about institutional matters makes them comparatively stronger. The language of the two Florida contracts is identical on this point: "5.2 Academic Freedom, within the context of the curriculum required by the University, is the freedom to discuss all relevant matters in the classroom, to explore all avenues of scholarship, research, and creative expression, to speak freely on all matters of university governance, and to speak, write, or act as an individual, all without institutional discipline or restraint." The key phrasing is "to speak freely on all matters of university governance."

The language is not as strong in the CUNY contract: "The Principles of Academic Freedom are recognized as applicable to . . . the formation of academic policy." But CUNY's is the only contract in which academic freedom is mentioned in an article on the discipline of personnel: "Members of the instructional staff may be disciplined by removal, suspension with or without pay, or any lesser form of discipline for one or more of the following reasons . . . (d) Conduct unbecoming a member of the staff: This provision shall not be interpreted so as to constitute interference with academic freedom." Such language captures, to a degree, the AAUP's recommended institutional regulation.

The Florida State University and University of South Florida contracts are also comparatively strong and distinctive in their inclusion of a clause that alludes to "the public good" in their academic freedom article: "5.1 Florida State University affirms the principles of academic freedom and responsibility, which are rooted in a conception of the University as a community of scholars united in the pursuit of truth and wisdom in an atmosphere of tolerance and freedom."

More explicit language about "the common good" is found in the academic freedom article (XIV) of the University of Rhode Island's contract: "Institutions of higher education are conducted for the common good and not to further the interests of either the individual or the institution as a whole. The common good depends upon the free search for truth and its free exposition. Academic Freedom is essential to these purposes and applies to both teaching and research." The contract further addresses the rights of graduate employees to academic freedom in their extramural speech, echoing the AAUP's language: "14.3 Graduate Assistants are employed as part-time teachers and researchers at an institution of higher education. When they write, or speak as citizens, they should be free from institutional censorship or discipline. As scholars, they should strive to be accurate, exercise appropriate restraint, should show respect for the opinion of others, and should make every effort to indicate they are not speaking for the institution."

Significantly, some contracts, such as those of the Graduate Assistants United bargaining unit at Florida A&M University and the University of Florida, speak of graduate assistants as "under the guidance of" either the department or their research supervisor, depending on whether the activity is teaching or research:

> It is the policy of the UBOT [University Board of Trustees] and UFF [United Faculty of Florida—the union affiliate] to encourage graduate assistants, in fulfillment of their assigned teaching responsibilities, to give their own interpretation of instructional materials used by them—whether self-chosen or prescribed by the teaching unit—within the bounds of knowledge and methodologies appropriate to the disciplinary field, under the guidance of the employing department or unit. In fulfilling assigned research duties, graduate assistants will be encouraged to exercise creativity and sound judgment in carrying out the theoretical, conceptual, and methodological design of the research under the guidance of the research supervisor.

Similarly, the University of Massachusetts, Amherst's contract reads, "Graduate student employees shall have reasonable latitude to exercise their professional judgment within their area of expertise in deciding how best to accomplish their assignments within the scope of the directions given by the individual's supervisor as well as fiscal and time constraints."

A particularly telling contract is that of the University of Rhode Island, which, by its language, takes a position on the status of graduate employees. A CBA from 2011 indicated that "graduate assistants are apprentices to a learned profession," whereas the latest contract (from 2018) dropped that phrase. But both contracts have "under the supervision" language: "Graduate students will have reasonable latitude to exercise their judgment in deciding how best to accomplish their teaching and research in their discipline under the supervision of the faculty of the department and college. They also are entitled to freedom in the classroom in discussion of their discipline, subject to the supervision of the faculty of the department and college."

Half of the contracts address academic freedom in extramural speech. One of the narrower of these is the contract from the University of Massachusetts, Amherst: "Within the provisions of applicable laws and University policies and subject to paragraph one above, graduate student employees are entitled to freely express in their work environment their political beliefs and/or affiliations." The narrowness of the "in their work environment" language is also found in Southern Illinois University, Carbondale's contract, which contains the same phrasing. By contrast, a more expansive reference to extramural speech appears in Rutgers University's contract, which invokes the AAUP's classic 1940 statement (Rutgers adopted it in 1967). The University of Rhode Island also makes reference more broadly to graduate employees' speech as citizens.

Finally, a total of four graduate employee contracts define academic freedom in relation to speech about institutional matters. For example, in the University of Florida contract, the phrasing is that graduate assistants have the right to "speak freely on all matters of university governance . . . all without institutional discipline or restraint." Florida State University and the University of South Florida have identical phrasing.

In unionized settings, part of ensuring academic freedom is language protecting bargaining unit members from discipline or retaliation due to their union membership or activity. Such language is generally found in non-discrimination clauses. Such clauses can also be seen as addressing the political affiliation or activity of bargaining unit members—similar to a protection of their right to engage in extramural speech. Non-discrimination articles are far more prevalent than academic freedom ones in the contracts of graduate employees. Twenty-nine of the thirty-two contracts have some sort of non-discrimination language that addresses either union affiliation and activity, or political affiliation and activity. All twenty-nine of them address discrimination against employees based on their *union affiliation*. Fewer (eighteen) mention *union activity*. Considerably less (thirteen) refer to *political affiliation*. And only one discusses *political activity*. This language provides some protection for bargaining unit employees to exercise their academic freedom to speak out on institutional matters. But it offers little to no protection for them to speak out about external political matters, even as this safeguard is one of the long-standing, central concerns of academic freedom.

Postdoctoral Employees and Academic Freedom

The third category in the contingent academy to be addressed here consists of postdoctoral employees. Of the five postdoc contracts, only two have academic freedom language. One of them (at the University of Massachusetts, Amherst) consists of one sentence in an appendix about grievances: "As in any grievance procedure, justice requires that the legal rights as well as the right to academic freedom of any complainant, the whistleblower, and the person who has allegedly violated the misconduct rules, the respondent, be fully assured." The second (at the University of Oregon) is a combined unit that includes tenure-stream faculty, contingent and adjunct faculty, and postdocs. The language ties academic freedom to "enrich[ing] the public" and indicates that "this policy establishes a robust view of academic freedom and freedom of speech in order to ensure that faculty have the freedom to conduct research, to teach, to engage in internal criticism, and to participate in public debate." Generally speaking, it is an expansive and strong articulation of academic freedom.

On non-discrimination clauses, all five of the contracts have language about union and political affiliation or activity. All of the clauses protect bargaining unit members with respect to their union membership, and four specifically protect their union activity. The ability to speak out about institutional matters is also an important safeguard for bargaining unit members. Further, there is sometimes whistleblower protection, as in the clause of the University of California's postdoc contract: "2. The University shall not retaliate against any Postdoctoral Scholar for identifying, and/or expressing concerns about safety-related issues." Yet only two of the contracts' non-discrimination clauses refer to political affiliation, and none to political activity. Thus there is no protection of postdocs' extramural speech.

Three of the contracts contain language about "independence." The wording in the University of Massachusetts's contract mirrors that of the National Academy of Sciences' report (NAS 2014) in defining a postdoc: "[A postdoctoral employee] is engaged in a temporary period, generally not exceeding six years, of mentored advanced training to enhance his/her professional skills and research and/or teaching independence needed to pursue an academic and/or research career." The University of Oregon's contract parallels that language, absent the term "independent." And the University of California's contract states that postdocs have "an individual development plan (IDP)," which "provides a planning process that identifies the Postdoctoral Scholar's general individual research goals, professional development and career objectives."

Strikingly, however, such provisions accord postdocs far less academic freedom than graduate employees. It is worth noting that in Canada, where larger proportions of academic employees are unionized, there are examples of postdocs having academic freedom protections. By way of example, the Université Laval contract ("Chapter 17" n.d.) for postdocs includes the following language: "While respecting the freedom of opinion of others, postdoctoral fellows shall enjoy the freedom of conscience inherent to a public academic institution such as the University. Such freedom may be restricted by the Employer only in accordance with the contractual obligations set out in the agreement. Postdoctoral fellows have the right to exercise their political freedoms in accordance with the contractual obligations set out in the agreement."

Conclusion

Throughout its history, academic freedom has been defined by a combination of elements: structures and norms of employment, such as tenure and shared governance; the collective actions of faculty in their national associations, such as the AAUP, the American Federation of Teachers, and unions; and the will of individual academic employees.

The prospects of academic freedom are similarly shaped by (a) the terms of employment that define increasing numbers of contingent academic employees; (b) the collective framing of possibilities by the more resourced, secure, and powerful segments of faculty, particularly the tenured class; and (c) the will of academic employees in all segments of their workforce to exercise, defend, and incorporate the varieties of academic personnel within the purview of academic freedom.

The core academic functions of higher education institutions are now largely performed by employees in contingent positions. Precarious terms of employment compromise academic freedom, as does "academic capitalism" and the culture wars of the times. Nowadays, "we are all contingent," not just metaphorically, but literally (Rhoades 2014b). This is evident in the restructuring of colleges and universities, which has led to the elimination of programs and tenure-stream positions. Put bluntly, those in the academy are, increasingly, "managed professionals" (Rhoades 1998).

But academic employees are also increasingly organizing to establish terms of employment that will secure greater levels of due process and academic freedom. Adjunct faculty have succeeded in establishing at least some statements and protections for academic freedom. There is considerable room, however, for strengthening such provisions, particularly in defining this freedom in the teaching of their courses, in embedding academic freedom protections in discipline and dismissal clauses, in addressing speech about institutional matters, and in ensuring greater job security through a presumption of reappointment. For their part, graduate employees have negotiated such safeguards in roughly half of their contracts. Again, though, there is room for considerably more and stronger provisions, including those that protect speech about institutional matters.

Finally, as the most vulnerable contingent of academic employees, postdocs have gained only quite limited protections. Most of their contracts do not address academic freedom. Baseline safeguards for postdocs refer more often to establishing some right to due process and to "independence." There is a need for these employees to have broader protections regarding academic freedom, for they are central to the research enterprise of universities. Further, postdocs and graduate employees are considerably more diverse in gender, ethnicity, and nation of origin than are tenure-stream professors. What are we conditioning in future faculty about the value of academic freedom, if such freedom goes unprotected for groups on whose labor major parts of institutions depend?

Tenured professors have a responsibility toward academic freedom that has yet to be sufficiently articulated, not just as individual advisors/mentors to graduate and postdoc employees and other contingent (as well as probationary) faculty, but also collectively, in helping to define rights possessed by these academic employees. Most importantly, the future of academic freedom is dependent on contingent employees' collective action, including the schooling of tenure-stream faculty. Lessons remain to be learned about how everyone benefits when academic freedom is a term of employment extended to all.

Note

1. See Cain (2018) for insight into the struggles between and within the AAUP and American Federation of Teachers over this statement and the length of the probationary period.

References

AAUP (American Association of University Professors). 2015. *Policy Documents and Reports*, 11th edition. Baltimore: Johns Hopkins University Press.

AAUP (American Association of University Professors). 2006. *Policy Documents and Reports*, 10th edition. Baltimore: Johns Hopkins University Press.

AAUP (American Association of University Professors) Committee A. 1980. "The Status of Part-Time Faculty." AAUP Reports & Publications, https://www.aaup.org/reports-publications/.

Baez, Benjamin and Sheila Slaughter. 2001. "Academic Freedom and Federal Courts in the 1990s: The Legitimation of the Conservative Entrepreneurial State." In John C. Smart (ed.), *Handbook of Theory and Research in Higher Education*, 73–118. Bronx, NY: Agathon Press.

Berry, Joe and Michelle Savarese. 2012. *Directory of U.S. Faculty Contracts and Bargaining Agents in Institutions of Higher Education*. New York: National Center for the Study of Collective Bargaining in Higher Education and the Professions.

Cain, Timothy R. 2018. "A Long History of Activism and Organizing: Contingent Faculty, Graduate Students, and Unionization." In Kim Tolley (ed.), *Professors in the Gig Economy: Unionizing Adjunct Faculty in America*, 46–68. Baltimore: Johns Hopkins University Press.

Camacho, Sayil and Robert A. Rhoads. 2015. "Breaking the Silence: The Unionization of Postdoctoral Workers at the University of California." *Journal of Higher Education* 86(2):295–325.

Cantwell, Brendan and Barrett J. Taylor. 2015. "Rise of the Science and Engineering Postdoctorate and the Restructuring of Academic Research." *Journal of Higher Education* 86(5):667–696.

"Chapter 17: Academic Freedom." n.d. Médias STEP, http://www.infostep.org/postdocs-en/collective-agreement-postdocs-en/.

Dougherty, Kristine A., Gary Rhoades, and Mark F. Smith. 2017. "The 'You're Fired' Era: Academic Freedom, Student Complaints, and Faculty Discipline." *The NEA 2017 Almanac of Higher Education*. Washington, DC: National Education Association.

Flaherty, Colleen. December 11, 2014. "Unsustainable Postdocs." *Inside Higher Ed*, https://www.insidehighered.com.

Hunter, James Davison. 1991. *Culture Wars: The Struggle to Define America*. New York: Basic Books.

Hutcheson, Philo A. 2000. *A Professional Professoriate: Unionization, Bureaucratization, and the AAUP*. Nashville, TN: Vanderbilt University Press.

Lewis, Lionel S. 1988. *Cold War on Campus: A Study of the Politics of Organizational Control*. New Brunswick, NJ: Transaction Books.

NAS (National Academy of Sciences). 2014. *The Postdoctoral Experience Revisited*. Washington, DC: National Academies Press.

National Research Council. 2005. *Bridges to Independence: Fostering the Independence of New Investigators in Biomedical Research*. Washington, DC: National Academies Press.

O'Neil, Robert M., Judith C. Areen, Matthew W. Finkin, Larry G. Gerber, William W. Van Alstyne, and Cary Nelson. 2009. "Protecting an Independent Faculty Voice: Academic Freedom after *Garcetti v. Ceballos*." *Academe* 95(6):67–80.

"Professors Assail Nearing Dismissal: Academic Freedom Violated by University of Pennsylvania, Committee Finds." May 27, 1916. *New York Times*, 6.

Rhoades, Gary. 2017. "Bread and Roses, and Quality too? A New Faculty Majority Negotiating the New Academy." *Journal of Higher Education* 88(5):645–671.

Rhoades, Gary. 2014a. "Extending Academic Capitalism by Foregrounding Academic Labor." In Brendan Cantwell and Ilkka Kauppinen (eds.), *Academic Capitalism in the Age of Globalization*, 113–136. Baltimore: Johns Hopkins University Press.

Rhoades, Gary. 2014b. "We Are All Contingent: Reorganizing Higher Education and Society." *On Campus* 33(4):2–4.

Rhoades, Gary. 2009. "From the General Secretary: What We Do to Our Young." *Academe* 95(3):56.

Rhoades, Gary. 1998. *Managed Professionals: Unionized Faculty and Restructuring Academic Labor*. Albany: State University of New York Press.

Robins, Edward E., Edwin R. A. Seligman, Edgar F. Smith, Simon N. Patten, Arthur O. Lovejoy, Davis R. Dewey, Henry W. Farnam, Franklin H. Giddings, and Roscoe Pound. 1916. "Part Two: Report of the Committee of Inquiry on the Case of Professor Scott Nearing of the University of Pennsylvania." *Bulletin of the American Association of University Professors* 2(3):5–57.

Rogers, Sean E., Adrienne E. Eaton, and Paula P. Voos. 2013. "The Effects of Unionization on Graduate Student Employees: Faculty-Student Relations, Academic Freedom, and Pay." *Industrial and Labor Relations Review* 66(2):487–510.

Schrecker, Ellen W. 1986. *No Ivory Tower: McCarthyism and the Universities*. New York: Oxford University Press.

Slaughter, Sheila. 1988. "Academic Freedom and the State: Reflections on the Uses of Knowledge." *Journal of Higher Education* 59(May/June):241–262.

Slaughter, Sheila. 1980. "The Danger Zone: Academic Freedom and Civil Liberties." *Annals of the American Academy of Political and Social Science* 448(March):46–61.

Slaughter, Sheila and Gary Rhoades. 2004. *Academic Capitalism and the New Economy: Markets, State, and Higher Education*. Baltimore: Johns Hopkins University Press.

Tolley, Kim and Kristen Edwards. 2018. "Reflections on the Possibilities and Limitations of Collective Bargaining." In Kim Tolley (ed.), *Professors in the Gig Economy: Unionizing Adjunct Faculty in America*, 187–202. Baltimore: Johns Hopkins University Press.

Turk, James L. 2014. *Academic Freedom in Conflict: The Struggle Over Free Speech Rights in the University*. Toronto: James Lorimer.

CHAPTER 7

The Challenges of Academic Freedom for Contingent Faculty

Eve Weinbaum and Dan Clawson

Where academic freedom is concerned, the focus is often centered on prominent colleges and universities. When a dispute arises about tenure-system faculty at Yale University, or Middlebury College, or the University of California-Berkeley, it can make national news. Scholars across the country may arguably be quicker to defend professors' rights to teach and pursue research when those faculty are respected experts in their fields, having distinguished profiles and prestigious appointments. Academic leaders may sign petitions and write op-eds defending their colleagues and their institutions from coercive measures to be taken against them.

But if a defense of academic freedom focuses only on tenure-system faculty, we overlook the largest share of those who teach in American higher education institutions. Higher education is in a process of transformation; the forces affecting it are the same as those reshaping the larger socioeconomy. Neoliberalism is the new order of the day. In the academy, the transformation involves a weakening of academic freedom, but for the most part this is collateral damage in the neoliberal campaign to shift costs, create insecurity, reinforce hierarchy, and magnify inequality. These changes are taking place throughout the world, from meatpacking plants to nursing homes, from auto manufacturing to the social services industry. Institutions of higher education are no exception.

Contingent Workers Are the New Faculty Majority

Discussions of academic freedom may typically focus on research universities and elite liberal arts colleges. These deliberations often center on threats to tenure-system faculty. Consequently, the discourse has not paid due accord to the larger segment of faculty today, to most student employees, and to many of the important issues pertaining to the freedoms that affect these two groups.

Ivy League institutions plus top-rated liberal arts colleges enroll 0.5 percent of all students in the United States (Clawson and Page 2011). When we add Research I universities, we are still left with but a small fraction of the higher education universe. More than a third of college enrollments are at two-year institutions (US Census Bureau 2009, table 269). As Steven Brint and Jerome Karabel (1989, v) have noted, "the majority of all degree-credit students entering the system of higher education have done so in a two-year institution." Moreover, large proportions of students are enrolled at lesser-known state colleges and universities—institutions filled with dedicated faculty and eager students, but not the sorts of places that generally receive media attention.

Further, we must not lose sight of the fact that a majority of the professoriate are employed today in contingent positions. From the 1940s through the 1970s, most faculty were in the tenure system, but academia has made a decisive shift toward contingent teaching employment since that time (Clawson 2009). In 1975, 35.9 percent of all faculty were full time and tenured; an additional 19.9 percent were full time, untenured, but on the tenure track. In total, 55.8 percent were full time in the tenure system. By 2007, only 20.9 percent of all faculty were full time and tenured, and only 9.7 percent were full time, untenured, but on the tenure track. Therefore, only 30.6 percent were full time and in the tenure system (Benjamin 2010). A focus on full-time, tenure-system faculty misses more than two-thirds of the people whose terms of employment may engender significant problems with academic freedom.

It is not easy to estimate precisely how quickly the tenure-track professoriate has been replaced by contingent faculty, in part because of the mix of terms and categories used for analysis. For many purposes, reliable federal data come from the integrated postsecondary education data system (IPEDS). These data, however, are based on counting the number of positions, not people. Thus, if an adjunct teaches at three different institutions, that person is tabulated three times. The current population survey (CPS) tallies individuals, but it "does not differentiate faculty by type of institution or by tenure status" (GAO 2017, 8). The differences between the two types of data can be substantial. For example, the CPS estimates that 31.7 percent of instructors work part-time, but "according to IPEDS data, part-time faculty held about 50.0 percent of instructional positions" (GAO 2017, 11). That is, the IPEDS estimate of the proportion of the professoriate who are part time is more than 50 percent higher than the CPS estimate, because IPEDS just counts the number of faculty positions instead of people.

These two key facts—where are the students, and who constitute the faculty—are, in turn, closely related. Part-time and temporary employment for teachers is most common at community colleges; the tenure system is strongest at elite institutions. As a general rule, the more prestigious the college or university, the higher the proportion of professors who are in the tenure system. "According to 2015 IPEDS data, contingent faculty fill 69.5 percent of the 1,444,774 postsecondary instructional positions across all institutions nationwide, including about 61.4 percent of instructional positions at 4-year institutions, 83.5 percent at 2-year institutions, and 99.7 percent at for-profit institutions" (GAO 2017, 10). Among four-year colleges, the larger ones tend to have a higher proportion of tenure-system faculty (GAO 2017). For-profit colleges and two-year institutions are staffed predominantly by contingent faculty, and even in four-year colleges, the number of contingent positions is greater than the number of tenure-system ones. All data sources are consistent in showing both that a large fraction of instructors are working in contingent positions, and that this proportion is increasing.

Contingent faculty come in many forms. At one end, a full-time, non-tenure-track professor on a long-term contract at a four-year institution may have a high degree of job stability and a range of protections. Some of these academics even have continuous appointments. Instead of signing a new contract every year, they are expected to remain in their positions, and specific reasons must be used to terminate their contracts. The possible reasons for firing a long-term, non-tenured professor may be spelled out in the institution's rules or in a union contract that requires "just cause." A continuous appointment does not have the full protection offered by tenure, but it can provide substantial job security.

At the other end, part-time faculty are hired by the course, as temporary workers. Even if they have been at the same institution and taught the same classes for several years, each course is—in principle and in practice—a new hire. There are no rules that guarantee a preference for the individual already in place, or that the course will continue to be offered. At many institutions, contingent faculty are explicitly banned from teaching more than a specified number of classes, because they would then be eligible for benefits or a continuing appointment.

Not only are there many different categories of non-tenure-system faculty (part time vs. full time, per course vs. salaried, long-term contracts vs. temporary hires), but their titles are also varied—and contested. Different faculty organizations, scholars, and administrators use alternative terms to refer to these academics. Even within our own university system in Massachusetts, faculty on one campus refer to themselves proudly as "adjuncts" and demand adjunct justice, while on another campus, instructors reject that term and see themselves as the heart of the teaching mission of the university. Some use the term "lecturer," as opposed to "professor," but others challenge that distinction, too, saying that lecturer is an inaccurate description of their work.

Some universities have non-tenure-track "teaching professors." On our campus, faculty initially preferred the term "contract faculty" to define those without tenure, but after the union won the right to continuing appointments after an individual had been employed for three years, they decided to call themselves "non-tenure-track (NTT) faculty." For the purposes of this chapter, we use these terms interchangeably. Contingent, adjunct, NTT, and contract faculty all refer to full- or part-time instructors who do not have the protections of tenure and are not on the tenure track.

How Academic Freedom Differs for Tenure-Track and Non-Tenure-Track Faculty

The comparative absence of academic freedom for contingent faculty matters not only because they are a large fraction of all academics, but also—and perhaps even more so—because the process of challenging and defending academic freedom differs significantly, based on the structural position of an instructor. The distinction between contingent and tenure-system faculty is not, in all likelihood, salient for those who attack a faculty member's statements or actions. For faculty, however, this distinction looms large, and not without reason. Most students and outside groups are hardly aware of what tenure means. For such people, attacks on academic freedom are essentially undifferentiated by the faculty member's structural position.

Yet the ways in which those in the professoriate are able to respond to attacks differ substantially. The social networks available to tenure-system faculty are usually wider, deeper, and more powerful. Such individuals typically have been at an institution longer, and, starting from their first day of employment, they work to develop networks, knowing that these will matter in achieving tenure and will endure over the long run. More-senior tenured professors generally are interested in cultivating networks with new tenure-system faculty, and invitations to coffee, lunch, or dinner are routine. Tenured academics rarely see a need to cultivate contingent faculty. The more years that tenure-system professors are in their positions, the more networks they are likely to have cultivated, which include those senior to them, those in roughly their own cohort, and those who are newly arriving junior colleagues.

Tenure-system academics' networks are also more structurally powerful. In comparison, contingent faculty may connect with tenure-system individuals, but many of their closest bonds probably are with other contingent faculty who, like themselves, have comparatively few resources to activate in times of trouble. Put simply, a tenure-system professor is likely to have a larger and more powerful social network as a resource that can be called upon for action.

Tenure-system faculty are also inclined to be more knowledgeable about, and have better access to, a variety of campus resources, ranging from the union, to the faculty senate, to the ombudsperson, to the equal opportunity office. Not only is a tenure-system professor more likely to know about these services, but also to be aware of which offices and resources have a demonstrated record of effectiveness, and which others are, for lack of a better way of putting it, paper tigers.

Most importantly, a tenure-system professor can draw on a major cultural resource: the widespread cultural sense—within academia and beyond—that such faculty *should have* academic freedom. The situation is analogous to Barbara Jeanne Fields's argument about why, in colonial America, after a period of contestation and uncertainty, Africans, but not English indentured servants, became permanently enslaved:

> Africans and Afro-West Indians had not taken part in the long history of negotiation and contest in which the English lower classes had worked out the relationship between themselves and their superiors. Therefore, the custom and law that embodied that history did not apply to them. To put it another way: when English servants entered the ring in Virginia, they did not enter alone. Instead, they entered in company with the generations who had preceded them in the struggle; and the outcome of these earlier struggles established the terms and conditions of the latest one. But Africans and Afro-West Indians did enter the ring alone. (Fields 1990, 104)

The American Association of University Professors (AAUP) is best known for defending academic freedom nationally through its policy statements, investigatory processes, and a well-publicized censure list. Faculty expect institutions to be committed to—and to defend—academic freedom. Any college or university that had a reputation for not doing so would risk losing prestige, and academics with choices about where to go for employment would tend to shun such a place. In theory, protections promulgated by the AAUP apply to contingent faculty. Their "Statement of Principles on Academic Freedom" (AAUP 1940) defines tenure by longevity: any full-time faculty member who has been reappointed for seven years has the protections of de facto tenure and cannot be fired without cause.

In practice, however, full-time professors without tenure are often let go—and part-time faculty or those with less longevity are even more vulnerable. An employer has many more tools available for getting rid of a contingent faculty member, and the academic community is rarely as outraged when this occurs as when a tenured professor is fired. When tenure-system faculty members say something offensive, an institution either has to live with them, buy them out (e.g., through an early retirement offer), or take actions that will lead to widespread and damaging charges that the institution has violated academic freedom.

By contrast, for contingent members of the professoriate, an employer simply can claim that such persons are not renewed for totally different reasons. This may violate AAUP policy positions, but it arguably happens often. For example, an administration can say that a termination has nothing to do with academic freedom; rather, the institution has decided not to offer a course again for "budgetary reasons" or other rationales. Thus an institution can violate academic freedom without admitting that it has done so. While the AAUP may investigate and, in rare cases, censure a college or university, there are, for all practical purposes, no other material consequences from the AAUP's involvement. Because an institution can claim a person was not fired, but simply was not renewed, and aver that the matter had nothing to do with academic freedom, it is more difficult to marshal on- and off-campus resources, including media and the public, in defense of those who have suffered this violation. Such faculty are almost never reinstated.

Understanding the degree of an academic's vulnerability affects the strength and character of attacks. For example, graduate students might express outrage at the comments of a non-tenure-track faculty member, but they might be reluctant to speak out against a full professor with a named chair and powerful connections in a field. A tenure-system professor has every reason to fight, and fight hard, for an appealing job. But contingent faculty members have good reasons *not* to fight. They are likely to be in need of another job (and probably still another one not long after that). Although certain colleagues might admire whatever defenses contingent faculty might undertake on behalf of their academic freedom, hiring decisions are ultimately made by administrators, and they are likely to avoid hiring individuals who might (in their eyes) "cause trouble." By rational choice, most non-tenure-track academics make the decision to stay quiet and look for their next job.

An Illustration: Two Racial Incidents

Two incidents about race in one department, taking place within a year of each other, help demonstrate how and why academic freedom is more problematic for contingent faculty.

Incident #1: An instructor, teaching an introductory course with graduate teaching assistants, discussed the treatment of American Indians in the Upper Midwest, specifically in the area where the faculty member had grown up. As part of that lecture, in an attempt to convey the attitudes of some local people toward these Natives, the instructor noted that in this area, Indians were often referred to as "prairie niggers." The use of this term was part of a lecture and clearly intended as an aspect of a teaching experience. At least one of the teaching assistants (TAs) for the course, however, raised an objection, stating that use of the "n-word" is always racist and unacceptable. The faculty member noted there was a good *instructional* reason to use the word—in fact, that individual was condemning its use—but, nevertheless, the instructor apologized personally and in writing to the TAs and the students.

Incident #2: Departmental offices were shuffled from one building to another. Graduate students and faculty received new keys and different office assignments. A black male graduate student was unsure of which room was his, and his key did not work for the office to which he thought he had been assigned. He went to try his key in other doors, looking for a place where the key worked and the room contained his belongings. The graduate student successfully opened an office and looked to see if his possessions were there. They weren't. As he exited the room, a white female faculty member who was moving out of that office encountered him. He explained he was a graduate student looking for his belongings, and the faculty member said all the items in that room were hers. The faculty member then crossed the hall to the office where the graduate student had just been and said that her purse was not where she had left it. The male reiterated that he was a graduate student and insisted he was not a thief. He opened the drawers of all the desks there, and the faculty member went into the room, checking to see that every drawer was empty. About ten minutes later the faculty member found her bag in her own new office, came back, and tried to apologize to the graduate student, who refused to accept the apology.

Which of these incidents raises the more serious concerns? Should people in one or both situations be subject to serious sanctions? Should either faculty member receive support from colleagues? Should the faculty member's status as either contingent or tenured shape that response?

In incident #2, the purse confrontation, the faculty member acknowledged in writing that her reaction had been racist. Graduate students organized protests and boycotted the department because of fallout from the incident. Nevertheless, there were no job ramifications for the professor's behavior. In fact, in a subsequent faculty meeting, she thanked her colleagues for their support. There is reason to believe that the situation would have been dramatically different if that person had not been a senior faculty member with tenure.

In incident #1, the individual was a full-time, non-tenure-track faculty member who used the "n-word" for pedagogical purposes. Despite the apology to everyone in the classroom, that person's contract was not renewed, although, before the incident, the instructor was informed of a pending contract with a continuing appointment. That individual never worked at the university again. The institution's stated reasons for non-renewal were scarce resources and departmental flexibility. No formal report of an academic freedom violation was made about the lecturer's non-renewal. An attempt to make an issue of it would almost certainly have had an unsuccessful outcome, as the university would claim the decision had nothing to do with the classroom speech, but rather was rendered on other grounds. Publicizing the issue most likely would have damaged the faculty member's future employability and might have led to that person being permanently labeled as "racially insensitive." This case, like many others, will never appear in any database attempting to track academic freedom issues.

How Common Are Academic Speech Incidents?

Reliable data on the number of non-tenure-track faculty who have been disciplined or fired because of speech that was considered political or in some way inappropriate are unavailable. Only cases that become public can be counted, and most academics who lose their jobs are unwilling to make their experiences generally known. On the contrary, they usually want to keep such episodes as quiet as possible as they search for another job. While tenured faculty may feel outrage and indignation when their academic freedom is violated, contingent faculty, by definition, have no right to long-term employment, so it is probably a rare exception for them to speak out about violations of their academic freedom.

The best available data on the matter were collected by Jeffrey Adam Sachs, a political scientist at Acadia University. Sachs compiled evidence from mainstream sources about US faculty who, between 2007 and 2018, were fired from their jobs for political speech. He showed that there was a significant uptick in the number of such firings, starting—perhaps coincidentally—around the time of Donald Trump's presidential election in 2016. Sachs (2018) created a database of fifty-nine identifiable academics who lost their jobs, and the data reveal that in 2017, there was a sharp increase in the number of terminations involving contingent faculty. Due to the inherent challenges of collecting such data, this number probably undercounts the phenomenon.

The data indicate that NTT faculty were most likely to lose their jobs because of political speech if they worked at religiously affiliated colleges and universities, where faculty are expected to adhere to the institution's spiritual tenets. Overall, the most common reason for being fired at these institutions was that a faculty member was "too liberal." For example, of twenty-six individuals fired or demoted in 2017, nineteen were politically liberal. We infer that this means they were (or were perceived as) anti-Trump, anti-police, anti-Christian, anti-white, anti-Israel, or pro-LGBTQ. When religious institutions are removed from the analysis, the disparity still persists. Liberal faculty members are more at risk of disciplinary actions than their conservative colleagues. From one point of view, this may not be surprising. Right-wing organizations are arguably well funded, well organized, and mobilized around the idea that professors are spreading left-wing ideologies on college campuses. Organizations such as Campus Reform, Turning Point USA, the Leadership Institute, Project Veritas, Students for Liberty, and other groups funded by conservative donors provide a network in which to disseminate stories and engage the media, in order to silence faculty whom they consider threatening.

Sachs (2018) also shows that the greatest rate of increase in firings occurs in public universities. One may contend that as the Right Wing gains strength, organizations have taken their campaigns from smaller private institutions—often religiously oriented and vulnerable to the opinions of alumni and donors—to large public institutions. It would appear that no campus is immune to these types of attacks.

The Invisibility of Non-Tenure-Track Academic Freedom Violations

When a faculty member with tenure is fired because of a political controversy, it is more likely to attract attention. This type of situation may also be relatively less ambiguous about what happened and why. Such conditions provide grounds on which to believe, however accurately or not, that there is some specific information about the circumstances surrounding the termination of a tenured faculty member.

By contrast, the situation is more ambiguous for non-tenure-track faculty members. Instructors can be fired in the middle of a contract; they can be suspended or taken out of the classroom and their contracts not renewed; or an administration can wait until their appointments expire and simply not rehire them. This last pattern is particularly difficult to track. When faculty are subject to sanctions short of termination—such as suspensions, demotions, reductions in teaching loads, or reassignments to non-teaching roles—it is even less likely that the cases are publicized. Yet the chilling effect on academic freedom is undoubtedly palpable.

To push this point, the examples from Sachs' (2018) data represent a small fraction of academic freedom violations within the population of NTT faculty. Sachs only tracks terminations, not lesser forms of punishment (or retaliation). In more than 90 percent of the cases where NTT instructors are fired or face serious job consequences, both the administration and the faculty member have strong incentives to remain silent about the matter, and even to deny that it happened. The individual who is involved prefers to keep anything controversial out of the press or social media. The administration does not want to be seen as caving in to pressure groups and seeks to avoid legal challenges. Arguably, in the majority of cases, the parties remain quiet and "move on."

Anecdotally, and by way of illustration, we have identified a number of instances in which NTT faculty were either fired or not renewed (when they had every expectation of renewal) because they said or did something that was either critical of their institution or controversial among students, alumni, donors, or organized political organizations. All of these acts, we contend, should be covered by academic freedom, but for most non-tenure-track faculty, the principle is meaningless if it cannot be materially applied.

Examples of Violations

Some people may not realize that free speech does not exist within the typical US workplace. Despite the First Amendment's protections of citizens' rights, a number of employees do not enjoy those same guarantees. Many of them are workers "at will" and can be terminated for behaviors and speech that disquiet their employer—a bumper sticker, a bad haircut, or a Facebook post. The same is true for faculty who do not have tenure or union protection. Non-tenure-track faculty may be terminated simply for displeasing their colleagues or their administration.

Lecturer Ruthie Robertson offended her employer, Brigham Young University, by a Facebook post: "I will always and forever stand up for the equality of the LGBT community. Sexuality and gender are not binary, they are on a spectrum and that's how we were made." BYU administrators called her in and asked her to "pray about the post," making it clear that they expected her to change the message. She was fired after refusing to take down her post. Although Robertson scrupulously ensured that her opinions never entered the classroom, her employer nevertheless had the legal right to fire her for expressing these views (Schmidt 2017a).

Similarly, according to the *Washington Post*, Katherine Dettwyler, an adjunct professor in anthropology at the University of Delaware, was fired after tweeting that Otto Warmbier, an American student arrested in North Korea after allegedly stealing a poster from his hotel, was "typical of the mindset of a lot of the young, white, rich, clueless males who come into my classes." "Is it wrong of me to think that Otto Warmbier got exactly what he deserved?" she wrote. Organizations described as right-wing distributed her post widely. Dettwyler recognized the way her tweets were being interpreted and erased the words that gave offense. But it was too late; the outcry led the university to fire her (Hawkins 2017). For Robertson and Dettwyler, and others, disagreeing with the political position of one's employer or bringing unwanted attention to one's college or university is enough to get one fired.

As some have argued, higher education institutions are increasingly motivated not by free speech or academic freedom, but rather by "risk management and brand management" (Reichman 2017). Lisa Durden, an adjunct professor at Essex County College in New Jersey, was invited to speak on Fox News about a Black Lives Matter celebration on Memorial Day in 2017. The organizing group advertised the event for "blacks only," and when the Fox hosts challenged Durden about that decision, she argued back against the newscasters' "white privilege." About forty-eight hours later, Essex suspended Durden and barred her from teaching her class, and two weeks later she was fired. The college's president released an extensive statement defending his decision. He said the administration was "immediately inundated with feedback from students, faculty and prospective students and their families expressing frustration, concern and even fear that the views expressed by a College employee (with influence over students) would negatively impact their experience on the campus . . . In consideration of the College's mission, and the impact that this matter has had on the College's fulfillment of its mission, we cannot maintain an employment relationship with the adjunct" (Schmidt 2017b).

When faculty members are fired after a controversial utterance, an institution is apt to find other reasons to justify their dismissal, sometimes citing student "fear" and families' "safety" concerns. College administrators typically insist that they are committed to freedom of expression, particularly in the past few years, when purportedly right-wing organizations have charged institutions of higher education with suppressing the speech of those who disagree with dominant views. Instead of addressing the utterances alleged to be offensive, administrators rely on a range of policies to discipline academics whose speech is thought to be troublesome. For example, faculty may be accused of violating a campus code of conduct or other institutional policies that demand "civility" and "respect." They may be accused of potential mental illness or deemed "unfit for duty." Faculty are often blamed for upsetting students and causing them to complain, which, administrators argue, is a violation of their employment contract. Institutional policies seemingly unrelated to academic freedom provide cover for administrations that are determined to remove a perceived troublemaker.

Kevin Allred, an adjunct professor at Rutgers University, was surprised when New York City police showed up at the door of his house in Brooklyn and carted him off to Bellevue Hospital. The day after Trump's election, Allred had posted a tweet that said, "If I see any Trump bumper stickers on the road today, my brakes will go out and I'll run you off the road." Ten days later, pointing out what he called a double standard, Allred tweeted, "Would conservatives care as much about the 2nd amendment if guns killed more white people?" Based on this tweet, which the Rutgers administration described as a threat, they decided to force Allred to undergo a psychiatric evaluation (Parascandola and McShane 2016). The administrators defended their action. "The Rutgers University Police Department responded to a complaint from a student and took all appropriate action," a spokesperson said (Tanenbaum 2016). Doctors at Bellevue found that Allred had no mental health issues and pronounced him healthy. Nevertheless, he was placed on immediate administrative leave and subsequently lost his job (Jaschik 2016b). Although New York, New Jersey, and Philadelphia newspapers covered the controversy over Allred's tweets, no one reported the fact that Allred lost his job because of his political speech. Evidently, the non-renewal of an NTT faculty member was not deemed newsworthy.

By illustrative contrast, when a full professor at the University of Tennessee wrote a tweet explicitly encouraging a similar kind of violence, he did not suffer any job-related consequences. Glenn Reynolds was well known for his provocative and, many would argue, offensive social media and blog posts. In the fall of 2016, when protesters in North Carolina blocked an intersection to protest police brutality and the killing of Keith Scott, an unarmed black man, Professor Reynolds, arguably conservative, tweeted that motorists in the area should "run them down." This call to violence was widely reported and condemned by political leaders and progressive groups, especially Black Lives Matter activists. The outcry caused the university administration to "investigate" the matter. In the end, Reynolds removed the offensive tweet (as had Dettwyler and Allred, discussed above). But, unlike the non-tenure-track faculty members, Reynolds's job was never threatened. He is still the Beauchamp Brogan Distinguished Professor of Law at the University of Tennessee (Flaherty 2016).

Barbara Madeloni was a full-time, long-term lecturer in the College of Education at the University of Massachusetts-Amherst. She was responsible for the high school teacher–training program at UMass, having been a high school teacher herself before coming to the university. When UMass was part of a field test of a new teacher-evaluation system, Madeloni protested. She spoke out against Pearson, the largest commercial company offering educational products and services in the world, as well as against the College of Education's proposed requirement that her graduate students send Pearson two ten-minute videos of themselves teaching. These were to become components of a new assessment system that Pearson was selling to the United States. Madeloni and her students resisted, as they were opposed to the privatization and corporatization of teaching, as well as to the idea that children and their student teachers were to be filmed without informed consent. Sixty-seven of her sixty-eight graduate students refused to participate in the pilot project. Madeloni was explicit about her class's critique of Pearson's education reform agenda. "We are putting a stick in the gears," she was quoted as saying (Winerip 2012).

A few days later, Madeloni was called in to meet with UMass administrators. She was warned not to speak for the university and not to coerce her students into protesting (she emphatically denied both claims). Shortly thereafter, Madeloni was informed that she would not have a job the following year; her contract would not be renewed. The university stated that, prior to the debacle, they had decided instead to hire a tenure-system faculty member. (Under her faculty union contract, this was the only reason the administration could use to terminate

Madeloni.) But Madeloni had little doubt about the situation: "It's clear to me this is an academic freedom issue. It's about me speaking back" (Carmichael 2012). Students and other supporters protested her termination and publicly requested the administration to reconsider, and 1,500 people signed an online petition supporting her stance against the Pearson project. Her union filed a grievance, stating that the administration had violated the collective bargaining agreement (CBA). After fighting her dismissal for a year, Madeloni agreed to settle with the university. But she never got her job back.

In contrast, Jacqueline Stevens, a full professor of political science at Northwestern University, also challenged her institution in a public way. Stevens researched her employer's ties to defense contractors, citing the corporatization of higher education and noting that "US government and economic elites distort research and teaching priorities." Stevens wrote widely about Northwestern's campus politics and led a protest against the appointment of Karl Eikenberry, a retired army general without a PhD, to lead a global studies institute at Northwestern. Stevens angered the administration with her repeated confrontations and challenges to their agenda.

In the fall of 2016, the university banned her from campus by citing campus codes of conduct and stating that her presence raised "safety concerns" among her colleagues. The Political Science Department's chair and associate chair accused Stevens of "gross incivility" and said "she seemed to be out of touch with reality," questioning her mental health. She was forbidden to have any contact with students and placed on immediate leave (Jaschik 2016a). Unlike Allred or Madeloni, however, Stevens had tenure. She and her colleagues were outraged about the infringement of her academic freedom. In her defense, Stephens disputed statements by the administration, protested her banishment, created a public blog, enlisted powerful faculty at other universities as allies, contacted media, and published articles about her unfair treatment. She was required to take a "fitness for duty" exam, similar to Allred's exam at Bellevue. But, unlike Allred, when Stevens was given a clean bill of health, the university allowed her to return to campus and resume teaching. As a tenured full professor, she rallied strong support from her colleagues and utilized resources that contingent faculty lack.

The Union Difference

Almost 20 percent of college and university teachers are covered by union contracts, if we include graduate student teachers, tenured and NTT faculty at public institutions, and adjuncts at private institutions. While they mostly join unions to campaign for decent wages and satisfactory working conditions, it is clear that faculty unions significantly improve academic freedom protections for everyone, including—and especially—contingent faculty.

The presence of a union can make significant differences in several ways. It advocates for the creation of the best possible jobs. For example, faculty unions seek to convert part-time adjunct positions into full-time non-tenure-track positions with benefits and job security, and to transmute full-time NTT positions into tenure-track ones. Strong unions resist the initial creation of part-time positions and specify rules limiting the conditions under which full-time NTT faculty may be utilized. A union thus works to improve the proportional mix of position types. De jure, it may be that everyone has academic freedom; de facto, the more secure the position, the greater the degree of academic freedom. Unions help create the better job security faculty need in order to be free to speak.

Further, unions increase academic freedom for everyone. They explicitly build this freedom into contracts and provide mechanisms to defend faculty who are under threat. Unions contest specific violations and offer the support of a lawyer and a grievance committee. They inform members of their rights. They publicize victories. They give members confidence that, if they are attacked, there will be organizational resources and organized individuals prepared to defend them.

Many faculty may believe their rights are protected by two sets of norms and laws: AAUP guidelines and the Constitution. On closer inspection, however, although both matter, neither, in our view, offers substantial protection. As the AAUP's famous "Statement of Principles" asserts, "Teachers are entitled to freedom in the classroom in discussing their subject, but they should be careful not to introduce into their teaching controversial matter that has no relation to their subject" (AAUP 1940). Faculty at public institutions have more protection than those at private colleges and universities under both the First Amendment, which safeguards speech, and the Fourteenth Amendment, which guarantees due process and makes it more difficult to fire public employees. But "extramural speech"—speech outside the classroom—is not protected by law. The AAUP guidelines covering "extramural speech"—a term that now has expanded to include Twitter, Facebook, blogs, and other electronic forms of speech in which a professor expresses an "opinion as a citizen"—state that such expression "cannot constitute grounds for dismissal unless it clearly demonstrates the faculty member's unfitness to serve" (AAUP Committee A 1965). The AAUP argues that "unfitness" can only be found through a due-process inquiry by a faculty committee—academe's version of a jury of one's peers—and the higher education institutions should protect extramural speech, even when it is found by some to be offensive. Of course, colleges and universities can regulate any speech that violates the law or presents an immediate threat, assuming that institutional policy clearly defines what constitutes a threat.

Without a union contract, however, neither the AAUP guidelines nor the US Constitution provide robust safeguards for faculty, and the protections they promise are difficult to enforce, as the above cases demonstrate. Nonetheless, academic unions affect balances of power in many concrete ways that expand the parameters of academic freedom for faculty. At a minimum, union contracts can incorporate the language from existing laws and policies, including the AAUP's policy statements. Administrators are often amenable to inserting existing legal guidelines into a CBA, and doing so creates a way for extant policies to be enforced. Such enforcement is possible because union contracts contain grievance procedures. When a CBA is violated, faculty members and their union have the right to file a grievance, which must be brought out in a formal hearing and may proceed to arbitration before a third party judge. The grievance procedure and arbitration can result in legally binding decisions. Equally importantly, administrators have an incentive to resolve grievances, rather than pursue a contentious process that could result in a costly or embarrassing judgment. By codifying AAUP guidelines and other professional norms, union contracts create enforceable rights. By providing access to attorneys and legal advice, unions help faculty defend themselves against actions that infringe on speech freedoms.

For example, anthropology lecturer Eric Canin at California State-Fullerton was accused of hitting a student during a rally and interfering with the Campus Republican students' free speech. The blogosphere lit up with calls for his termination, and the administration fired him after a short investigation. The California Faculty Association (the campus union) filed a grievance. After losing the initial hearings, the union brought the case to arbitration. It turned out that video footage of the event showed Canin had not so much as touched a student, let alone "assaulted" one. The union won the arbitration and Canin got his job back (Flannery 2017). Without a union and its access to attorneys, we surmise that Canin would not have been reinstated.

Faculty union contracts often go beyond existing policies to create more-extensive entitlements to academic freedom and political activities. For instance, the Massachusetts Society of Professors (MSP), the union of faculty and librarians at the University of Massachusetts-Amherst, negotiated language that guarantees academic freedom "inside and outside the classroom," thus protecting extramural speech. According to this language, no one can be disciplined or fired for tweeting or blogging or posting on Facebook. The contract also specifies that university service, in addition to teaching and research, is covered by academic freedom.

Firing or punishing someone for controversial speech or activity is made more difficult when a union represents workers. In forty-three states, an employee who is not a union member can be fired for almost any reason, or for no reason at all, which is consistent with at-will employment. Union contracts, by contrast, require that the employer demonstrate just cause before terminating an employee. Thus, for academics, the burden of proof is placed on the administration. With a contract, employees at institutions of higher education are innocent until proven guilty, a principle that does not hold in most US workplaces. A union contract in academe also guarantees progressive discipline, meaning that an administration must thoroughly investigate suspected wrongdoing and provide an individual with opportunities to address it. If problematic behavior persists, supervisors must provide a series of warnings—usually a verbal warning, and then one or more written notifications—before suspending or firing someone.

Just cause and progressive discipline are strong protections for full-time faculty. Many unions provide continuing appointments and just cause for non-tenure-track as well as tenured faculty. Continuing appointments at UMass-Amherst, for example, require just cause to be applied after three years of employment. This was a major victory for the union. During the contract negotiations, the administration argued that just cause was equivalent to tenure, which they did not want to offer to NTT faculty. When the union won the right to just cause for an individual after three years of employment, NTT faculty did not explicitly get tenure, but their academic freedom was given strong protection. Part-time or short-term contingent instructors do not have the just cause standard, so they generally remain at-will employees. Even for these faculty, however, when a union contract ensures academic freedom, no one in the bargaining unit—not even adjuncts—can legally be terminated for exercising their academic freedom. In Article 18.5.1, the MSP contract states:

> Just cause for dismissal will be related to the fitness of the faculty member or librarian in his or her professional capacity, and may include, but not be limited to, demonstrated substantial and manifest neglect of duty or failure to perform one's duty, severely inadequate performance, or egregious misconduct that substantially impairs the individual's fulfillment of his or her institutional responsibilities. In all cases of substandard performance, the University will make attempts at remediation prior to invoking dismissal procedures. Dismissal procedures will not be used to restrain faculty members or librarians in the exercise of

> their academic freedom, or in the exercise of any other rights they possess as members of society. (MSP 2020, 36)

Union contracts also specify procedures in the event that an administration considers suspending or terminating a faculty member. After a progressive disciplinary process has been completed, termination is possible only through a transparent faculty governance process. In most union contracts, termination requires a decision by a jury of one's peers—that is, a faculty panel must decide that termination is warranted. In strong union contracts, NTT faculty have this right, and only a faculty committee can terminate a lecturer protected by just cause. An over-zealous supervisor, or administrators under pressure from the public, boards of trustees, large donors, or politically connected organizations, do not have the power to terminate faculty covered by a sound CBA.

Finally, faculty unions protect academic freedom by educating, organizing, and mobilizing their members. A de jure right to speak is not worth anything if faculty remain quiet out of fear of adverse consequences. Unions operate against such fear. They educate members about their rights, including protections in the CBA, as well as about laws and professional norms. Union protections can also inspire individual courage. By speaking out, filing grievances, and actively defending their members, unions give individuals the confidence to speak and an awareness that they have safeguards. When faculty know they are organizationally represented, with access to legal recourse, they are more likely to exercise academic freedom. Academic freedom thus becomes a de facto right.

Conclusion

In the past decade, contingent faculty have started unions at more than sixty private colleges and universities, and they have joined faculty unions at many public institutions (Edwards and Tolley 2018). The relative ease with which contingent faculty can be abused with regard to the basic necessities of academic employment demonstrates the urgency of an organized movement on behalf of academic freedom for these majority members of the academy.

The perception that only those with tenure warrant strong academic freedom represents an obstacle to both thought and action. As Clausen and Swidler (2013) state, "Treating tenure and its protection of academic freedom as a scarce faculty reward—a 'badge of merit' rather than a routine support for academic endeavor—endangers the academic freedom of the community as a whole." Because the professoriate is increasingly a contingent workforce, we must effectively break the conceptual link between *tenure* and *academic freedom*. Faculty, especially those without the protection of tenure, need the support of both tenured professors and their institutions. As we have sought to demonstrate, if we are to challenge the groups that call for faculty to be punished or fired for their utterances, we will need strong unions to extend the valued principles on which authentic academic work relies.

References

AAUP (American Association of University Professors). 1940. "1940 Statement of Principles on Academic Freedom and Tenure." AAUP Reports and Publications, https://www.aaup.org/reports-publications.

AAUP (American Association of University Professors) Committee A. 1965. "Committee A Statement on Extramural Utterances." *AAUP Bulletin* 51(1):29.

Benjamin, Ernst. 2010. "The Eroding Foundations of Academic Freedom and Professional Integrity: Implications of the Diminishing Proportion of Tenured Faculty for Organizational Effectiveness in Higher Education." *AAUP Journal of Academic Freedom* 1, https://www.aaup.org/reports-publications/.

Brint, Steven and Jerome Karabel. 1989. *The Diverted Dream: Community Colleges and the Promise of Educational Opportunity in America, 1900–1985*. New York: Oxford University Press.

Carmichael, Mary. September 21, 2012. "UMass Lecturer Says School Is Punishing Her." *Boston Globe*, https://www.bostonglobe.com.

Clausen, Jan and Eva-Maria Swidler. 2013. "Academic Freedom from Below: Toward an Adjunct-Centered Struggle." *AAUP Journal of Academic Freedom* 4, https://www.aaup.org/reports-publications/.

Clawson, Dan. 2009. "Tenure and the Future of the University." *Science* 324(5931):1147–1148.

Clawson, Dan and Max Page. 2011. *The Future of Higher Education*. New York: Routledge.

Edwards, Kristen and Kim Tolley. June 3, 2018. "Do Unions Help Adjuncts?" *Chronicle of Higher Education*, https://www.chronicle.com.

Fields, Barbara Jeanne. 1990. "Slavery, Race and Ideology in the United States of America." *New Left Review* 181:95–118.

Flaherty, Colleen. September 23, 2016. "Run Them Down." *Inside Higher Ed*, https://www.insidehighered.com.

Flannery, Mary Ellen. July 23, 2017. "Cal State Lecturer Reinstated, Victory for Academic Freedom." *NEA Today*, https://www.nea.org/publications/.

GAO (Government Accountability Office). 2017. "Contingent Workforce: Size, Characteristics, Compensation, and Work Experiences of Adjunct and Other Non-Tenure-Track Faculty." Report to Congressional Requesters. GAO-18-49. Washington, DC: US Government Accountability Office.

Hawkins, Derek. June 26, 2017. "Professor Who Said 'Clueless White Male' Otto Warmbier Got 'What He Deserved' Won't Be Rehired." *Washington Post*, https://www.washingtonpost.com.

Jaschik, Scott. September 6, 2016a. "Banned from Campus." *Inside Higher Ed*, https://www.insidehighered.com.

Jaschik, Scott. November 21, 2016b. "Professor's Incendiary Rhetoric in the Age of Donald Trump." *Inside Higher Ed*, https://www.insidehighered.com.

MSP (Massachusetts Society of Professors). June 30, 2020. "2017–2020 Contract." https://umassmsp.org/contract/.

Parascandola, Rocco and Larry McShane. November 16, 2016. "Rutgers University Professor Taken for Psych Evaluation after 'Threatening' Gun Control, Flag Burning Tweets." *New York Daily News*, http://www.nydailynews.com.

Reichman, Hank. October 19, 2017. "Two Welcome Contributions to the Conversation on Academic Freedom and Free Speech." *Academe Blog*, https://academeblog.org.

Sachs, Jeffrey Adam. April 27, 2018. "There Is No Campus Free Speech Crisis: A Close Look at the Evidence." *Niskanen Center* (blog), https://niskanencenter.org.

Schmidt, Samantha. July 19, 2017a. "Mormon University Instructor Fired after Facebook Post Supporting LGBT Rights, She Says." *Washington Post*. https://www.washingtonpost.com.

Schmidt, Samantha. June 26, 2017b. "Professor Fired after Defending Blacks-Only Event to Fox News." *Washington Post*, https://www.washingtonpost.com.

Tanenbaum, Michael. November 17, 2016. "Rutgers Professor Forced into Psych Evaluation over Second Amendment Tweets." *Philly Voice*, http://www.phillyvoice.com.

US Census Bureau. 2009. *Statistical Abstract of the United States: 2010*, 129th edition. Washington, DC: US Bureau of the Census.

Winerip, Michael. May 6, 2012. "Move to Outsource Teacher Licensing Process Draws Protest." *New York Times*, https://www.nytimes.com.

CHAPTER 8

Academic Freedom and Institutional Review

Laura Stark

This chapter examines the conceptual relationship between institutional review and academic freedom. Defenders of academic freedom have long seen institutional review boards (IRBs) as a threat. A substantial body of scholarship has explored the empirical connection between the actions of specific universities' IRBs and academics' freedom in research. This chapter clarifies the premises and implications of that conceptual link, as yet left unexamined. In doing so, it establishes grounds for resisting institutional review as a threat to academic freedom and amplifies the opportunities to appropriate institutional review as a tool to expand academic freedom.

The American Association of University Professors (AAUP) takes as its mission the protection of academic freedom, and it has long worked to study and advocate for a more appropriate research oversight system. The first section of this chapter explains the emergence of IRBs as a locus of concern, both for academic freedom and for the AAUP specifically. The writing of former AAUP president Cary Nelson sets the tempo of critique over the past six decades. In its second section, the chapter provides broader legal and conceptual foundations of institutional review in the United States. In the 1970s, the federal government empowered committees at local research institutions to make ethical decisions about researchers' studies. This shift in the legal location of moral judgment—from the researcher to an IRB—yielded debates among scholars, as well as in the AAUP, about what form of expertise was ethically needed for sound scientific judgment. The third section pinpoints the need to adjudicate between just and unjust uses of power by institutional review processes. It is important to establish the relationship between academic freedom and institutional review if the principle is to ground the critiques—and the creative appropriations—of this entrenched bureaucratic process. Most importantly, the section demonstrates the conceptual link between academic freedom and institutional review by expanding on the theory of "expert professional speech," as articulated by legal scholar David M. Rabban. The chapter closes by amplifying the liberating potential of institutional review.

Institutional Review in Theory and Practice

The relationship between IRBs and faculty researchers has changed substantially since 1974, when the US Congress passed the first federal laws on the treatment of human subjects and mandated local institutional review. What began in the 1970s as begrudging adherence (by most bioscience researchers) or blissful ignorance (by many social scientists) shifted in the early 2000s to active criticism across the disciplines, if for different reasons (Babb 2020). Many professional organizations corralled faculties' complaints into collective political action.

The experiences of AAUP's former president Cary Nelson, who served from 2006 to 2012, dramatize the broad shift in academic sensibilities about institutional review over this period. Nelson published an academic memoir in 2004 in which he recounted his own experiences as a college student serving as a human subject for medical research at the US National Institutes of Health (NIH). I interviewed him in 2010 about his part in a project on the emergence, during the twentieth century, of a global market for healthy civilians to serve in medical experiments (Stark 2010). In our conversation, as well as in his book, *Office Hours*, Nelson described a mixed experience at NIH (Nelson 2004, 74; Stark 2012).

That episode provided a lifetime of stories, but he felt researchers took advantage of him in some aspects. He was pressured to participate in studies, and he was uncomfortable in ways he had not anticipated. For example, Nelson described an incident with NIH researchers who were interested in doing odor-detection studies on him, which required taking spinal fluid (Stark n.d.). They acknowledged that such a procedure could cause infection and also paralysis. "I refused," Nelson recounted. "Then the pressure began." As he explained: "It was not, of course, until two years later, in 1966, that NIH—under orders from the US Surgeon General—introduced a committee system to evaluate the ethics of human subject research. The hospital had a preliminary system to review the general plans for research with normal controls in 1964, but no full-scale ethical oversight."[1] His experiences as a "normal control" in 1964 appeared to him to call for better research oversight and a rebalance of power in research contexts—one that would shift power from the opportunistic researcher to an advocate and watchdog for participants like the young Cary Nelson, who was then still a minor. It seemed, in other words, to call for a more muscular ethics review board. In his view, NIH's weak oversight of researchers in the 1960s was a serious problem. "Suffice it to say that it would have been very nice to have had an institutional review board in place in 1964," Nelson (2004, 70) wrote forty years later.

At the time I interviewed him about his experiences as a human subject, Nelson was working in the opposite direction. He was leading the major US organization (the AAUP) that advocated on behalf of academics to limit the power and reach of institutional review boards and return to researchers the academic freedom that, the AAUP argued, IRBs had restricted. As Nelson explained, in practice, "the admirable moral imperatives propelling an IRB forward become entangled with legal constructs that compromise fairness and sanity, not to say academic freedom." The fixes to the ethical missteps that Nelson experienced in the 1960s had produced a new set of problems. "It serves to protect the rights of individual research subjects and to safeguard the institution against suits and regulatory reprisals. It also entails more institutional responsibility and liability." As a result, "IRB surveillance thus simultaneously mitigates and enhances legal risk," and so the past becomes present again. "At some point we enter the airless world of NIH in 1964" (Nelson 2004, 74). By the 2000s, Nelson's sensibility about institutional review was characteristic of the research professoriate, which layered resistance to the process (as it was practiced) atop support for the process (in theory).

Any effort to understand, critique, and improve protections for research participants always has two dimensions. The first orients to the law that is on the books—whether the rules, in theory, are appropriate, practicable, equitable, and well justified. The second brings into view the law as it is in practice—that is, how the regulations are interpreted. This second dimension is the site of researchers' most intense frustrations, because the rules on the books describe the method through which they must be interpreted—namely, through a procedure in which a committee carries out "institutional review." In doing so, the rules shift authority about the research in question (specifically, its compliance with law and ethics) from the researcher to institutional review board committee members.

Research Experts, Rule Experts, and Amateurs

What once seemed to be frustrations among researchers about IRBs are now being framed as violations of a protected right for many researchers—namely, academic freedom. This threat to academic freedom stems from the locus of authority in decision making within IRBs. To be sure, at universities, IRB members are mostly fellow academics, but IRBs are required to have at least one member unaffiliated with the institution, commonly called a "community representative" (Stark 2012). In addition, IRB administrators attend meetings, often contributing to evaluations of research, even though their formal role is record keeping. According to the regulations, this combination of academics, community members, and administrators, if properly assembled, will produce a group that is "sufficiently qualified through the experience and expertise of its members, and the diversity of the members, including consideration of race, gender, and cultural backgrounds and sensitivity to such issues as community attitudes, to promote respect for its advice and counsel in safeguarding the rights and welfare of human subjects" ("Federal Policy" 2016, 134).[2]

Yet, in the AAUP's judgment, "there is no reason for believing that IRB members are especially competent to assess practices," such as protecting research data. "Doing that calls for experts" (AAUP 2011, 11). But who is the expert on the ethics and regulatory compliance of researchers' planned work? Some scholars use the term "amateur" to refer to faculty members on IRBs and reserve the language of "expert" to refer to professional IRB administrators who are versed in the rules (Babb 2020). This divide is ultimately unhelpful, because it fails to address institutional review as practice. I, instead, consider the issue of expertise—and, specifically, expert professional speech—in an effort to critically and productively understand how we may conceptually tie academic freedom to institutional review.

Although many legal scholars agree that academic freedom is protected through the Constitution, it is a matter of debate whether that protection coheres in the First Amendment, is implied in a composite of several amendments, or is merely a "work place policy" (Brest 1987; Getman and Mintz 1987; Ellis 2018). It is unclear whether those freedoms are guaranteed for all academic laborers, only for professors, or for academic groups and institutions, rather than individuals (see Metzger 1988). As a result of the ambiguity about the meaning and boundaries of academic freedom, the link between academic freedom and institutional review itself is rendered still more complex.

Sociologists and legal scholars have attempted to clarify that link. From a legal perspective, it is a difficult task, given the dearth of case law. Sociologist Jack Katz (2007) has argued that institutional review is a form of prior restraint, which is a restriction on a person's expression before it has taken place. Citizens are protected from prior restraint by the First Amendment, and Katz argues that critics of human subjects overreach can get some traction on these grounds (also see Feeley 2007). Yet legal scholars who share Katz's broad sympathies—that is, frustration with IRBs and a commitment to innovate within, if not overturn, the system—have suggested that prior restraint is a weak legal argument when applied to IRBs.[3] Thus an appropriate and productive frame through which to understand the relationship between academic freedom and institutional review would have to be found elsewhere.

To be sure, researchers, including sociologists, have published critical scholarly pieces on the injustices, as well as the flawed logic, of institutional review for the professoriate and for people participating in research (e.g., De Vries and Forsberg 2002; Bosk and De Vries 2004; Bozeman and Hirsch 2005; Bradburd 2006; Bledsoe et al. 2007; Feeley 2007; Katz 2007; Lederman 2007a; 2007b; Heimer and Petty 2010; Schrag 2010; Mamo and Epstein 2014; Stark 2016; Van den Hoonaard and Hamilton 2016). Interest in the disjuncture between research rights and institutional review is strong enough to support several academic journals devoted to research regulation, including the *Journal of Empirical Research on Human Research Ethics*, *Ethics and Human Research*, and *Accountability in Research*. Critical, scholarly analysis of institutional review spans geographic regions and continues to yield dissertations on the review process from across the globe (Eyal 2017; Jacobs 2018). Academic and mass market presses have recognized the ongoing frustration with IRBs, and publications on the topic have held strong (Angell 2016). Moreover, academic professional organizations, most notably the AAUP, have continued over the decades to write important policy reports on academic freedom and institutional review. As the association explained to the federal agency that oversees and enforces regulations on institutional review boards, "since 1981, the AAUP has expressed concern about the potential for human subjects research protections to interfere with academic freedom" (AAUP 2011).

Yet most of this work, important as it is, sets aside the question of the character of the relationship through which institutional review can threaten academic freedom. Instead, empirical studies and critical analyses tend to start from the assertion that IRBs, in the words of the

AAUP, simply represent an "encroachment on academic freedom" (AAUP Committee A 2013, 3). As part of its efforts, in 2013 the AAUP published a valuable analysis of "what has most troubled those [researchers] who must live under the regulations" (AAUP Committee A 2013, 3) The AAUP analyzed the main concerns of social science organizations that provided public comments to the 2011 federal advance notice of public rulemaking ("Human Subjects" 2011), which announced that the US Department of Health and Human Services would be overhauling the original legislation—the National Research Act (1974)—that mandated institutional review. In its report, the AAUP organized these concerns into seven themes: (1) inappropriate reporting, (2) excessive reporting, (3) consent, (4) confidentiality, (5) the appeal process, (6) unnecessary regulation of minimal risk methods, and (7) regulation of non–federally funded projects. Based on my own empirical research, these themes aptly represent the *content* of issues that produce the most troublesome interactions between researchers and IRBs (Stark 2012). Still, the *character* of the relationship between academic rights and institutional review has remained unspecified.

To address the problems of institutional review as a threat to academic freedom, it is thus crucial to consider two questions. What is the relationship between academic freedom and institutional review? And what is it about this relationship that should cause concern?

Intramural Speech and Peer Review

Legal scholar David M. Rabban has made a compelling suggestion that the link between academic freedom and institutional review is best understood in terms of peer review (Rabban 2018). This frame is appealing, because IRBs are one among a set of groups, including funding panels, that carry out practices of "valuation" in the sciences using peer review (Lamont 2010; 2012). It is worth noting that in addition to being a legal scholar, Rabban was also chair of the AAUP's Committee A on Academic Freedom and Tenure, which oversaw the Subcommittee on Academic Freedom and Institutional Review that produced several reports and analyses. Consequently, his analysis is not independent of the recent tensions between the professoriate and IRBs that are of interest here. In general, Rabban shares the view of other scholars that academic freedom is constitutionally protected, as well as that the most basic features of this right are still matters of disagreement, which makes academic freedom difficult to safeguard. His aim is to develop a First Amendment theory of academic freedom.

To do so, Rabban builds on the AAUPs "1915 Declaration of Principles on Academic Freedom and Academic Tenure" (AAUP 2015) to propose that professors have a special right, compared with other citizens protected through the Constitution, in the form of expert professional speech. Because the job of academics is to produce and disseminate knowledge, activities related to this work are a protected form of speech—both in teaching and in research. Such speech deserves to be valued and safeguarded, because it underpins democratic decision making. By Rabban's theory, this form of speech derives from specific expertise on the topic addressed, as opposed to speech on any topic that happens to be carried out by a faculty member.

Expert professional speech includes the judgments that professors offer in intramural speech—that is, in the evaluations that academics make as part of their jobs within universities that stem from their expertise as researchers and educators, such as the assessments rendered when serving on tenure and promotion committees. (Rabban is less convinced that academic freedom as expert professional speech holds for institutions, rather than individuals, and he is not fully persuaded that the *political* positions professors express about the universities that employ them are protected, because such positions rarely extend from a specific form of academic expertise.)

Building on these AAUP principles, Rabban's theory stipulates that legitimate expert professional speech is determined by the peer review model. One implication is that professors must be encouraged to discuss whether the judgments their colleagues make as part of university work—such as serving on IRBs—are within their areas of professional expertise or beyond them. By allowing the possibility to frame the relationship between researchers and IRB members as one of peer review, Rabban creates concrete grounds on which to debate—and resolve—the differences in professional expert judgments that may arise between the expert under review (i.e., the researcher) and the expert(s) serving on IRBs. The question becomes, Who holds the professional expertise for authoritative judgment on a given protocol? (Another matter is whether political biases come into play, a particular concern in the relatively small communities that are college campuses.)

Framing academic freedom and institutional review as a matter of peer review may empower researchers as experts in their own fields. This framework demands that local IRBs clarify what it is, exactly, about board members' professional training, as well as their "race, gender, and cultural backgrounds and sensitivity to such issues as community attitudes" that constitute a form of expertise, according to the regulations ("Federal Policy" 2016, 134). That is to say, What is the relationship between "expertise" and life or work "experience"?

The framework may also raise unhappy possibilities for some researchers. Protection of expert professional speech, using the peer review model, means that researchers would be only one of the sets of actors with a legitimate claim to academic freedom. Professors serving on IRBs—the researchers' peers—would also have the freedom to express and make decisions based on their expert judgments, even if they conflict with the judgment of the proposed project's researchers. The specific point of debate is whether any given IRB member is, in the words of the US government, "sufficiently qualified through the[ir] experience and expertise" to trump the researcher's expertise ("Federal Policy" 2016, 134). In addition, when put into action, IRBs may find that the best protection of expert professional speech is to restrict wider access to reviewers' evaluations, in order to protect anonymity, such as in journal or grant reviews, or in tenure and promotion deliberations. This formalization stifles communication between evaluators and those being judged. This outcome would undermine the spirit of open, expert debate that the peer review framework is designed to encourage. Nonetheless, in principle, the peer review model opens IRBs to a more productive and precise debate about the legitimacy of professors' judgments in carrying out research.

Conclusion

Researchers' frustrations with institutional review boards have been well documented, and, despite recent changes in federal law, the tensions continue unabated (Stark 2012). My aim in this chapter has been to address how scholarly communities might best respond to that tension. A reply is necessary at this moment, because new federal regulations for human subjects protections were passed in 2017 ("Federal Policy" 2017) and published in final revised form the following year ("Federal Policy" 2018), the first substantial overhaul in forty years. The consequences of these new, purportedly more flexible regulations are still being felt and assessed.[4]

The answer to the question of who should have greater power in institutional review and research ethics decisions—the (ideally responsible) researcher or the (one hopes well-functioning) IRB—is not straightforward. The appeal of understanding the link between academic freedom and institutional review as a process of peer review is that it removes the need to ultimately invest authority in any one source, whether it be the reviewers or the researcher. Institutional review can be more aptly envisioned as relational and situational, rather than asymmetric between actors, and transposable across cases. Interactions of researchers and IRB members can be understood as an ongoing relationship that is open to change over time. Authority is centered on the collective assessment of researchers' and board members' expertise in a given review.

What remains, then, is to expose the relationships between reviewers and researchers—the specific, tangible interactions on paper and in person—in order to understand the terms on which they operate. We will need to discover how professional expertise is grounded, granted, denied, and challenged through institutional review. Logistically, exposing these interactions to critical scrutiny would mean making public more of the communications already used to arrive at decisions—such as email and preliminary reviews—and the spaces of deliberation, including meeting rooms. Institutional review as peer review awaits a full operationalization. It is an *experiment* in the making, in the best sense of the term, whose results remain not fully known.

Notes

1. The NIH's Clinical Center had a proto-IRB called the Clinical Research Committee, which was required to review all studies on healthy human subjects but only studies of sick patients that were considered "hazardous."

2. The regulations continue: "In addition to possessing the professional competence necessary to review specific research activities, the IRB shall be able to ascertain the acceptability of proposed research in terms of institutional commitments and regulations, applicable law, and standards of professional conduct and practice. The IRB shall therefore include persons knowledgeable in these areas. If an IRB regularly reviews research that involves a vulnerable category of subjects, such as children, prisoners, pregnant women, or handicapped or mentally disabled persons, consideration shall be given to the inclusion of one or more individuals who are knowledgeable about and experienced in working with these subjects" ("Federal Policy" 2016, 134). The law also suggests how expertise would be recognized in the details of an IRB member's profile that the government considers relevant, including: "earned degrees; representative capacity; indications of experience such as board certifications, licenses, etc. sufficient to describe each member's chief anticipated contributions to IRB deliberations" ("Federal Policy" 2016, 133).

3. Hamburger (2004, 276) argues that institutional review is unconstitutional because it violates the government's spending and licensing doctrine, which prevents the government from using these powers to limit speech. In doing so, "the regulations establish a new, soft kind of censorship. Instead of harshly imposing the force of law on individuals, this censorship seeks only the cooperation of institutions; instead of attempting to repress popular opinion, it appeals to the moral sensibilities of a majority. Indeed, rather than aim at political or religious ends, this censorship aspires to be bureaucratic, and rather than threaten civil liberties, it attempts to protect them."

4. In 2011, the federal government proposed revisions ("Human Subjects Research Protections" 2011) to 45CFR46 (also known as the Common Rule)—which was an updated version of regulations originally adopted in the 1970s following the National Research Act (1974)—and asked for public comment on the proposed revisions. The government received more than 1,100 responses from individuals and organizations, including academic professional associations, such as the AAUP. The federal government passed the final rules in the last days of the Obama administration ("Federal Policy" 2017), and they were published in final revised form the following year ("Federal Policy" 2018). It remains a matter of disagreement whether the new rules constitute a wholesale rethinking and replacement of the former regulations or are best described as a revision—that is, a gentle polishing of the edges of a poorly constructed law. Among the most important changes for social scientists are the addition of categories that exempt or excuse more research from regulation, and the

ability of researchers to determine for themselves whether their research is exempt from regulation by using an online "decision tool," rather than applying for an exemption from their IRB.

References

AAUP (American Association of University Professors). 2015. "1915 Declaration of Principles on Academic Freedom and Academic Tenure." *Policy Documents and Reports*, 11th edition, 3–12. Baltimore: Johns Hopkins University Press.

AAUP (American Association of University Professors), submitted by B. Robert Kreiser. 2011 "Comments in Reply to 'Human Subjects Research Protections: Enhancing Protections for Research Subjects and Reducing Burden, Delay, and Ambiguity for Investigators.'" Regulations.gov, https://www.regulations.gov/document?D=HHS-OPHS-2011-0005-0371/.

AAUP (American Association of University Professors) Committee A. March 2013. "Regulation of Research on Human Subjects: Academic Freedom and the Institutional Review Board." AAUP Reports & Publications, https://www.aaup.org/file/IRB-Final-Report.pdf.

Angell, Marcia. December 3, 2015. "Medical Research on Humans: Making It Ethical." *New York Review of Books*, http://www.nybooks.com.

Babb, Sarah. 2020. *Regulating Human Research: IRBs from Peer Review to Compliance Bureaucracy*. Stanford, CA: Stanford University Press.

Bledsoe, Caroline H., Bruce Sherin, Adam G. Galinsky, Nathalia M Headley, Carol A. Heimer, Erik Keldgaard, James Lindgren, Jon D. Miller, Michael E. Roloff, and David H. Uttal. 2007. "Regulating Creativity: Research and Survival in the IRB Iron Cage." *Northwestern University Law Review* 101(2):593–641.

Bosk, Charles L. and Raymond G. De Vries. 2004. "Bureaucracies of Mass Deception: Institutional Review Boards and the Ethics of Ethnographic Research." *Annals of the American Academy of Political and Social Science* 595:249–263.

Bozeman, Barry and Paul Hirsch. 2005. "Science Ethics as a Bureaucratic Problem: IRBs, Rules, and Failures of Control." *Policy Sciences* 38(4):269–91.

Bradburd, Daniel. 2006. "Fuzzy Boundaries and Hard Rules: Unfunded Research and the IRB." *American Ethnologist* 33(4):492–498.

Brest, Paul. 1987. "Protecting Academic Freedom through the First Amendment: Raising the Unanswered Questions." *Texas Law Review* 66:1359–1362.

De Vries, Raymond G. and Carl Forsberg. 2002. "What Do IRBs Look Like? What Kind of Support Do They Receive?" *Accountability in Research* 9(3–4):199–216.

Ellis, Lindsay. July 24, 2018. "What Is Academic Freedom? Statement That Alarmed Professors at U. of Texas Sets Off Debate." *Chronicle of Higher Education*, https://www.chronicle.com.

Eyal, Hedva. 2017. "Medical Experimentation on Humans in Israel: The Dynamic of Power, Knowledge and Regulation." PhD diss., Hebrew University of Jerusalem.

"Federal Policy for the Protection of Human Subjects." June 19, 2018. *Federal Register* 83(118):28597–28620.

"Federal Policy for the Protection of Human Subjects." January 19, 2017. *Federal Register* 82(12):7149–7274.

"Federal Policy, Part 46—Protection of Human Subjects." October 1, 2016. *Code of Federal Regulations*, 45CFR46, 128–148.

Feeley, Malcolm. 2002. "Response to Comments." *Law & Society Review* 41(4):811–818.

Getman, Julius G. and Jacqueline W. Mintz. 1987. "Foreword: Academic Freedom in a Changing Society." *Texas Law Review* 66:1247–1264.

Hamburger, Philip. 2004. "The New Censorship: Institutional Review Boards." *Supreme Court Review* 2004:271–354.

Heimer, Carol A. and JuLeigh Petty. 2010. "Bureaucratic Ethics: IRBs and the Legal Regulation of Human Subjects Research." *Annual Review of Law and Social Science* 6:601–26.

"Human Subjects Research Protections: Enhancing Protections for Research Subjects and Reducing Burden, Delay, and Ambiguity for Investigators." July 26, 2011. *Federal Register* 46(143):44512- 44531.

Jacobs, Noortje. 2018. "Ethics by Committee: Governing Human Experimentation in the Netherlands, 1945–2000." PhD diss., Maastricht University, Netherlands.

Katz, Jack. 2007. "Toward a Natural History of Ethical Censorship/Response to Comments." *Law & Society Review* 41(4):797–810.

Lamont, Michele. 2012. "Toward a Comparative Sociology of Valuation and Evaluation." *Annual Review of Sociology* 38:201–21.

Lamont, Michele. 2010. *How Professors Think: Inside the Curious World of Academic Judgment*. Cambridge, MA: Harvard University Press.

Lederman, Rena. 2007a. "Comparative 'Research': A Modest Proposal Concerning the Object of Ethics Regulation." *PoLAR: Political and Legal Anthropology Review* 30(2): 305–327.

Lederman, Rena. 2007b. "Educate Your IRB: An Experiment in Cross-Disciplinary Communication." *Anthropology News* 48(6):33–34.

Mamo, Laura and Steven Epstein. 2014. "The Pharmaceuticalization of Sexual Risk: Vaccine Development and the New Politics of Cancer Prevention." *Social Science and Medicine* 101:155–65.

Metzger, Walter. 1988. "Profession and Constitution: Two Definitions of Academic Freedom in America." *Texas Law Review* 66:1265–1291.

National Research Act. July 12, 1974. Public Law 93-48, https://uscode.house.gov/statutes/pl/93/348.pdf.

Nelson, Cary. 2004. *Office Hours Activism and Change in the Academy*. New York: Routledge.

Rabban, David M. August 23, 2018. "First Amendment Academic Freedom." University of Chicago School of Law. Unpublished manuscript.

Schrag, Zachary M. 2010. *Ethical Imperialism: Institutional Review Boards and the Social Sciences, 1965–2009*. Baltimore: Johns Hopkins University Press.

Stark, Laura. 2016. "The Language of Ethics: How Ethics Review Creates Inequalities for Language Minorities in Research." In Will C. Van den Hoonaard and Ann

Hamilton (eds.), *The Ethics Rupture: Exploring Alternatives to Formal Research-Ethics Review*, 91–105. Toronto: University of Toronto Press.
Stark, Laura. 2012. *Behind Closed Doors: IRBs and the Making of Ethical Research*. Chicago: University of Chicago Press.
Stark, Laura. May 24, 2010. Oral history interview with Cary Nelson, Champaign, Illinois.
Van den Hoonaard, Will C. and Ann Hamilton (eds). 2016. *The Ethics Rupture: Exploring Alternatives to Formal Research-Ethics Review*. Toronto: University of Toronto Press.

CHAPTER 9

Reclaiming Harvard Law School

An Expression of Student Academic Freedom

Philip Lee

Part I: Reclaim Harvard Law School

Founded in 1817, Harvard Law School (HLS) has become an icon of American legal education. From popular movies, such as *The Paper Chase*, *Love Story*, and *Legally Blonde*, this institution has been imprinted on the public's imagination as what a law school looks and feels like. HLS has also been a mechanism for entrée into the upper echelons of power. For example, four of the nine sitting US Supreme Court Justices attended HLS (US Supreme Court n.d.).

HLS is the oldest continually existing law school in the country ("History" n.d.). This influential institution of higher education has had a long history that overlaps with one of the vilest practices in America—the legally sanctioned enslavement of people of African descent. As one of the most visible contemporary symbols of this interaction, the official HLS coat of arms, or shield, has contained the family crest of an eighteenth-century slaveowner, Sir Isaac Royall, Jr., since 1937 ("Harvard Law School Shield" n.d.). Royall left an early bequest to HLS that funded the law school's first endowed chair. In order to honor his donation, HLS derived its shield, containing three sheaves of wheat, from the Royall family's crest. For eighty years, the HLS coat of arms was used without much awareness of its link to slavery.

Daniel Coquillette and Bruce Kimball (2015) have helped change this. These historians were on a mission to excavate the forgotten origins of HLS, which included its previously ignored ties to slavery and the Confederacy (Arnett 2016). Their book project began in the late 1990s, after receiving a grant from the Spencer Foundation. In their extensive research, the authors sought to unearth more details about the life of Sir Isaac Royall, who settled in Medford, Massachusetts, by way of Antigua, an island in the Lesser Antilles.

Coquillette and Kimball (2015) found that the Royall family's wealth—including the money that Sir Isaac Royall, Jr., left to fund HLS's first endowed chair—was based on the labor of that family's slaves. They also learned that the punishment for these slaves' resistance to the era's economic system and sociopolitical order was swift and terrible. After the plans for a slave revolt in Antigua were discovered, "five slaves were 'broken on the wheel,' six gibbeted alive, and seventy-seven burned at the stake, including Hector, the trusted head slave, or 'driver,' of the Royall family. Within a year, the Royalls decided to leave for Massachusetts, bringing at least twenty-seven slaves with them" (Coquillette and Kimball 2015, 82).

The revelations about Sir Isaac Royall, Jr., and his family in Coquillette and Kimball's book, *On the Battlefield of Merit*, did not go unnoticed. On October 20, 2015, HLS students took to social media to initiate a Royall Must Fall campaign, which allied itself with the Rhodes Must Fall movement in South Africa and England. Using the hashtags #HectorMustRise, #RoyallMustFall, and #HLSBurntAlive, the Royall Must Fall Facebook page explained, "We are a movement of students calling for the decolonization of our campus, the symbols, the curriculum and the history of Harvard Law School" (Royall Must Fall n.d.). The group's Twitter page, Royall Must Fall (@RoyallMustFall) (n.d.) did the same.

On November 18, 2015, Royall Must Fall published an open letter to the dean of Harvard Law School, Martha Minow, demanding the removal of the Royall family crest from the law school shield. The student activists explained, “Physical symbols are an expression of who we are and what we value as a community. From the portraits of professors on the second floor of Wasserstein, to the paintings in the library, to the current composition of the faculty, the law school is filled with visual reminders that this school was created by, and for, white men. The most ubiquitous of these symbols, the seal—which adorns all of our buildings, apparel, stationery, and diplomas—honors a slaver and murderer” (Royall Must Fall 2015).

The very next day, an unknown person or persons placed black tape across the faces of many of the African American professors' portraits contained in one of the law school's buildings. The law school then held a community meeting with students, faculty, and administrators to discuss the black-tape incident, where Dean Minow acknowledged that racism was an issue in both the law school and the country (Bidgood 2015).

The students subsequently formed a new group, called Reclaim Harvard Law School, to align itself with similar movements across the country (Mack n.d.). Reclaim Harvard Law broadened the students' demand to change the law school's crest to also encompass (1) establishing a critical race theory program; (2) changing the existing curriculum to include the integration of marginalized narratives and a serious inquiry into how racism and imperialism are creating and perpetuating the existing legal order; (3) creating an Office of Diversity and Inclusion, aimed at curtailing organizational hierarchy; (4) improving affordability and financial access by marginalized students; (5) sustaining a commitment to recruiting, retaining, and promoting professional staff of color; (6) requiring cultural competency training for all staff; and (7) creating a Harvard Law School Diversity Committee (composed of students, faculty, and staff) to implement the listed demands (“Reclaim Harvard Law Demands” 2015).

During the next semester, the students would make their voices heard. Beginning at 8 p.m. on Monday, February 15, 2016, students in Reclaim Harvard Law began their occupation of the fireside lounge in Wasserstein Hall ("Reclaim Harvard Law Occupies Fireside Lounge" 2016). They renamed the space Belinda Hall, in honor of Belinda Sutton, a former slave who had successfully petitioned the Massachusetts General Court for a pension from the Royall estate ("Belinda Sutton" n.d.). For the next four months, Reclaim Harvard Law would be a continual presence in Belinda Hall and would conduct teach-ins and group discussions on perspectives the students felt were missing from the curriculum, such as critical race theory, feminist theory, and queer theory. Reclaim Harvard Law explained its occupation of the law school's space on its blog: "Reclaim Harvard Law claims the space of Belinda Hall for those who are marginalized by HLS. We are creating our own Office of Diversity and Inclusion there. We are engaging in the Critical Race Theory and contextualization discussions lacking in our classrooms. We will continue to promote the availability of such opportunities for all students. For now we are engaging in self-teaching and learning, in an environment that seeks to welcome everyone" ("Frequently Asked Questions" n.d.). In sum, the students took their education into their own hands and sought to learn things they thought were missing from the classroom.

Shortly after the black-tape incident in November 2015, Dean Minow appointed a committee to address the first of the students' demands ("Committee Exploring" 2015). The committee was charged with studying the HLS shield and recommending to the Harvard trustees whether to continue or discontinue the shield's use. Chaired by legal historian Bruce H. Mann, the committee eventually consisted of twelve faculty members, alumni, students, and staff members (Mann et al. 2016). The committee solicited feedback from the larger HLS community by email and through two open discussion meetings. It heard directly from over 1,000 people.

On March 3, 2016, ten committee members, with two dissenting votes, recommended that the shield be retired (Shammas 2016). The majority's recommendation first noted that the committee was unanimous in acknowledging that Harvard must recognize its past association with slavery, in order to understand slavery's continuing impact on the school (Mann et al. 2016). But the committee members disagreed about what was to be done. The majority of the committee concluded, "We believe that if the Law School is to have an official symbol, it must more closely represent the values of the Law School, which the current shield does not" (Mann et al. 2016, 9). In a dissenting recommendation that was joined by an HLS student on the committee, legal historian Annette Gordon-Reed wrote that Royall's crest should be retained, because it would force people to confront HLS's connection to slavery (Gordon-Reed 2016). She suggested that instead of being retired, the shield should be modified by "making explicit our debt to the enslaved and our commitment, in their memory, to the cause of justice"—perhaps by adding the word *justitia* ("justice") to the shield by leaving the sheaves of wheat but making them smaller to accommodate that word (Gordon-Reed 2016, 2).

Eleven days later, the university's president and the Fellows of the Harvard Corporation adopted the majority's recommendation (Faust and Lee 2016). The sheaves of wheat would no longer symbolize the law school. Later that day, Royall Must Fall (@RoyallMustFall) (2016) announced on Twitter, "Royall has fallen!" The fight for their other demands, however, would continue.

Amid this student activism, a question arises. What does academic freedom have to do with these students' right to engage in such protest activities? The answer depends on how one perceives the students' role in their own learning. One viewpoint is that academic freedom is reserved solely for professors, because students do not contribute to systematic learning (Byrne 1989). Another perspective is that students are protected by academic freedom, because faculty and students have had a symbiotic relationship, so this freedom extends to both parties as members of a collective learning community (Metzger 1988). The former belief was how student academic freedom was conceived in the early years of American higher education. The latter conviction, however, became the foundation for a stronger formulation of students' academic freedom rights, starting in the 1960s.

Part II: Learning Theory and Academic Freedom

Michael Ryan and Gretchen Martens articulated a difference between two types of learning: passive and active. These scholars observed: "Passive learning takes place when students take on the role of 'receptacles of knowledge'; that is, they do not directly participate in the learning process. One common passive instructional mode is the ever-popular lecture. Active learning is more likely to take place when students are doing something besides listening" (Ryan and Martens 1989, 20).

Early views of student academic freedom envisioned university students as passive learners who were merely receiving information from faculty experts. For example, when the American Association of University Professors (AAUP) promulgated its highly influential "Declaration of Principles on Academic Freedom and Academic Tenure," student freedom was an afterthought (Seligman et al. 1915). The declaration discussed two separate types of academic freedom: freedom for teachers to research and teach (*Lehrfreiheit*), and freedom for students to learn (*Lernfreiheit*). The declaration then stated, however, "It need scarcely be pointed out that the freedom which is the subject of this report is that of the teacher" (Seligman et al. 1915, 20). It proceeded to elaborate on what academic freedom should mean for professors by discussing the scope and basis of the power of academic boards of trustees, the nature of the professorial calling, and the function of the university.

The focus on teacher freedom made sense in the early years of universities. This was a time when a college matriculant was still a child. For example, the average age of a freshman in the University of Pennsylvania's class of 1852 was fourteen (University of Pennsylvania n.d.). Therefore, universities were seen as acting in the place of a parent, or in loco parentis (Lee 2011). Daniel Coit Gilman, in his first address as president of Johns Hopkins University in 1876, noted: "The College implies, as a general rule, restriction rather than freedom . . . The college theoretically stands in loco parentis; it does not afford a very wide scope" (Johns Hopkins University n.d.). Therefore, in the context of early universities, students exercised very little freedom, because they were viewed as children who needed to be reined in by their substitute parents—that is, their professors. An expression of this paternalism is evidenced in the AAUP declaration's admonishment that a professor "be especially on his guard against taking unfair advantage of the students' immaturity by indoctrinating him with the teacher's own opinions" (Seligman et al. 1915, 35). Inherent in this warning was the belief that the flow of information and learning went in one direction—from professor to student. Students were not viewed as being in a position to contribute to either their own learning or the learning of others. This would change in the 1960s.

In loco parentis ended during the height of the civil rights movement, when young adults on college campuses started successfully claiming their right to speak out against racial injustice (Lee 2011). At that point, there was a greater societal acknowledgement of students' rights and freedoms. Adapting to the changing times, the AAUP, along with other higher education organizations, jointly authored a new document that revisited the issue of what student academic freedom entails (AAUP et al. 1967). The joint statement recognized that "freedom to teach and freedom to learn are inseparable facets of academic freedom. The freedom to learn depends upon appropriate opportunities and conditions in the classroom, on the campus, and in the larger community" (AAUP et al. 1967, 365–66). It then detailed these elements.

Of particular relevance in this statement were the necessary conditions for student freedom to flourish, which implied that students are co-producers of knowledge with other members of the university community. It noted, for example, that "students should be free to take reasoned exception to the data or views offered in any course of study and to reserve judgment about matters of opinion" (AAUP et al. 1967, 366). This was a break from the days of in loco parentis, when it would be taboo—and even a punishable offense—for students to disagree with their professors. The joint statement also acknowledged: "Students bring to the campus a variety of interests previously acquired and develop many new interests as members of the academic community. They should be free to organize and join associations to promote their common interests" (AAUP et al. 1967, 366). This was a recognition of the value that students' prior experiences have in enriching campus life.

Next, the joint statement noted, "Students and student organizations should be free to examine and discuss all questions of interest to them and to express opinions publicly and privately" (AAUP et al. 1967, 366–67). Thus the expression of student voices was viewed as an important component of student freedom. Further, the statement addressed student participation in institutional governance by explaining, "As constituents of the academic community, students should be free, individually and collectively, to express their views on issues of institutional policy and matters of general interest to the student body" (AAUP et al. 1967, 367). Therefore, students were not mere passive receptacles of learning. Instead, they were considered to be valued stakeholders, with something meaningful to contribute to how their educational institutions were governed.

As for student publications, the joint statement opined that they "are valuable aids in establishing and maintaining an atmosphere of free and responsible discussion and of intellectual exploration on the campus" and "are a means of bringing student concerns to the attention of the faculty and the institutional authorities and of formulating student opinion on various issues on the campus and in the world at large" (AAUP et al. 1967, 367). Once again, students' voices were seen as an important component of academic freedom.

Finally, the joint statement recommended, "Faculty members and administration officials should ensure that institutional powers are not employed to inhibit such intellectual and personal development of students as is often promoted by their exercise of the rights of citizenship both on and off campus" (AAUP et al. 1967, 367). This is particularly important for two reasons. First, it recognized that the intellectual and personal growth of students occurs when they exercise their freedom. Second, it urged that the students' ability to do this should be protected, in order to enable such growth. In modern educational terminology, these conditions, taken together, would amount to a freedom to engage in active learning.

Part III: Student Protest as an Expression of Active Learning

Along with the shift in how the AAUP and other higher education organizations viewed students, learning theory was evolving to emphasize active over passive learning. Active learning has its roots in constructivist learning theory. This theory posits that learning is a contextualized process of *creating* knowledge, rather than passively acquiring it. John Dewey set forth a major tenet of constructivist thought when he explained what differentiates "education based upon experience from traditional education" (Dewey 1938, 79). Dewey wrote that one of the useful outcomes of experiential learning, a type of learning he considered superior to its traditional counterpart, is that "it arouses in the learner an active quest for information and for production of new ideas" (Dewey 1938, 79).

Another tenet of constructivism is Jean Piaget's (1954) idea that learning takes place through a process of constructive deduction—meaning that young learners actively engage with the world around them in order to make sense of it. An additional tenet of constructivism is L. S. Vygotsky's (1978) idea of social development. He studied the relationship between cognitive processes and social activities and emphasized the sociocultural dimension of learning. Vygotsky theorized that learning takes place when students solve problems beyond their developmental level with the support of their teachers or peers.

Active learning is also associated with the work of Paulo Freire, in his critique of what he called "the banking model" of education (Freire 2018, 72). Under the banking model, "the teacher's task is to organize a process which already occurs spontaneously, to 'fill' the students by making deposits of information which he or she considers to constitute true knowledge. And since people 'receive' the world as passive entities, education should make them more passive still, and adapt them to the world" (Freire 2018, 76).

Thus the banking model assumes that students are mere passive receptacles of knowledge. Freire further contended that this model was oppressive, because it placed teachers in a position of absolute power over their students' learning. He wrote that the banking concept "attempts to control thinking and action, leads women and men to adjust to the world, and inhibits their creative power" (Freire 2018, 77). He argued that active learning, in contrast, is a form of liberation and empowerment. Students should be viewed as active co-producers of knowledge, along with their teachers, "so that both are simultaneously teachers *and* students" (Freire 2018, 72, emphasis in original). Therefore, Freire believed that education, at its best, was a continual process in which students and teachers were engaged in learning from each other.

In a seminal text on active learning, Charles Bonwell and James Eison (1991, iii) defined active learning as "instructional activities involving students in doing things and thinking about what they are doing." Active learning encompasses the following characteristics (Bonwell and Eison 1991, 2):

- Students are involved in more than listening.
- Students are engaged in activities (e.g., reading, discussing, writing).
- Less emphasis is placed on transmitting information and more on developing students' skills.
- Students are involved in higher-order thinking (analysis, synthesis, evaluation).
- Greater emphasis is placed on students' exploration of their own attitudes and values.

What Reclaim Harvard Law School accomplished in banning the school's shield was consistent with all of these characteristics. First, the students did more than listen to classroom lectures and dialogue. They were active learners who learned by doing. They had to, in order to demand a meaningful change in their legal education that would be heard and taken seriously. Through readings outside of their syllabi, they were able to connect the history of HLS with the legacy of slavery. By studying new historical scholarship on the subject, the students were able to apply their knowledge and press for institutional change. They were willing to take responsibility for their own learning by conducting reading groups and inviting guest speakers. The students of

Reclaim Harvard Law School proclaimed: "We will assume the burden of educating ourselves and others in spite of this institution and not because of it. We will force this institution to become the educational environment which it has hitherto only pretended to be" ("Reclaim Harvard Law Occupies" 2016). They transformed the discourse at HLS to focus on racial injustice.

This transformation was lauded by faculty and staff. In a letter published on December 9, 2015, thirty-three HLS professors and staff members wrote the following about the student activists: "We have been inspired by their efforts, and we are grateful for the courage, intelligence, dignity, and resiliency that they have exhibited in calling for reform in our School and in our nation . . . Moreover, we think that the time has come for our institutional conversation to shift to the task at hand: real, concrete and timely action. In signing this letter, we are taking one small step to make clear our strong support for making those investments" (Ardalan et al. 2015).

Although the students received much support from other students and faculty and staff, this was not unanimous. The issues that the students' activism brought to the fore also generated disagreement and vigorous debate. For example, the controversy over the HLS shield produced diverging views on what to do with the shield from students, alumni, faculty, and staff (Mann et al. 2016). As we have seen, the official resolution of the controversy produced two well-reasoned but conflicting recommendations on whether the shield should be retired. Also, some students publicly disagreed with Reclaim Harvard Law's tactics.

Further, faculty and staff members engaged in public debates about the students' activism. For example, Professor Randall Kennedy (2015) wrote in the *New York Times* that he was neither alarmed nor hurt by the black tape placed over his portrait. Kennedy proceeded to caution the students not to exaggerate their claims of racism when there is no clear proof of racial animus, or minimize their own strength and the victories that they had already achieved. Professor John Hanson and the program director of the Systemic Justice Project, Jacob Lipton, responded in a blog that Professor Kennedy's piece missed the point the students were trying to make, because while Kennedy was focusing on explicit racism, the students were trying to bring attention to systemic racism (Hanson and Lipton 2015). Finally, when seven faculty members felt the criticism of the dean was unreasonable, they wrote a letter to laud the goals of the students but denounce some of their tactics (Cohen et al. 2016). This disagreement was not a sign of failed student activism. On the contrary, this vigorous exchange of differing views, driven by students voicing their concerns, was higher education at its best. It was a recognition that student voices mattered and could make a difference.

Second, the students developed new skills by engaging in activism. Just as they needed to learn about HLS's historical connection to slavery, in order to challenge the continuing use of the HLS shield, they had to further research the history of activism at HLS to connect the past with the present, so as to guide their future activities. Students in Reclaim Harvard Law School wrote: "Our recent efforts are intellectually descended from the numerous student movements that have arisen time and again at HLS, because of a long-true reality: Harvard Law School is not an inclusive institution. It does not promote diversity. It is not a leader in promoting racial justice. Instead, it is a leader in the further entrenchment of the status quo" ("Reclaim Harvard Law Occupies" 2016). Such student movements included the Third Word Coalition that pushed for increased diversity in the faculty and in curricular selections in the early 1980s; the Coalition for Civil Rights that sued the law school for increased faculty diversity in the early 1990s; the Griswold 9, who occupied the dean's office for twenty-four hours in protest of the lack of diversity on the faculty in the early 1990s; and others ("Timeline" n.d.).

The students also learned how to draft demands to the HLS administration, while collaborating with multiple constituents. Reclaim Harvard Law members worked with various student organizations in getting their message out to the community. They discovered how to align with others whom they interacted with every day. For example, when the HLS cleaning staff, whom one of the students described as "black and brown people like me," arrived early in the morning to "disrupt and dismantle" Belinda Hall, the students realized that their goals of equity and justice overlapped with these laborers (Raymond 2016). Avoiding an unnecessary confrontation between themselves and workers, the students assisted the staff in cleaning up the space. Reclaim Harvard Law participants acquired presentation and negotiation skills through multiple meetings with the dean and other members of the administration. Lastly, the students found out how to bring their message to a broader audience than those who physically attended their meetings. They managed the communication of their activism through social media, such as Twitter and Facebook, and traditional media, including opinion pieces with local and national newspapers, as well as interviews on national television news programs.

Third, the students engaged in higher-order thinking, including a broad analysis of inequality in society, by discussing topics such as mass incarceration, the prison-industrial complex, and the school-to-prison pipeline. They proceeded to evaluate the shortcomings of the current law school curriculum, in order to change the status quo. Most importantly, they engaged in a synthesis of their analysis and evaluation by subsequently exploring different ways to fill the gaps in their learning to address various forms of injustice. One student occupier of Belinda Hall explained:

> In Belinda Hall, I and others have engaged in political education, comparing the writings of Stokely Carmichael and Bayard Rustin. I've seen critical race theorists like Native American Professor Gerald Torres and Latina Professor Margaret Montoya expand students' imaginations. I've watched films that deal with challenging topics of race, religion, gender, and sexual orientation like *Brother Outsider* and *Omar*. I've even enjoyed the comedy routine of Palestinian Professor Amer Zahr. And as I write this, I see classmates preparing for a student-led discussion of Ta-Nehisi Coates' *Between the World and Me* and James Baldwin's *The Fire Next Time* (Raymond 2016).

Many more speakers and events would follow. Thus, through personal accountability for their own education and intellectual engagement with others, Reclaim Harvard Law members applied various critiques of the current legal system to undergird their activism.

Fourth, the students emphasized their own attitudes and beliefs about social justice and inclusion in pressing for change. They realized that the curriculum diverged from their own values and took responsibility for their learning in a way that was consistent with their beliefs. In the spring of 2016, these students made their voices heard. Through their activism, they took ownership of their education and made their opinions matter. They generated dialogue and vigorous debate. They placed a focus on an important issue and changed the way people thought. They transformed their learning space. This was part of their freedom to learn. Henry Reichman, writing as the chair of Committee A—the AAUP committee charged with investigating violations of professorial academic freedom—observed the following about student academic freedom: "Faculty members should welcome the challenges the protesting students have posed. Student movements offer countless opportunities for students—as well as their teachers—to learn. To approach them in this way, in the spirit of the student academic freedom proclaimed and defined by the AAUP and its collaborators back in 1967, is therefore simply to fulfill our responsibility as educators" (Reichman 2015).

Simply put, the students in Reclaim Harvard Law School exercised their academic freedom to learn and, while they did so, others learned, too. Student academic freedom, therefore, gave the protesters the strongest protections for what they did.

Part IV: The First Amendment?

Amid the students' activism, another question arises. Why not just rely on First Amendment principles to protect the HLS students' right to protest? First Amendment free speech rules are insufficient for several reasons. At a private institution like Harvard, the First Amendment would not take the students very far. The relevant words of the amendment are: "Congress shall make no law . . . abridging the freedom of speech." The US Supreme Court later interpreted this to mean that governmental action—either at the federal or state level—is required for the First Amendment to be violated (*Gitlow* 1925). Since Harvard is a private institution, First Amendment protections would not apply to the law students if the institution decided to punish them for their activism. Nonetheless, some plaintiffs have brought suit against HLS for constitutional violations arguing that it is an arm of the state. For example, a law school applicant sued HLS, arguing that his denial of admission was a constitutional violation (*Krohn* 1977). He contended that HLS was a state actor, because of its historic connections to the Commonwealth of Massachusetts. The applicant lost. The federal court noted, "While [the applicant] has written a fascinating historical review of the founding of Harvard University, we agree with the district court that he has failed to show a sufficient present day relationship between Harvard and the Commonwealth to treat the school as a public institution subject to federal jurisdiction" (*Krohn* 1977, at 23).

Even assuming that First Amendment rules apply to student activists—for example, if the students were at a public university—these rules would fall short in protecting their right to voice their opinions and participate in the governance of the school. In at least one case (*Healy* 1972), the US Supreme Court has applied a free speech rule that arose from a dispute at a public high school and middle school in Des Moines, Iowa (*Tinker* 1969).

In *Tinker*, one junior high school student and two high school students decided to wear black armbands in support of a truce during the Vietnam War. When school officials learned of this, they imposed a rule prohibiting the wearing of any armbands in school. The students, nonetheless, wore their bands and were sent home. They subsequently challenged the armband policy as a violation of the First Amendment. They won. The US Supreme Court stated, "The District Court recognized that the wearing of an armband for the purpose of expressing certain views is the type of symbolic act that is within the Free Speech Clause of the First Amendment. As we shall discuss, the wearing of armbands in the circumstances of this case was entirely divorced from actually or potentially disruptive conduct by those participating in it. It was closely akin to "pure speech" which, we have repeatedly held, is entitled to comprehensive protection under the First Amendment" (*Tinker* 1969, at 506–7). The court, however, also articulated the applicable standard for free speech in public schools, stating that "conduct by the student, in class or out of it, which for any reason . . . materially disrupts classwork or involves substantial disorder or invasion of the rights of others is . . . not immunized by the constitutional guarantee of freedom of speech" (*Tinker* 1969, at 513). Forty years after *Tinker* was decided, confusion in the lower courts exists as to which rules would apply to public universities in free speech disputes.

On the one hand, some courts have followed *Healy* and applied the *Tinker* standard to free speech disputes at colleges and universities. For example, in *DeJohn v. Temple University*, the US Court of Appeals for the Third Circuit applied *Tinker* to a free speech challenge to the university's sexual harassment policy. The court, however, acknowledged that under *Tinker*, colleges and universities "are granted *less leeway* in regulating student speech than are public elementary or high school administrators" (*DeJohn* 2008, at 316).

On the other hand, other courts have disagreed that *Tinker* applies to higher education disputes at all. Amanda Tatro, a mortuary science student at the University of Minnesota, received a failing grade in her required anatomy laboratory course because she posted status updates on her Facebook account that included statements about the cadaver she and her group were dissecting. Tatro described the statements as a "satirical commentary and violent fantasy about her school experience" (*Tatro* 2012, at 511). She subsequently failed the course for not complying with academic program rules. Tatro challenged these sanctions on First Amendment grounds. The Minnesota Supreme Court, however, refused to apply *Tinker* as the proper test governing this dispute, noting, "The *Tinker* substantial disruption standard does not fit the purposes of the sanctions here" (*Tatro* 2012, at 519–20).

In *Tatro*, the University of Minnesota argued that an additional First Amendment rule arising from a free speech dispute at a Missouri public high school pertained to the situation at hand. That case involved a group of high school students' free speech challenge to the principal's decision to remove two articles from a student newspaper that he deemed inappropriate. The US Supreme Court held for the school principal, noting that "educators do not offend the First Amendment by exercising editorial control over the style and content of student speech in school-sponsored expressive activities so long as their actions are reasonably related to legitimate pedagogical concerns" (*Hazelwood* 1988, at 273). Disagreement exists as to whether *Hazelwood* applies to higher education disputes.

The US Court of Appeals for the Ninth Circuit subsequently adopted the *Hazelwood* test in a higher education dispute involving a master's student challenging the rejection of his thesis, because it rebuked the graduate school dean and other staff in an expletive-laden "Disacknowledgements" section (*Brown* 2002). In *Tatro*, however, the Minnesota Supreme Court went in a different direction and rejected *Hazelwood* as the proper First Amendment test to apply in higher education. The *Tatro* court observed that applying *Hazelwood* "would give universities wide-ranging authority to constrain offensive or controversial Internet activity by requiring only that a school's actions be 'reasonably related' to 'legitimate pedagogical concerns'" (*Tatro* 2012, at 518). The Minnesota Supreme Court was worried that *Hazelwood* would vest too much power in higher education administrators toward regulating the speech of their students. As an alternative, the court adopted a strict scrutiny standard that took into account the mortuary science student's professional obligations, stating that "any restrictions on a student's Facebook posts must be narrowly tailored and directly related to established professional conduct standards" (*Tatro* 2012, at 521).

Tatro's rejection of both *Tinker* and *Hazelwood* as the proper tests in the context of higher education makes sense for a number of reasons. First, different pedagogical purposes exist for primary and secondary schools (K–12) and higher education institutions. The former principally exist to inculcate societal values. The US Supreme Court, in writing about public school education, noted: "It is the very foundation of good citizenship. Today it is a principal instrument in awakening the child to cultural values . . . and in helping him to adjust normally to his environment" (*Brown* 1954, at 493). In a later case that involved a school disciplining a student for offensive speech at a school event, without running afoul of the Constitution, the court wrote: "The process of educating our youth for citizenship in public schools is not confined to books, the curriculum, and the civics class; schools must teach by example the shared values of a civilized social order" (*Bethel* 1986, at 683). In contrast, colleges and universities, at their best, encourage their students to question their understanding of the world around them and develop new ways of seeing. The US Supreme Court has acknowledged this critical purpose:

> To impose any strait jacket upon the intellectual leaders in our colleges and universities would imperil the future of our Nation. No field of education is so thoroughly comprehended by man that new discoveries cannot yet be made . . . Scholarship cannot flourish in an atmosphere of suspicion and distrust. Teachers and students must always remain free to inquire, to study and to evaluate, to gain new maturity and understanding; otherwise our civilization will stagnate and die. (*Sweezy* 1957, at 250)

Therefore, since higher education encourages students to challenge their a priori assumptions about the world, students in this context should have more freedom to speak than they do in elementary, middle, and high schools.

Second, different maturity levels exist between students in primary and secondary schools and those in higher education institutions. While public school students are typically children below the age of majority, college and university students are usually adults. Thus, as adults, these students should be given more freedom to speak than the children in public schools.

Third, related to the prior two reasons, public schools have a duty to act in loco parentis on behalf of their students (*Bethel* 1986, at 684). They have broad disciplinary authority, akin to what parents have over their children. By contrast, colleges and universities have not had this legal relationship with their students since the early 1970s (Lee 2011). Thus higher education students should be given more freedom to speak than those whose schools are acting as parents in relation to them.

If *Tinker* and *Hazelwood* are not the proper doctrines in higher education, then the student activists could turn to general free speech principles that apply outside the school context. One of the most relevant would be the true threat doctrine. In *Watts v. United States*, the US Supreme Court stated, "What is a threat must be distinguished from what is constitutionally protected speech" (*Watts* 1969, at 707). In *Watts*, a man was convicted for threatening the president of the United States, because he stated that if he was forced into the military, the president would be the first person he would put in his sights. The court held that this statement was constitutionally protected speech, because it did not constitute a true threat, but, rather, was "a kind of very crude offensive method of stating a political opposition to the President" (*Watts* 1969, at 708). Another relevant principal under general free speech law would be the application of strict scrutiny in cases of content-based speech regulation. This principle declares that such speech restrictions must be "narrowly tailored to serve a compelling state interest" (*Austin* 1990, at 655). While both the true threat doctrine and strict scrutiny afford students in colleges and universities more protection than *Tinker* and other school law cases, they are still lacking, because they do not consider the special context of higher education. A better approach would be to explore how students' academic freedom gives them a right to protest.

Such an approach provides benefits over a First Amendment course of action. First, student academic freedom is not limited by the strictures of the free speech framework created by school law cases like *Tinker* and *Hazelwood*. While *Tinker* allowed speech regulations if school officials could reasonably forecast substantial disruption, and *Hazelwood* permitted regulation of school-sanctioned speech on the basis of legitimate pedagogical concerns, a student academic freedom framework would take the students' freedom to learn into account. It would recognize that students are active participants in their own education and give them more leeway to engage in activist speech and actions as a function of that learning.

Second, student academic freedom overcomes the limitations of general First Amendment principles, such as the true threat doctrine and strict scrutiny. While these free speech protections, which apply outside of a school context, offer more safeguards than the school law cases, these doctrines do not take into account the unique contributions that college and university students can make in their learning environments. Instead of asking whether a student is making a true threat by saying certain things, or if a university is regulating speech in a way that is narrowly tailored to meet a compelling objective, a student academic freedom analysis would give the students more agency, viewing them as co-producers of knowledge in a collective learning environment. Under this framework, the most relevant question for a university dealing with student activism would be, How does the students' speech enhance the campus learning environment?

Third, unlike the First Amendment, student academic freedom applies to both private and public institutions. This is a crucial difference. Even with the limitations of First Amendment law at public institutions, it is still better than the nonexistent constitutional protections at private universities. Student academic freedom would fill in the gap between public and private institutions of higher education and provide better protection at both places than is currently supplied by constitutional law. This freedom could be codified in institutional rules and policies by incorporating the AAUP et al.'s (1967) joint statement on student academic freedom. Furthermore, this freedom could be legally enforced through contract law (Lee 2018) or by AAUP investigations into student academic freedom violations, similar to the work the AAUP's Committee A has done for professorial academic freedom violations since 1915 (Lee 2015).

Conclusion

By March 15, 2016, the HLS shield started coming down from public display (Svrluga 2016). The students made this happen by occupying and renaming the student center; issuing written demands and putting pressure on the administration; conducting teach-ins; and engaging in other forms of protest. They were active learners who took part of their education into their own hands. In so doing, these students exercised their academic freedom. They made their university a better place.

References

AAUP (American Association of University Professors), US National Student Association, Association of American Colleges, National Association of Student Personnel Administrators, National Association of Women Deans and Counselors, American Association for Higher Education, Jesuit Education Association, et al. 1967. "Joint Statement on Rights and Freedoms of Students." *AAUP Bulletin* 4(December): 365–368.

Ardalan, Sabi, Ona Balkus, Roger Berlting, Cheryl Bratt, Esme Caramello, Stephanie Davidson, Fernando Delgado, et al. December 9, 2015. "An Open Letter to the Harvard Law School Community." *The Justice Blog*, https://systemicjusticeblog.wordpress.com/2015/12/09/.

Arnett, Dugan. March 15, 2016. "Meet the Coauthor Who Shined a Light on the Harvard Law Crest Controversy." *Boston Globe*, https://www.bostonglobe.com.

Austin (*Austin v. Mich[igan] Chamber of Comm[erce]*). 1990. 494 U.S. 652. Justia, https://supreme.justia.com.

"Belinda Sutton and Her Petitions." n.d. Royall House & Slave Quarters, http://www.royallhouse.org/slavery/belinda-sutton-and-her-petitions/.

Bethel (*Bethel Sch[ool] Dist[rict] v. Fraser*). 1986. 478 U.S. 675. Justia, https://supreme.justia.com.

Bidgood, Jess. November 19, 2015. "Tape Found over Portraits of Black Harvard Professors." *New York Times*, https://www.nytimes.com.

Bonwell, Charles C. and James A. Eison. 1991. *Active Learning*. ASHE-ERIC Higher Education Report No. 1. Washington DC: George Washington University, School of Education and Human Development.

Brown (*Christopher Todd Brown, Plaintiff-appellant, v. Charles Li et al., Defendants-appellees*). 2002. 308 F.3d 939 (9th Cir.). Justia, https://law.justia.com.

Brown (*Brown v. Board of Education of Topeka*). 1954. 347 U.S. 483. Justia, https://supreme.justia.com.

Byrne, J. Peter. 1989. "Academic Freedom: A 'Special Concern of the First Amendment.'" *Yale Law Journal* 99:251–340.

Cohen, Glen, Randall Kennedy, Richard Lazarus, Todd Rakoff, Carol Steiker, Kristen Stilt, and David Wilkins. March 21, 2016. "An Open Letter to the Harvard Law School Community." *Harvard Law Record*, http://hlrecord.org.

"Committee Exploring Whether Harvard Law School Shield Should Be Changed." November 30, 2015. *Harvard Law Today*, https://today.law.harvard.edu.

Coquillette, Daniel R. and Bruce A. Kimball. 2015. *On the Battlefield of Merit: Harvard Law School, the First Century*. Cambridge, MA: Harvard University Press.

DeJohn (*Christian M. DeJohn v. Temple University; David Adamany; Richard Immerman; Gregory J. W. Urwin*). 2008. Case No. 07-2220. United States Court of Appeals for the Third Circuit, http://www2.ca3.uscourts.gov/opinarch/072220p.pdf.

Dewey, John. 1938. *Experience and Education*. New York: Touchstone.

Faust, Drew and William F. Lee. March 14, 2016. "Dear Dean [Martha] Minow." *Harvard Law Today*, https://today.law.harvard.edu/wp-content/uploads/2016/03/Harvard_Corp_letter_shield.pdf.

Freire, Paulo. 2018. *Pedagogy of the Oppressed*. New York: Bloomsbury Academic.
"Frequently Asked Questions." n.d. *Reclaim Harvard Law School* (blog), https://reclaimharvardlaw.wordpress.com/frequently-asked-questions/.
"Gilman's Inaugural Address." n.d. Johns Hopkins University, https://www.jhu.edu/about/history/gilman-address/.
Gitlow (*Gitlow v. New York*). 1925. 268 U.S. 652. Justia, https://supreme.justia.com.
Gordon-Reed, Annette. March 3, 2016. "A Different View." *Harvard Law Today*, https://today.law.harvard.edu/wp-content/uploads/2016/03/Shield_Committee-Different_View.pdf.
Hanson, Jon and Jacob Lipton. November 29, 2015. "A Response to Randall Kennedy." *The Justice Blog*. https://systemicjusticeblog.wordpress.com/2015/11/29/a-response-to-randall-kennedy/.
"The Harvard Law School Shield: A Timeline." n.d. Harvard Law School Shield Exhibit, Harvard Law School Library, https://exhibits.law.harvard.edu.
Hazlewood (*Hazelwood Sch[ool] Dis[trict] v. Kuhlmeier*). 1988. 484 U.S. 260. Justia, https://supreme.justia.com.
Healy (*Healy v. James*). 1972. 408 U.S. 169. Justia, https://supreme.justia.com.
"History of Harvard Law School." n.d. Harvard Law School, https://hls.harvard.edu/about/history/.
Kennedy, Randall. November 27, 2015. "Black Tape at Harvard." *New York Times*, https://www.nytimes.com.
Krohn (*Kenneth B. Krohn, Plaintiff-appellant, v. Harvard Law School et al., Defendants-appellees*). 1977. 552 F.2d 21 (1st Cir.). Justia, https://law.justia.com.
Lee, Philip. 2018. "Student Protests and Academic Freedom in an Age of #blacklivesmatter." *Ohio State Law Journal* 79(2):223–278.
Lee, Philip. 2015. *Academic Freedom at American Universities: Constitutional Rights, Professional Norms, and Contractual Duties*. Lanham, MD: Lexington Books.
Lee, Philip. 2011. "The Curious Life of In Loco Parentis in American Universities." *Higher Education in Review* 8:65–90.
Mack, Kenneth W. n.d. "Royall Must Fall: The Shield is Retired." Harvard Law School Shield Exhibit, Harvard Law School Library, https://exhibits.law.harvard.edu.
Mann, Bruce H., James E. Bowers, Tomiko Brown-Nagin, Janet Halley, Rena Karefa-Johnson, Robert J. Katz, Samuel Moyn, et al. March 3, 2016. "Recommendation to the President and Fellows of Harvard College on the Shield Approved for the Law School." *Harvard Law Today*, https://today.law.harvard.edu/wp-content/uploads/2016/03/Shield-Committee-Report.pdf.
Metzger, Walter P. 1988. "Profession and Constitution: Two Definitions of Academic Freedom in America." *Texas Law Review* 66:1265.
Piaget, Jean. 1954. *The Construction of Reality in the Child*. New York: Basic Books.
Raymond, Jordan. March 4, 2016. "Why I'm Sleeping in Belinda Hall." *Harvard Crimson*, https://www.thecrimson.com.
"Reclaim Harvard Law Demands." December 4, 2015, *Reclaim Harvard Law School* (blog). https://reclaimharvardlaw.wordpress.com/demands/.

"Reclaim Harvard Law Occupies Fireside Lounge." February 16, 2016. *Harvard Law Record*, http://hlrecord.org.

Reichman, Henry. December 4, 2015. "On Student Academic Freedom." *Inside Higher Ed*, https://www.insidehighered.com.

Royall Must Fall. November 18, 2015. "An Open Letter to Dean Minow from Students of Harvard Law School: Royall Must Fall." *Harvard Law Record*, http://hlrecord.org.

Royall Must Fall. n.d. "About." Facebook, https://www.facebook.com/pg/RoyallMustFall/about/?ref=page_internal/.

Royall Must Fall (@RoyallMustFall). March 14, 2016. "Royall has fallen!" Twitter, https://twitter.com/RoyallMustFall/status/709477612741984256/.

Royall Must Fall (@RoyallMustFall). n.d. "Information About." Twitter, https://twitter.com/RoyallMustFall.

Ryan, Michael P. and Gretchen G. Martens. 1989. *Planning a College Course*. Ann Arbor: University of Michigan, National Center for Research to Improve Postsecondary Teaching and Learning.

Seligman, Edward R. A., Charles E. Bennett, James Q. Dealey, Richard T. Ely, Henry W. Farnam, Frank A. Fetter, Franklin H. Giddings, et al. 1915. "General Report of the Committee on Academic Freedom and Academic Tenure." *Bulletin of the American Association of University Professors* 1(1):15–43.

Shammas, Michael. March 4, 2016. "After Months of Advocacy and Debate, Harvard Law Recommends Shield Change." *Harvard Law Record*, http://hlrecord.org.

Svrluga, Susan. March 15, 2016. "The Harvard Law Shield Tied to Slavery Is Already Disappearing, after Corporation Vote." *Washington Post*, https://www.washingtonpost.com.

Sweezy (*Sweezy v. New Hampshire*). 1957. 354 U.S. 234. Justia, https://supreme.justia.com.

Tatro (*Amanda Tatro, Appellant, v. University of Minnesota, Respondent*). 2012. 816 N.W.2d 509 (Minn.). Leagle, https://www.leagle.com/decision/inmnco20120620392.

"Timeline of Student Activism for Diversity and Inclusion." n.d. *Reclaim Harvard Law School* (blog), https://reclaimharvardlaw.wordpress.com/timeline-of-student-inclusion-requests/.

Tinker (*Tinker v. Des Moines Independent Community School District*). 1969. 393 U.S. 503. Justia, https://supreme.justia.com.

University of Pennsylvania. n.d. "Selected Class Histories: College Class of 1852." Penn University Archives & Records Center, https://archives.upenn.edu.

US Supreme Court. n.d. "About the Court." Supreme Court of the United States, https://www.supremecourt.gov/about/biographies.aspx.

Vygotsky, L. S. 1978. *Mind in Society*. Cambridge, MA: Harvard University Press.

Watts (*Watts v. United States*). 1969. 394 U.S. 705. Justia, https://supreme.justia.com.

PART IV

LESSONS FROM HISTORY

CHAPTER 10

Academic Freedom and Its Useful Past

Timothy Reese Cain

Academic freedom has deep European roots, but in the United States it began to come of age with changes in views of knowledge and institutional structures in the decades after the Civil War. The professionalization of the faculty and increasing reliance on expertise were key features in its development, as was the growing ability of faculty to work together across institutions. The 1915 founding of the American Association of University Professors (AAUP) and then the release of its 1915 "Declaration of Principles on Academic Freedom and Academic Tenure" were signal events (Seligman et al. 1915), as were the beginnings of its investigations into alleged violations of faculty rights. Significant restrictions on faculty activities during World War I were followed by religiously inspired attacks on the teaching of science and repeated Red Scares. As the AAUP sought to establish academic freedom as a core value of US higher education, it was joined by a handful of other organizations, most notably the American Federation of Teachers (AFT), which took a more activist approach to the issues. The 1940 "Statement of Principles on Academic Freedom and Tenure"

(1940/1970), jointly agreed upon by the AAUP and the Association of American Colleges (AAC), helped codify and institutionalize understandings of and protections for academic freedom, though the widespread attacks on faculty during the McCarthy period (Hutcheson 1997; Schrecker 1986), and, later, the dismissal of multiple faculty for their civil rights work (Williamson-Lott 2018), demonstrated that this freedom is frail and constantly renegotiated. Just as the epistemological shifts of the late nineteenth century spurred the development of academic freedom, those of the late twentieth century, which were conjoined with the changing makeup of the faculty, necessitated new ways of thinking about it. Those changes also fostered and revealed fissures in the professoriate and in the larger society that have proven intractable. The challenges that they have posed have only been exacerbated by the centralization of administrative authority and the pressures of the neoliberal university. For over more than a century, faculty have navigated these challenges, made public their principled stands, and negotiated rights. At the same time, others have quietly succumbed to more mundane forces working against their independence in expression, research, and teaching.

The history of academic freedom, only very briefly sketched above, is not prescriptive. It does not tell us how to act or what to do. It cannot provide definitive answers to modern problems. As Reubén Donato and Marvin Lazerson noted while reporting on a conference on the future of the history of education: "Few historians think in terms of immediate 'lessons.' Neither their disciplinary training nor their historical findings prepare them to offer concrete and specific solutions." Yet, they continued, "most educational historians believe . . . that their work can and should inform current policy debates" (Donato and Lazerson, 2000, 9). Such is the case with the history of academic freedom. It provides background, deepens understandings, and highlights ways in which ideas developed and how social and professional norms came into existence. As participants in a "Forum on Academic Freedom" (2018) argued, the history of academic freedom can inform thinking and raise crucial issues.[1] The cases discussed below are complex, as are most that involve academic freedom, and this chapter neither tells the entire story nor provides a full history of the development of that freedom in the United States. Rather, it uses historical examples to highlight enduring issues that remain important as we look to the future of academic freedom.

"A Tyranny of Public Opinion"

On April 23, 1899, Sam Hose was lynched in Newnan, Georgia. It was a particularly horrific and brutal incident in a thoroughly horrific and brutal practice that swept the South, as well as being applied elsewhere. Throngs of white Georgians took trains to Newnan to participate in the spectacle. News reports counted 2,000 participants and onlookers, some of whom left with souvenirs cut from Hose's body. Among those disgusted by the event was Andrew Sledd, who had elsewhere witnessed multiple mobs gathered to perform similar acts of violence (Arnold 2009). A professor at Emory College in Georgia and the son-in-law of the institution's still-influential former president, Warren A. Candler, Sledd soon recounted these events as part of a larger critique of lynching and a call for better treatment for Black Americans. Sledd's article, although well short of a claim for equality, argued that Blacks were inferior to Whites, but he attributed that status to conditions of slavery and claimed that Blacks maintained inalienable rights (Sledd 1902). The article, after being rejected by several outlets, was published in the Boston-based *Atlantic Monthly*.

The piece initially received little attention, but in early August, Rebecca Latimer Felton—daughter of slaveowners, defender of lynching, and Candler antagonist—wrote a letter to the editor of the *Atlanta Constitution* decrying Sledd's treason against the South. Calling the article "'rot' that Mr. Andrew Sledd has vomited into the columns of the Atlantic Monthly," she warned that Sledd might be lucky to escape the South uninjured (Felton 1902). Felton's letter caused an uproar, including in Covington, the town closest to Emory College. People were surprised by Sledd's argument, irate that he had localized his criticisms to Georgia by discussing Hose's lynching, and offended that he had published the critique outside of the region. In the *Atlanta Journal*, one

Covington resident called the article "malicious," while another warned that southerners would no longer be comfortable sending their sons to Emory ("Emory Professor" 1902). Newspapers editorialized for Sledd's dismissal (Editorial 1902), and Felton received laudatory letters encouraging her to continue her attacks (Johnson to Felton 1902), including one predicting that students would "mutiny and refuse absolutely to receive instruction from this maligner of the South" (Renfroe to Felton 1902). Another letter questioned Sledd's motives, called him "half-crazy," and exclaimed, "He is realizing what a fearful thing he has done and I hope he fears for his life" (Johnson to Felton 1902). On August 5, two straw dummies were burned in effigy in Covington. One was intended to represent Sledd, and the other an unidentified Black man ("Bad Boys" 1902).

The situation was fast moving and turned quickly as public pressure mounted and newspapers stoked anti-Sledd sentiment. The first public comments by Emory's new president, James E. Dickey, defended Sledd's right to publish his article, but, amid the uproar, he acted to appease the populace. As controversy engulfed the college, donors threatened to withdraw, newspapers across the state lambasted Sledd, and letter writers called for boycotts of the institution. Dickey demanded Sledd's resignation. After initially declining, Sledd submitted it later that evening, claiming that he was doing so in an attempt to protect the institution (Reed 1988, 471–81; Matthews 2003, 8–12). He wrote to Candler: "I am cramped and stunted by the atmosphere that prevails. I had thought to be able to bring about a better state of things; but the people and the College will have none of it" (Sledd to Candler 1902, cited in Williamson 1984, 260.).

Sledd's forced resignation is just one example of the role that public sentiment has played in shaping restrictions on college faculty, and on teachers more broadly. We might think about specific cases, such as that involving Ward Churchill, after his commentary linking victims of the September 11, 2001, terrorist attacks to Nazi war criminal Adolf Eichman (*Churchill* 2012), or, more broadly, about anti-communist hysteria during several Red Scares, but the possible examples are far too numerous to even attempt to outline. The landmark 1915 "Declaration of Principles" identified this public pressure as the "most serious difficulty" involving academic freedom: "Public opinion is at once the chief safeguard of a democracy, and the chief menace to the real liberty of the individual. It almost seems as if the danger of despotism cannot be wholly averted under any form of government. In a political autocracy there is no effective public opinion, and all are subject to the tyranny of the ruler; in a democracy there is political freedom, but there is likely to be a tyranny of public opinion" (Seligman et al. 1915, 31–32).

In the AAUP's terms, the difficulty of maintaining the university as an "inviolable refuge" from such tyranny remains pronounced in the twenty-first century and has been exacerbated by the ubiquity of social media, which spreads information—truthful or otherwise—far faster and more widely than the newspapers of Sledd's era. Simple statements that faculty make, including as private citizens, are now amplified and, at times, taken out of context and twisted. Well-funded pressure groups shape opinion and direct animus at both individuals and the professoriate as a whole. Faculty have been dismissed not only for what they have said online, but also for what others have claimed they posted. In some cases, fear of public opinion has led to draconian rules, including those imposed by the Kansas Board of Regents after a faculty member's controversial tweet about the National Rifle Association in the aftermath of a mass shooting (Lowry 2014). In a politically and culturally fractured country, overcoming this tyranny of public opinion remains central to any efforts to secure faculty freedoms to both do their work *and* enjoy the rights of citizenship. Moving forward, the challenge is not just defending academic freedom as a right in the moment of an attack, but also educating people about how vital it is to the work of higher education. AAUP leaders recognized that such education, and the shaping of public opinion, were central to their work from the organization's earliest days. Three of the first four AAUP presidents explicitly mentioned it in their presidential addresses (Haberler 2015, 66). It remains just as vital a century later.

Public Reprobation Can, However, Bolster Academic Freedom

Just over a year after Sledd's resignation, a faculty member at Trinity College in Durham, North Carolina, likewise challenged southern racial norms and also faced calls for his dismissal. The two cases shared many similarities, including their implication of broader political battles and disagreements within the Methodist Church. Yet the outcome in Durham was different, in part because of Sledd's removal from Emory College and the way that it was viewed across the nation. Although Emory acted explicitly with an eye toward public opinion, the backlash against its action was severe. In the North and West, numerous papers critiqued the college and used it to question the state of education and freedom in the South. Donors withdrew, enrollments declined, and the institution faced financial difficulties. Rather than saving the institution, removing Sledd endangered it (Reed 1988, 481–84; Matthews 2003, 11–12). Trinity College's president, John C. Kilgo, like Candler a leader in the Methodist Church, wrote to Candler about his dismay at the harm done by Sledd's removal, noting: "I am pained to see our Methodist colleges, one after another, yield to this crowd of freedom-haters. Now old Emory . . . falls down before this set and surrenders forever the old College into their hands. It is enough to make the Angels weep. Trinity stands alone now in this conflict, and the struggle deepens" (Kilgo to Candler 1902, quoted in Porter 1964, 100).

The case at Trinity College centered on John Spencer Bassett, a professor and the editor of the *South Atlantic Quarterly*. As Bassett finalized his article, "Stirring Up the Fires of Race Antipathy," for publication in the October 1903 issue of his journal, he added a sentence designed to attract attention. To the piece, which was written in response to sensationalized coverage of Booker T. Washington and other Black members of a traveling party being served dinner before Whites, as well as the broader racial conditions in the South, he inserted the following: "Now Washington is a great and good man, a Christian statesman, and take him all in all the greatest man, save General Lee, born in the South in a hundred years" (Bassett 1903, 299). Later, in a letter to Charles Francis Adams on November 3, 1911, Bassett noted, "It was not a sudden thought. Putting it into the article, however, was sudden" (quoted in Stephenson 1948, 439). It led to substantial difficulties for Bassett and Trinity but eventually resulted in a strong statement in defense of academic freedom.

Bassett's critique of the coverage of Washington's dinner pointed squarely at Josephus Daniels, the publisher of the Raleigh *News and Observer*, and Daniels responded. For more than a month, his paper attacked Bassett and roused increasing sentiment that the professor was unfit for a position in the South. Criticism of Bassett grew in other newspapers and spread beyond the press to include such things as the Smithfield Methodist Episcopal Church petitioning for Bassett's removal; letters of condemnation sent to Bassett and Trinity; calls for a student boycott; and a note slid under Bassett's door, warning that he could be lynched. Yet as attacks on Bassett and Trinity grew, an undercurrent of support did, as well. The western part of the state, which had a smaller Black population, was more inclined to defend Bassett, and both national newspapers and a handful of North Carolina ones editorialized on his behalf (Garber 1937, 239–66; Morrison 1962; Porter 1964, 110–31; Williamson 1984, 262–66). Influential alumni lobbied the institution, including journalist Walter Hines Page, who explicitly referenced the damage done to Emory and argued in a letter to Benjamin N. Duke on November 26, 1903, that if Bassett were retained, "liberal people all over the United States will rejoice and congratulate the college. Every really great & free institution in the whole country will rejoice; and Trinity will stand higher than it could be made to stand by many years of good quiet work" (quoted by Garber 1937, 263).

In early December, Trinity's governing board met to decide Bassett's future, amid rumors that the president and faculty might resign if academic freedom was not protected. Indeed, all had written resignation letters, but they were to be kept private unless there was an adverse ruling. Over the course of seven hours, the trustees heard an impassioned plea for Bassett's retention from Kilgo; a resolution from alumni studying at Columbia University, urging that the institution protect its reputation by keeping Bassett; and even lengthy quotes from Dickey's earlier support for Sledd in his case at Emory (Garber 1937; Porter 1964, 131–33; Williamson 1984, 266–67). A resolution from the faculty argued that the case was of national importance with Trinity's future hanging in the balance: "Other colleges have been called upon to face the same issue which you are to decide. Such as have failed have been disgraced in the eyes of the academic world" ("Memorial" 1904, 65). At 3 a.m., the trustees endorsed a prepared statement that disassociated the institution from Bassett's views but defended his right to assert them: "Liberty may sometimes lead to folly; yet it is better that some should be tolerated than that all should think and speak under the deadening influence of repression. A reasonable freedom of opinion to a college is the very breath of life; and any official throttling of the private judgment of its teachers would destroy their influence, and place upon the college an enduring stigma" ("Statement of the Trustees" 1904, 63).

Concerns about perception, especially within higher education, informed the decision, and the college was gratified by the response it received. Retaining Bassett brought it national respect ("A Notable Victory" 1904). Although North Carolina papers editorialized against the act, publications outside the region lauded the decision and proclaimed it a great event for the South. In 1905, US President Theodore Roosevelt visited Trinity and praised it for its defense of academic freedom. Page's forecast of the value of defending academic freedom proved true.

Trinity is not the only institution to gain new standing through defending academic freedom, and Emory is not the only one to be chastised for violating it. As Zachary Haberler (2013) argued, and Hans-Joerg Tiede (2014; 2015) echoed, publicity was central to the formative years of academic freedom, as newspapers played important roles in conveying events, raising concerns, and enflaming opinion. The need for public scrutiny of institutional actions informed the work of the AAUP from its earliest days. Investigative reports, launched with Arthur O. Lovejoy's pioneering inquiry into the University of Utah (Mower and Mogren 2014), were designed to bring the facts of alleged violations to light and build a form of academic freedom case law. The implementation of what became known as censure following egregious political interference into public institutions in Mississippi in the 1930s was likewise designed to bring attention to administrations that violated its principles. The AFT and American Civil Liberties Union (ACLU) used publicity even more aggressively in the 1930s. These efforts were not always successful, but concerted public attention to the necessity of academic freedom and critiques of institutions that violated it helped form modern understandings of the principle (Cain 2012; Haberler 2013; Tiede 2014; Tiede 2015, 37–38). Such attention is still needed today, as well as in the future, to help extend the protections of academic freedoms to the full range of instructors in higher education.

Collective Faculty Action Is Important, Though Not Always Present

The potential for negative attention was central to the ultimate adjudicating of the Bassett affair, but other elements were also at play. Whereas the faculty at Emory sided against Sledd, academics at Trinity rallied behind their colleague when he was attacked. The defense of Bassett was one case within a larger phenomenon that has proved to be important. As late nineteenth-century events involving the emerging discipline of economics demonstrate, faculty defense actions—which were conveyed in the expanding press—increasingly but inconsistently played important roles in the early development of academic freedom.

In 1894, both the University of Wisconsin's Richard T. Ely and his former student, Edward W. Bemis of the University of Chicago, ran afoul of their institutions for publicly expressing progressive views on unions and related issues. Their ideas were deemed radical, though Richard Hofstadter and Walter P. Metzger argued that both men might better be understood as "meliorists in social reform and gradualists in social action, rejecting the anarchist's method and the socialist's total panacea." They continued, "Ely, attacked for his heterodox views, was tried, acquitted, and vindicated; Bemis, attacked for his heterodox views, was dismissed without formality" (Hofstadter and Metzger 1955, 425–26). The divergent outcomes in these two cases can be partially explained by the different ways in which other academics responded to them. Ely, long established if somewhat controversial, received support from not only his university's president, but also from well-known faculty across the country. Highly respected professors led his defense campaign, publicized his cause, and testified on his behalf: "Their agitation aroused the entire profession; social scientists everywhere rallied to Ely's defense" (Hofstadter and Metzger 1955, 432). Bemis did not have Ely's standing and, despite Ely's efforts to help, few defended him. Support for Bemis was equivocal, and those who would have been most valuable refrained from offering any assistance. Some who had backed Ely actively worked against Bemis. Ely's case resulted in Wisconsin's Board of Regents famously proclaiming: "In all lines of academic investigation it is of the utmost importance that the investigator should be absolutely free to follow the indications of truth wherever they may lead. Whatever may be the limitations which trammel inquiry elsewhere we believe the great state University of Wisconsin should ever encourage that continual and fearless sifting and winnowing by which alone the truth can be found" (Herfurth 1998, 66–67). Bemis's academic career sputtered and later ended after he was dismissed in a politically motivated purge after a brief stint at Kansas State Agricultural College (Hofstadter and Metzger 1955, 425–36; Furner 1975, 147–98).

The defense of Ely was important, though deployed outside of organizational channels. In the ensuing years, professional associations increasingly involved themselves when academic freedom was challenged. The American Economic Association (AEA) led the way. When Brown University economist and president Elisha Benjamin Adams was told to restrict his public statements on free silver in 1897, he resigned. Academics rallied to his defense and pressed the institution to decline his resignation and protect academic freedom. Some in the AEA pushed for an official response, but in a compromise move to counter fears of overreach, those on a committee of leading members were invited to sign a petition on Adams's behalf. Others soon followed, and when the board finally met to consider his resignation, a stack of petitions and letters of support more than a foot high was presented. Adams was retained. Three years later, when Jane Lathrop Stanford ordered the removal of Edward A. Ross from Stanford University, the reaction of social scientists was even more pronounced. It included multiple professors resigning from the institution and substantial national response. The AEA again acted informally but did so resolutely, under the guidance of Columbia University economist E. A. Seligman. The result was the first report of its kind on a violation of academic freedom. Again, leading faculty from prestigious institutions endorsed the report. Seligman and others also recognized the necessity of securing Ross's future and facilitated his faculty position at the University of Nebraska, lectures at Harvard University, and, eventually, full resuscitation at the University of Wisconsin. Proposed boycotts of Stanford University failed, but the collective action of its faculty took a toll on the institution, provided Ross with a path to continue his career, and helped establish both the principles and the means of defending them (Furner 1975, 205–59).

These early endeavors would inform later efforts for collective action, including the creation of the AAUP and the ensuing work of its Committee A as an investigatory body. These have been crucially important in the longer history of faculty rights, as have been those of other organized faculty, notably the AFT. Yet, as the failure to boycott Stanford University and the decision of Ross's colleagues outside of the social sciences to support the institution over the individual highlight, concerted collective action has been inconsistent and incomplete (Furner 1975, 251–56; Cain 2007). A decade after the Ross case, author John Jay Chapman condemned faculty timidity by noting, "The average of this species will look on at an act of injustice done to a brother professor by their college president with the same unconcern as the rabbit who is not attacked watches the ferret pursue his brother up and down the warren to predestinate and horrible death" (Chapman 1910, 7). That timidity was on full display amid some of the most dramatic challenges to academic freedom the industry of higher education has seen. During the anti-communist attacks of the late 1940s and early 1950s, for example, the faculty largely failed to defend academic freedom, and the AAUP was quiet until the worst of the challenges were over. As Ellen W. Schrecker (1986, 308) wrote: "In most cases, it was not so much what these people did that upset the blacklisted professors as it was what they did not do. They did not organize; they did not protest; they did not do anything that reversed the tide of dismissals."

In the modern era, collective faculty action remains inconsistent. The profession is split in numerous ways, including (but not only) by discipline, institutional type, and kind of appointment. The significant epistemological shifts and divergences dating to the 1960s have also divided the professoriate. A weak job market in multiple fields and the de-tenuring of faculty place pressures that limit collective action and mimic some of those in the Ross case. In that instance, faculty who were not well positioned to find suitable employment elsewhere stayed at Stanford or took the recently vacated jobs there. Moreover, even those who advocate for collective action in perhaps its strongest form, unionization, can find that action to be difficult. Legislation limits bargaining rights in many states, with a recent trend toward greater restrictions. Moreover, US Supreme Court rulings from *NLRB* (1980), denying tenure-line faculty at private institutions bargaining rights, to *Janus* (2018), depriving unions of representation fees, further inhibit faculty organizing.

Historical evidence cannot provide clear direction on how faculty might overcome the challenges to working collectively, but it does point to the importance of such efforts. Academic freedom is the "key legitimating concept of the entire enterprise" of higher education (Menand 1996, 4). Yet its practice has always been politically contested and negotiated amid changing power relationships. It is therefore necessary for faculty to reestablish their collective power so that college instructors as a whole, rather than individual well-positioned professors, can achieve academic freedom in the twenty-first century managerial university.

Not All Threats Are External to the Faculty

While concerted faculty action is paramount, it is important to acknowledge that threats can also come from within the faculty. Schrecker (1986, 105–10), for example, argued that in addition to fear, one of the reasons that faculty did not stand up against McCarthyist investigations was because many agreed that those who were members of the Communist Party (CP) did not deserve their jobs. Faculty, such as Sidney Hook, attacked communist professors from within higher education and worked to legitimize the purges. He argued that CP membership was itself antithetical to academic freedom and, therefore, disqualifying (Nemeth 2017). Arthur Lovejoy, one of the most important people in the development of academic freedom, concurred. In the aftermath of the University of Washington's 1948 dismissal of three faculty members for communist activity, he argued, "No one . . . who desires to maintain academic freedom in America can consistently favor that movement, or give indirect assistance to it by accepting as fit members of the faculty of universities, persons who have voluntarily adhered to an organization one of whose aims is to abolish academic freedom" (Lovejoy 1949).

Perhaps less remembered than the challenges of the late 1940s and early 1950s were those that occurred during World War I. Faculty were so vocal in their advocacy for entry into the war that the *New Republic* later claimed they were the professionals most responsible for the United States' intervention. James McKeen Cattell's dismissal from Columbia University is the most famous case from that period, but the situation at the University of Michigan is more instructive on this point. That university first emphasized a neutrality policy for its faculty, students, and visiting speakers, but, as the United States' intervention approached, it put its full backing behind the war effort. For example, students were forbidden to reside in a boarding house after its proprietor allegedly spoke favorably about Germany, and at least one student who was alleged to support the German cause was dismissed. More central here, though, are the widespread and lasting attacks on University of Michigan faculty whose loyalty was or could plausibly be questioned, including those pressed by geologist William Hobbs. A leader of the hyperpatriotic National Security League (NSL) and a member of the AAUP's Committee A, Hobbs repeatedly probed his colleagues' loyalty, pushed the institution to remove those he found wanting, and generated evidence that could be used against his peers.

For example, he gathered dubious student testimonials of inappropriate classroom statements and argued that a young child's comment in support of Germany was evidence that the child's father should be dismissed. Hobbs was perhaps the NSL's most vociferous advocate of that organization's call for all colleges and universities to investigate their faculties and purge those whose loyalty could not be confirmed. He was joined in his efforts by other Michigan faculty, including professor of German John W. Scholl, future university president Alexander Grant Ruthven, and historian Claude Van Tyne (Gruber 1975, 163–212; Cain 2011, 304–23; "Who Willed American Participation?" 2017). Van Tyne's efforts to further war hysteria were such that Peter Novick (1988, 120) argued, "Few went so as far as Van Tyne in his avowed renunciation of traditional scholarly norms." In all, more than a dozen faculty and staff members lost their positions at the university due to allegations about their loyalty, with institutional leaders specifically noting that actual evidence of disloyalty was not needed if suspicions were strong enough. While not all of the blame falls on the faculty, and a few actually worked on behalf of their threatened colleagues, professors were central to the purges (Cain 2011).

As these events highlight, despite the dangers of public opinion, academic freedom cannot be conceived of as a battle between faculty and others, or institutional members and outsiders. Restrictions on academic freedom are a problem affecting the profession, but they can also be promulgated by members *of* the profession. It is especially pernicious when tenured faculty use their positions of authority to inappropriately influence the work and livelihood of those without the protections of tenure, whether or not those individuals are on the tenure track. More than 100 years ago, in his critique of the AAUP's 1915 "Declaration of Principles," Amherst College president and free speech advocate Alexander Meiklejohn made a similar point. He warned of elite professors who could control the fates of those below them in the academic hierarchy:

> The evil here is closely akin to the institution known as "head of the department." I have heard a good deal about the despotism of college

> presidents and trustees but I do not believe that it compares with that of the so-called "heads" who are in charge of subordinate teachers . . . They block the way of advancement of all younger men; in large measure they determine what shall be taught and how it shall be taught by their subordinates; and my impression is that their "points of view" are rather important and that conflicting "points of view" sometimes have to give way before them. Such a form of organization is, I think, hostile to academic freedom. (Meiklejohn 1916, 184–85)

To be clear, this is not to suggest that faculty should not play significant roles in assessing their colleagues' work; in hiring, tenuring, and promoting other faculty; or in creating and enacting academic policy. Based on their disciplinary and methodological expertise, they are uniquely qualified to render judgment on academic work and professional qualifications. They are best prepared and positioned to design and enact curricula and assess student outcomes. As such, it is vital that they maintain—or, in some cases, gain—central academic decision-making roles that push against the administration-centric reshaping of higher education. Moreover, they must do so with commitments to academic freedom, academic values, and professional ethics.

Focusing on Sensational Cases Is Misleading

Meiklejohn's critique of the AAUP's 1915 "Declaration" included another observation that remains relevant: "If one were, as a college president, to set about limiting academic freedom, he would be very foolish to attempt it by the dismissal of professors who have attracted public attention by the freedom of their utterances. To do that is to invite public condemnation, to arouse clamor, and to ensure that contempt and distrust of all the men who are left upon the teaching staff." Instead, he argued, those set on restricting academic freedom and limiting the range of faculty views would be better served by doing so at the point of hiring, as it "can be done in secret; it arouses no public discussion, it gives no basis for hostility on [the] part of teachers previously chosen" (Meiklejohn 1916, 183). Meiklejohn identified one aspect of the larger problem of focusing on sensational cases when we think about academic freedom. It is something that Hofstadter and Metzger (1955, ix) likened to writing a history of unionization by only discussing strikes. Those cases might capture our attention and prove to be important in teasing out larger issues, but they are only part of the story of academic freedom. Others among them are the development of policies and protections, the evolution of ideas about academic freedom, and the role they have played in shaping higher education.

Focusing more narrowly on challenges to and violations of sitting professors' academic freedom, the publicly known cases still only provide a glimpse into a larger situation. Faculty lose their positions without fanfare and under false pretenses, and sometimes institutions wait until after the spotlight has receded to act against an allegedly troublesome faculty member. In 1909, for example, the University of Michigan was faced with calls to remove William E. Bohn for being a socialist revolutionary. Cognizant of potentially negative public reaction, a professor wrote to the institution's leader of his "hope that nothing will be done which will have the appearance, or can easily be given the appearance, of dismissing a man because he is a Socialist" (Cooley to Hutchins 1909). President Harry Burns Hutchins responded that "no sudden or ill-advised action" would be taken, but that Bohn would soon be removed (Hutchins to Cooley 1909). When Hutchins, fearful of losing both legislative support and private donations, pushed Bohn out a few months later, the institution denied that his political views had anything to do with it, and public attention was short lived (Cain 2012, 26–27). Almost a decade later, during the purges of faculty members discussed above, the University of Michigan frequently offered public justifications that hid the true reasons behind the dismissals. Hutchins also convinced a faculty member to take a leave of absence for the duration of the war, which the board made permanent without informing the professor (Cain 2011, 306–9). Concurrently, the University of Illinois investigated five members of its faculty for "disloyalty." A special investigatory committee cleared them, and they retained their positions. Within three years, however, all but one was quietly forced out of the institution, and its president assured a worried trustee that he had removed the most radical members of the faculty. The only one of the accused professors who survived the purge later admitted that he was allowed to keep his position because the institution needed "display liberals," and that he lied for the administration (Feer 1950, 79; Tap 1992, 10–19; Solberg 2004, 76).

Academic freedom is undermined in additional ways that fall short of restrictions in hiring and outright dismissal of heterodox professors. There are academic equivalents of the "freeway therapy" that US Deputy District Attorney Richard Ceballos experienced when he was critical of his office's handling of evidence. As punishment for his public speech while in his job, Ceballos was denied a promotion and transferred to a distant office, to make his work more onerous (*Garcetti* 2006). Similar acts against faculty include removing an instructor from a specific class, assigning undesirable committee work, or denying privileges and opportunities afforded to others. Broader shifts in higher education impinge on academic freedom in different ways that may be even more pressing. For example, the prioritization of research grant dollars over scholarly contributions changes value structures and shapes the very work that professors can be supported in doing. So, too, do grant and contract agreements that fund institutional programs in ways that take appropriate oversight out of the hands of faculty. The quiet non-renewal of instructors working without the protections of tenure is and will remain a fundamental challenge to academic freedom. Taken together, these and other pressures implicate John Dewey's 1902 contention that "subtle and refined danger is always, more to be apprehended than a public and obvious one . . . Ability to talk freely is an important thing, but hardly comparable with the ability to work freely. Now freedom of work is not a matter which lends itself to sensational newspaper articles. It is an intangible, undefinable affair; something which is in the atmosphere and operates as a continuous and unconscious stimulus" (Dewey 1902, 9–10). In short, the sensational cases that capture our attention are "the pathology of the problem" (Hofstadter and Metzger 1955, ix). Understanding them provides insight, but it can also miss persistent challenges that must be addressed in order for academic freedom to be secured.

Shared Governance Is Intertwined with Academic Freedom

Ceballos's experiences in the district attorney's office, as well as broader harassment that extended beyond it, led him to pursue legal action in a case that ultimately reached the US Supreme Court. In its 2006 *Garcetti v. Ceballos* ruling, the court found against Ceballos: "When public employees make statements pursuant to their official duties, the employees are not speaking as citizens for First Amendment purposes, and the Constitution does not insulate their communications from employer discipline." The challenges posed by the *Garcetti* ruling were apparent from the start. The majority opinion ambiguously nodded toward academic freedom in noting, "We need not, and for that reason do not, decide whether the analysis we conduct today would apply in the same manner to cases involving speech related to teaching." In his dissent, Justice Souter was more direct: "The ostensible domain beyond the pale of the First Amendment is spacious enough to include even the teaching of a public university professor, and I have to hope that today's majority does not mean to imperil First Amendment protection of academic freedom in public colleges and universities, whose teachers necessarily speak 'pursuant to official duties.'" (*Garcetti* 2006). In the years since, lower courts have issued inconsistent rulings on whether *Garcetti* applies to faculty, and the US Supreme Court has not heard a case that would provide further clarity. Moreover, its broader rulings are, as Robert C. Post (2012, 207) argued, "incoherent." What is clear, however, is that the courts offer only partial protections for academic freedom, and that faculty speech related to intramural utterances and governance functions is the most vulnerable.

Faculty members' right to speak freely on internal matters has long been a source of contention. The formulation of academic freedom offered in the 1915 "Declaration of Principles" had three elements: freedom of teaching, freedom of research and dissemination, and freedom of extramural utterances. The document's calls for faculty involvement in reappointment decisions, and its claim that "trustees hold an essential and highly honorable place, but . . . faculties hold an independent place, with quite equal responsibilities—and in relation to purely scientific and education questions, the primary responsibility," suggest a faculty voice in governance (Seligman et al. 1915, 26–27). Still, there was no explicit discussion of what Matthew Finkin and Robert Post (2004, 113) call the "freedom of intramural expression": "faculty speech that does not involve disciplinary expertise but is instead about action, policy, or personnel of a faculty member's home institution." Yet freedom of intramural speech was involved in the first AAUP investigation at the University of Utah (Mower and Mogren 2014) and was increasingly so as the association created "soft law" through its ensuing reports. Among the first ninety-four Committee A investigations finding fault with an administration, "in almost a two thirds, the issues were intramural and largely personal, hinging on the jealousy between a president and a professor, or the conflict between strong personalities, or the petty vindictiveness of someone in high office, or . . . the decision to cut down the staff in an effort to economize. In 52 cases, the subcommittee found the president to have been autocratic and arbitrary. At one place, a professor and four colleagues were dismissed for having submitted a proposal recommending greater faculty participation in the governing of the college" (Hofstadter and Metzger 1955, 492).

The experiences of John Ervin Kirkpatrick, the aggrieved professor in the above quote, are instructive here. In the late 1910s, Washburn College was a small institution, highly dependent upon the local business community for its viability. Its president, Parley Paul Womer, prioritized fundraising over academic quality. Amid ongoing struggles between the faculty and Womer, Kirkpatrick openly advocated for both salary increases and changes in the institutional governance structure (Kirkpatrick 1919). He pushed for a greater faculty role in governance and led a small group of colleagues in proposing a new organizational plan that would provide this. Womer denounced and rejected the proposals. At an ensuing faculty meeting, however, Womer suggested a compromise, called for a new period of cooperation, and offered several proposals that hewed closely to the ones that he had just rejected. The faculty agreed to his proposals, including the creation of a joint committee of faculty and administrators to help advise the president, greater job security for faculty, and protections against "willful and capricious action" (Wheeler n.d., 257). The board of trustees approved the new plan of cooperation and dismissed Kirkpatrick for his efforts in trying to bring it about (Kirkpatrick 1919; Lovejoy et al. 1921; Cain and Gump 2011, 7–14).

Kirkpatrick continued his career with several short-term appointments before accepting a seemingly more stable position at Olivet College in Michigan. He also deepened his efforts for faculty governance in numerous publications, some based on research into the history of college and university organization, others on his contemporary observations (Cain and Gump 2011, 25–30). For example, he argued that "the faculty is the only group in the college that is sufficiently trained and experienced to enable it to formulate and to administer successfully the most important affairs of the school," and that "'Presidentitis' can be cured only by faculty responsibility" (Kirkpatrick 1920, 22, 23). He likewise worked for reform at Olivet. He found that the college welcomed faculty input in significant ways, but it still had a governing board that he viewed as too powerful. In June 1926, just weeks before the publication of his *American College and Its Rulers*, which both complemented Olivet's progressive policies and critiqued the influence of a powerful trustee (Kirkpatrick 1926), he was dismissed. The letter informing him of the decision paradoxically noted that it was "not because of any inefficiency on your part as a classroom teacher but because your views of college administration, which views you have always been free to express and advocate, are not in harmony with the views of the Board of Trustees and of the substantial friends of Olivet not on the board who are giving financial support to Olivet College" (*Olivet College Echo* 1926). The AFT's *American Teacher* opined, "No case could do more to fully substantiate Dr. Kirkpatrick's assertion as to the real ruler of American colleges than does Dr. Kirkpatrick's own" ("Attacks on Tenure" 1926, 17).

Kirkpatrick's dismissal from Olivet shows how issues involving intramural speech sometimes overlap with those concerning research and extramural speech. His scholarship on university governance was conjoined with his efforts for organizational change. Such occurrences are just one reason to take an expansive view of academic freedom for intramural utterances. As Matthew Finkin argued:

> When before speaking, the professor must first question the capacity in which the speech is uttered—Am I engaged in specifically disciplinary discourse and so I have academic freedom? Am I speaking as employee and so may find myself utterly without protection unless my speech is upon a matter of political, social, or other concern to the community at large (and even then does not fall afoul of some balance later to be struck)?—there is no doubt that in an institution presided over by an aspiring despot the majority, being risk adverse, will tend to steer clear of the forbidden zone" (Finkin 1988, 1342–43).

Kirkpatrick's firing from Washburn more clearly involved intramural speech and, further, points to the importance of protections. In its report on the situation, the AAUP emphasized that the issue is "not less serious than a charge of unwarrantable restriction of freedom of teaching. If leadership in the attempt to alter existing conditions and to introduce a greater degree of representative government into the organization of a college or university is to be punished by dismissal . . . the processes making for reform in the internal constitution of American colleges are threatened at their point of origin, and the teaching profession is deprived of the right of even urging changes which it may believe to be needful" (Lovejoy et al. 1921, 68).

Kirkpatrick's dismissals from both Washburn and Olivet Colleges were just two of the numerous incidents that demonstrate the extent of governance controversies in academic freedom's formative years. The AAUP report (Lovejoy et al. 1921) on his dismissal from Washburn was among those that it used to make a claim for a greater faculty voice in institutional affairs. Those efforts took place alongside the work of the association's Committee T on the Place and Function of Faculties in University Governance and Administration, founded in 1917, to study and promote faculty governance. Yet despite widespread provisions for shared governance, including those endorsed by the AAUP, the American Council on Education, and the Association of Governing Board of Colleges and Universities in their "Statement of Government of

Colleges and Universities" (AAUP et al. 1966), the relationships between academic freedom and shared governance remain, at one and the same time, in dispute and utterly clear.

Scholars differ on whether and what type of intramural faculty speech is covered by traditional notions of academic freedom, especially in relation to constitutional considerations of academic freedom. Finkin and Post (2009, 125), for example, offered a robust understanding of intramural speech as one of four main elements of academic freedom, though they conceded that while it "does not entitle faculty to participate in actual institutional decision making, such an entitlement would be the logical outgrowth of the idea of institutional citizenship on which this aspect of academic freedom rests." Judith Areen (2009, 947) argued, "Academic freedom, properly understood, has what I will call a 'governance dimension.' It is not only about faculty research and teaching; it is also about the freedom of faculties to govern their institutions in a way that accords with academic values." Cary Nelson (2010, 32) called academic freedom "an empty concept" without shared governance, while Larry Gerber (2011), echoing AAUP language, claimed that they are "inextricably linked." Mark Yudoff (1988) and Michael Olivas (1993, 1845) are among those who have questioned why faculty should have speech rights not afforded other workers. Stanley Fish (2014, 37–44) has queried whether shared governance is an academic value at all, much less one supported by academic freedom.

Like Areen (2009), I argue that it very much *is* an academic value, one that dates to communities of scholars that preceded the modern university and gets to the core of the very mission of college and universities. Beyond that, the freedom of intramural utterances is a necessary precondition for shared governance. Faculty cannot play an effective role without it. As the AAUP argued in Kirkpatrick's case (Lovejoy et al. 1921), if questioning academic policy can lead to dismissal, faculty are silenced, and shared governance is precluded. This is the situation for the increasing numbers of non-tenure-line faculty who are frequently denied the opportunity to contribute to the governance of their institutions. The ongoing restructuring of higher education necessitates new and robust protections that will allow the full range of the professoriate to participate in governance without fear of reprisal.

Access to Academic Freedom

On April 23, 1899, Sam Hose was lynched in Newnan, Georgia, one instance of a despicable practice that swept the South but also took place elsewhere. Sam Hose died a violent death. He was brutalized, dismembered, and burned alive. Parts of his body were taken as souvenirs and, for years, were the source of racist humor in the South (Arnold 2009, 172). Andrew Sledd lost his job because he wrote about the event and censured the South for its traditions, practices, and belief structures. As critics of his dismissal argued at the time, he should have been defended, rather than attacked. Nonetheless, Sledd left Emory University with enough money to undertake graduate study at Yale, went on to become president of what is now the University of Florida, and later returned to Emory as a professor.

Academic freedom is vitally important, as it enables colleges and universities to do the work that they are charged with undertaking. It has, though, too often been disconnected from larger considerations of discrimination and stratification in American society and US higher education. Sledd's academic freedom was violated. Sam Hose's being was. While Sledd and John Spencer Bassett (1903) called for better treatment of Black people, neither called for equality, much less argued that the academic positions and freedom they sought for themselves should be extended to members of other races. As James Anderson (1993, 153–54) wrote: "Until 1941 no African American scholar, no matter how qualified, how many degrees he or she had earned, or how many excellent articles and books he or she had published, was hired in a permanent faculty position at any white university in America. The absence of African Americans from these positions reflected at least one form of racial discrimination that was common to both the North and South." Moreover, even Black faculty who found positions at historically Black colleges and universities faced substantial restrictions on their work, based on the larger issues of societal racism, stratification, and institutional needs to appease public and private funders. Efforts toward Black academic freedom were most dangerous (e.g., Gasman 1999; Williamson-Lott 2018, 48–57, 112–15).

It is not only discrimination against members of particular racial and ethnic groups that has restricted employment opportunities in higher education—and therefore the rights of academic freedom that they would possess. Among many examples, we can point to the discrimination that contributed to a drop in the percentage of women on US faculties in the mid-twentieth century (Graham 1978), and to what Sheila Slaughter (1994, 84) called the "pervasiveness of gender issues in 1980s academic freedom cases" (also see Porwancher 2013, 278). Others are the purges of lesbian, gay, and bisexual faculty, undertaken both on the broad scale of Florida's Johns Committee in the 1960s (Graves 2009; Braukman 2012, 72–82) and in specific cases, such as that of Martha Deane, forced to resign from UCLA in the 1950s because of her sexuality. These events highlight different means of access to faculty positions and the various experiences encountered once such jobs are acquired (Weiler 2007). Moreover, the attacks on academic freedom associated with the culture wars of the 1990s were assaults on both scholarly fields that examine gender, race, and sexuality and those that benefited from such examination. As Christopher Newfield (2008, 65) colorfully noted (attributing the phrasing to sociologist Avery Gordon), they "allowed the Red menace to be replaced by a rainbow menace."

The point is not to conflate academic freedom and broader issues of discrimination, but instead to emphasize that broader constraints on freedom necessarily impact those who have academic freedom and the ways in which it can be used. Our notions of academic freedom developed within a larger, stratified system. It was and has been conceived and defended on the basis of the expertise of professors in institutions of higher education, but neither access to that expertise nor to those positions is evenly distributed. More than two decades ago, Sylvia Tamale and J. Oloka-Onyango examined gender and academic freedom in Africa and asked, "How can women be deemed really free actors when the academy is itself riddled with prejudices that derive from the exercise of power in an institution that is traditionally authoritarian and isolationist?" (Tamale and Oloka-Onyango 1997, 15) Much more recently, John Higgins considered great disparities of access to education in South Africa and inquired, "What does the right to academic freedom mean in a society where the material foundations for practice are lacking or unevenly distributed because of material inequalities?" (Higgins 2019, cited in Scott 2019, 12). Evidence of structural racism, as well as bias on the basis of gender and sexual orientation, calls on us to ask similar questions in the United States.

Conclusion

To paraphrase historian of higher education John Thelin (1982), academic freedom has a useful past. As he would argue, specific cases become parts of institutional sagas—the stories that institutions tell about themselves and how they came to be. Duke University, for example, celebrates the Bassett affair as a key moment in its development from Trinity College into a world-class university (Porter 1964). The University of Wisconsin memorializes its "sifting and winnowing" statement (Herfurth 1998), although, amid Governor Scott Walker's attempts to remake the institution, opposing sides have both invoked it. When told in full, the history of academic freedom can provide a depth of understanding unavailable when modern issues are examined without insight into the way that ideas developed, policies were negotiated and renegotiated in politicized contexts, and faculty freedoms were violated as well as protected. Even when looked at in brief, history can point to longstanding concerns and highlight areas to which faculty—and, indeed, anyone with a stake in higher education—need to be attuned.

What are these issues, and what might we expect in moving forward? The "tyranny of public opinion" will remain a primary challenge, especially when the internet makes it easy to strip context, distort messages, and intentionally generate backlash. The politicized public sphere and some politicians' readiness to attack, rather than support, higher education only makes that tyranny more dangerous. The inclination, in some quarters, to deny the credibility of science likewise creates conditions inhospitable to academic freedom. As noted at the outset of this chapter, the rise of expertise a century ago helped contribute to the formulation of academic freedom. The rejection of science and expertise threatens it. Colleges and universities will demonstrate their values by how they respond to such efforts to silence faculty.

There is little reason to believe that the shift toward a predominantly non-tenure-line faculty will be reversed in the near future. Such a repositioning fundamentally undercuts the faculty in institutional affairs: in its capacity to actually do academic work, and in its ability to speak freely. As was argued more than 100 years ago, at-will faculty employment essentially undermines the system of higher education by allowing the pursuit of knowledge to be beholden to market and political conditions, and by making intramural speech more dangerous. Moreover, the economic collapse associated with COVID-19 can only be expected to strip more money from higher education and augur more managerial practices in it. Retrenchment has been a significant part of the reshaping of higher education in the past, and it is again underway at the time of this writing. As Slaughter (1994) demonstrated, it is often undertaken in ways that both undercut the collective faculty voice and eliminate specific members who are deemed troublesome. The intersection of money and academic freedom will remain a pressing issue that deserves more attention as we go forward.

Considering these and related challenges, faculty collective action will retain, and even gain, importance. Whether through unions, professional associations, or local bodies, academics will need to reassert a shared voice to help mitigate the pressures of managerialism that undermine their roles. Doing so will be difficult, in light of the fracturing of the professoriate. C. P. Snow (1959) warned of the misunderstandings between the "two cultures" of scientists and humanists. Burton Clark (1987, 42) identified the twin considerations of institution type and discipline that help define and differentiate faculty and their careers. Now, the diffuse kinds of appointments have added a third axis to Clark's "professorial matrix," turning it into an array that further works against faculty unity. If academics, especially tenured professors in well-resourced institutions, protect only their own positions and work conditions, then academic freedom for most faculty will become more restricted. Ironically, perhaps the extent of the shift to non-tenure-line faculty offers the best hope for a reckoning. Those in the academy can either work together for collective rights—as well as for the benefit of higher education and the society it serves—or allow it to be further undermined.

More broadly, observers will probably continue to focus on the dramatic cases and controversial events that raise political issues or are clearly antithetical to academic freedom. The future of higher education would be better served if we also attend to quieter and subtler—but nevertheless dangerous—challenges to academic freedom: the prioritization of efficiency over academics; reward structures that value countable units over exploration; litigation that bogs down or dissuades research; a reliance on grant dollars that transfers academic judgment from faculty to funders; a misuse of power over graduate students and postdocs in their instructional and research roles; and a preference for student satisfaction over learning outcomes. At the same time, some of the most important issues are dramatic and eye opening. As history has repeatedly demonstrated, and as the discussion throughout this chapter has made clear, structural racism and broader discriminatory practices are societal problems that affect access to academic freedom. Academic freedom is a principle that undergirds higher education. As long as access to it is unequal—due to religion, race, gender, sexual orientation, appointment types, political beliefs, or other reasons—it will remain an ideal, more than a reality.

Note

1. Some of the ideas sketched here build on my own contribution to that forum (Cain 2018).

References

AAUP (American Association of University Professors). 1940/1970. "1940 Statement of Principles on Academic Freedom and Tenure." AAUP Reports & Publications, https://www.aaup.org/reports-publications.

AAUP (American Association of University Professors), American Council on Education, and Association of Governing Board of Colleges and Universities. 1966. "Statement of Government of Colleges and Universities." AAUP Reports & Publications, https://www.aaup.org//reports-publications.

"A Notable Victory for Academic Freedom." 1904. *World's Work* 7(3):4284–4287.

"Attacks on Tenure and Academic Freedom." 1926. *American Teacher* 11(3):16–17.

Anderson, James D. 1993. "Race, Meritocracy, and the American Academy during the Immediate Post–World War II Era." *History of Education Quarterly* 33(2): 151–175.

Areen, Judith C. 2009. "Government as Educator: A New Understanding of First Amendment Protection of Academic Freedom and Governance." *Georgetown Law Journal* 97(4):945–1000.

Arnold, Edwin T. 2009. *What Virtue There Is in Fire: Cultural Memory and the Lynching of Sam Hose*. Athens: University of Georgia Press.

"Bad Boys Burn Sledd in Effigy." August 7, 1902. *Atlanta Constitution*, 4.

Bassett, John Spencer. 1903. "Stirring Up the Fires of Race Antipathy." *South Atlantic Quarterly* 2(4):297–305.

Braukman, Stacy. 2012. *Communists and Perverts under the Palms: The Johns Committee in Florida, 1956–1965*. Gainesville: University Press of Florida.

Cain, Timothy Reese. 2018. "'Friendly Public Sentiment' and the Threats to Academic Freedom." *History of Education Quarterly* 58(3):428–435.

Cain, Timothy Reese. 2012. *Establishing Academic Freedom: Politics, Principles, and the Development of Core Values*. New York: Palgrave Macmillan.

Cain, Timothy Reese. 2011. "'Silence and Cowardice' at the University of Michigan: World War I and the Pursuit of Un-American Faculty." *History of Education Quarterly* 51(3):297–329.

Cain, Timothy Reese. 2007. "For Education and Employment: The American Federation of Teachers and Academic Freedom, 1926–1941." *Perspectives on the History of Higher Education* 26:67–102.

Cain, Timothy Reese and Steven E. Gump. 2011. "John Ervin Kirkpatrick and the Rulers of American Colleges." *AAUP Journal of Academic Freedom* 2, https://www.aaup.org/reports-publications/.

Chapman, John Jay. July 1, 1910. "Professorial Ethics." *Science* 32(809):5–10.

Churchill (*Churchill v. University of Colorado at Boulder*). 2012. CO 54 No. 11SC25. Justia, https://law.justia.com.

Clark, Burton R. 1987. *The Academic Life: Small Worlds, Different Worlds*. Princeton, NJ: Carnegie Foundation for the Advancement of Teaching.

Cooley, Charles H. to H. B. Hutchins. December 14, 1909. Box 1, Hutchins Papers, Bentley Historical Library, University of Michigan.

Dewey, John. 1902. "Academic Freedom." *Educational Review* 23:1–14.

Donato, Rubén and Martin Lazerson. 2000. "New Directions in American Education History: Problems and Prospects." *Educational Researcher* 29(8):4–15.

Editorial. August 7, 1902. *Cedartown Standard*, 2.

"Emory Professor Excites Indignation." August 4, 1902. *Atlanta Journal*, 1.

Feer, Robert A. 1950. "Academic Freedom at State Universities: The University of Illinois 1867–1950, a Case Study." BA thesis, Harvard University.

Felton, Mrs. W. H. [Rebecca Latimer]. August 3, 1902. "Letter to the Editor." *Atlanta Constitution*, B4.

Finkin, Matthew W. 1988. "Intramural Speech, Academic Freedom, and the First Amendment." *Texas Law Review* 66(7):1323–1349.

Finkin, Matthew W. and Robert C. Post. 2009. *For the Common Good: Principles of American Academic Freedom*. New Haven, CT: Yale University Press.

Fish, Stanley. 2014. *Versions of Academic Freedom: From Professionalism to Revolution*. Chicago: University of Chicago Press.

"Forum on Academic Freedom." 2018. *History of Education Quarterly* 58(3):420–474.

Furner, Mary O. 1975. *Advocacy and Objectivity: A Crisis in the Professionalization of American Social Science, 1865–1905*. Lexington: University Press of Kentucky.

Garber, Paul Neff. 1937. *John Carlisle Kilgo: President of Trinity College, 1894–1910*. Durham, NC: Duke University Press.

Garcetti v. Ceballos. 2006. 547 U.S. 410. Justia, https://supreme.justia.com.

Gasman, Marybeth. 1999. "Scylla and Charybdis: Navigating the Waters of Academic Freedom at Fisk University during Charles S. Johnson's Administration." *American Educational Research Journal* 36(4):739–758.

Gerber, Larry G. 2011. "'Inextricably Linked': Shared Governance and Academic Freedom." *Academe* 87(3):22–24.

Graham, Patricia Albjerg. 1978. "Expansion and Exclusion: A History of Women in American Higher Education." *Signs: Journal of Women in Culture and Society* 3(4):759–773.

Graves, Karen L. 2009. *And They Were Wonderful Teachers: Florida's Purge of Gay and Lesbian Teachers*. Urbana: University of Illinois Press.

Gruber, Carol S. 1975. *Mars and Minerva: World War I and the Uses of the Higher Learning in America*. Baton Rouge: Louisiana State University Press.

Haberler, Zachary. 2015. "Publicity and the American Association of University Professors." *Perspectives on the History of Higher Education* 31:49–78.

Haberler, Zachary. 2013. "Liberty but Not License: Publicity, Academic Freedom and the Professionalization of the Professoriate, 1890–1929." PhD diss., University of California-Riverside.

Herfurth, Theodore. 1998. "Sifting and Winnowing: A Chapter in the History of Academic Freedom at the University of Wisconsin." In W. Lee Hanson (ed.), *Academic Freedom on Trial: 100 Years of Sifting and Winnowing at the University of Wisconsin-Madison*, 58–89. Madison: Office of Publications at the University of Wisconsin-Madison.

Higgins, John. 2019. "Abstract Human Right or Material Practice? Academic Freedom in an Unequal Society." In Crain Soudien, Ingrid Woolard, and Vasu Reddy (eds.), *State of the Nation: Poverty and Inequality; Diagnosis, Prognosis and Responses*. Cape Town, South Africa: Human Sciences Research Council Press.

Hofstadter, Richard and Walter P. Metzger. 1955. *The Development of Academic Freedom in the United States*. New York: Columbia University Press.

Hutcheson, Philo A. 1997. "McCarthyism and the Professoriate: A Historiographic Nightmare?" In John C. Smart (ed.), *Higher Education: Handbook of Theory and Research*, vol. 12, 435–460. Bronx, NY: Agathon Press.

Hutchins, H. B. to Charles H. Cooley. December 15, 1909. Box 1, Hutchins Papers, Bentley Historical Library, University of Michigan.

"Indignation at Covington." August 5, 1902. *Atlanta Constitution*, 6.

Janus (Mark Janus v. AFSCME [American Federation of State, County, and Municipal Employees] et al.). 2018. 585 U.S. ___, Docket No. 16-1466, https://supreme.justia.com.

Johnson, Lily to Mrs. Felton. August 6, 1902. Rebecca Latimer Felton Papers, Hargrett Rare Books and Manuscript Library, University of Georgia, http://dlg.galileo.usg.edu/guan/0081/pdfs/harg0081-004-007.pdf.

Kilgo, J. C. to W. A. Candler. August 14, 1902. Trinity College Papers, Duke University Archives.

Kirkpatrick, J. E. 1926. *The American College and Its Rulers*. New York: New Republic.

Kirkpatrick, J. E. 1920. "The Place of the Faculty in the Organization and Government of Colleges." *School and Society* 12(288):22–23.

Kirkpatrick, J. E. 1919. "The Why of Academic Unrest." *School and Society* 10:52–53.

Lovejoy, Arthur O. 1949. "Communism versus Academic Freedom." *American Scholar* 18(3):332–337.

Lovejoy, Arthur O., Grace Van S. Baur, Raymond G. Gettel, Edgar James Swift, and U. G. Weatherly. 1921. "Report of the Committee of Inquiry on Conditions in Washburn College." *Bulletin of the American Association of University Professors* 7(1–2):66–137.

Lowry, Bryan. May 14, 2014. "Kansas Regents Adopt Revised Social Media Policy." *Kansas City Star*, http://www.kansascity.com.

Matthews, Terry L. 2003. "The Voice of a Prophet: Andrew Sledd Revisited." *Journal of Southern Religion* 6:1–13.

Meiklejohn, Alexander. 1916. "Discussion." *Association of American Colleges Bulletin* 2(3): 179–187.

"Memorial from the Faculty to the Trustees." 1904. In "Trinity College and Academic Liberty." *South Atlantic Quarterly* 3(1):65–68.

Menand, Louis. 1996. "The Limits of Academic Freedom." In *The Future of Academic Freedom*, 3–20. Chicago: University of Chicago Press.

Morrison, Joseph L. 1962. "Josephus Daniels and the Bassett Academic Freedom Case." *Journalism Quarterly* 39(2):187–195.

Mower, Allyson and Paul Mogren. 2014. "A Collision of Rights." In *When Rights Clash: Origins of the University of Utah Academic Senate*, chapter 2, https://whenrightsclash.lib.utah.edu/?p=191/.

Nelson, Cary. 2010. *No University Is an Island: Saving Academic Freedom*. New York: New York University Press.

Nemeth, Julian. 2017. "The Case for Cleaning House: Sidney Hook and the Ethics of Academic Freedom during the McCarthy Era." *History of Education Quarterly* 57(3): 399–426.

Newfield, Christopher. 2008. *Unmaking the Public University: The Forty-Year Assault on the Middle Class*. Cambridge, MA: Harvard University Press.

NLRB [National Labor Relations Board] v. Yeshiva Univ. 1980. 444 U.S. 672. Justia, https://supreme.justia.com.

Novick, Peter. 1988. *That Noble Dream: The "Objectivity Question" and the American Historical Profession*. New York: Cambridge University Press.

Olivas, Michael A. 1993. "Reflections on Professorial Academic Freedom: Second Thoughts on the Third 'Essential Freedom.'" *Stanford Law Review* 45(6):1835–1858.

Olivet College Echo. June 16, 1926.

Porter, Earl W. 1964. *Trinity and Duke, 1892–1924: Foundations of Duke University*. Durham, NC: Duke University Press.

Porwancher, Andrew. 2013. "Prying the Gates Wide Open: Academic Freedom and Gender Equality at Brown University, 1974–1977." *Pedagogica Historica* 29(2):273–292.

Post, Robert C. 2012. "Discipline and Freedom in the Academy." *Arkansas Law Review* 65(2):203–215.

Reed, Ralph E., Jr. 1988. "Emory College and the Sledd Affair of 1902: A Case Study in Southern Honor and Racial Attitudes." *Georgia Historical Quarterly* 72(3):463–492.

Renfroe, J. W. to Rebecca Latimer Felton. July 5, 1902. Rebecca Latimer Felton Papers, Hargrett Rare Books and Manuscript Library, University of Georgia, http://dlg.galileo.usg.edu/guan/0081/pdfs/harg0081-004-007.pdf.

Schrecker, Ellen W. 1986. *No Ivory Tower: McCarthyism and the Universities*. New York: Oxford University Press.

Scott, Joan Wallach. 2019. *Knowledge, Power, and Academic Freedom*. New York: Columbia University Press.

Seligman, Edwin R. A., Charles E. Bennett, James Q. Dealey, Richard T. Ely, Henry W. Farnam, Frank A. Fetter, Franklin H. Giddings, et al. 1915. "General Report of the Committee on Academic Freedom and Academic Tenure." *Bulletin of the American Association of University Professors* 1(1):15–43.

Slaughter, Sheila. 1994. "Academic Freedom at the End of the Century: Professional Labor, Gender, and Professionalization." In Philip G. Altbach, Robert O. Berdahl, and Patricia J. Gumport (eds.), *Higher Education in American Society*, 3rd edition, 73–100. Amherst, NY: Prometheus Books.

Sledd, Andrew. July 1902. "The Negro: Another View." *Atlantic Monthly* 90:65–73.

Sledd, Andrew to Warren A. Candler. August 27, 1902. Warren A. Candler Collection, Emory University.

Solberg, Winston U. 2004. "William Abbott Oldfather: Making the Classics Relevant to Modern Life." In Lillian Hoddeson (ed.), *No Boundaries: University of Illinois Vignettes*, 69–87. Urbana: University of Illinois Press.

Snow, C. P. 1959. *The Two Cultures and the Scientific Revolution*. Cambridge: Cambridge University Press.

"Statement of the Trustees." 1904. In "Trinity College and Academic Liberty." *South Atlantic Quarterly* 3(1):62–64.

Stephenson, Wendell H. 1948. "The Negro in the Thinking and Writing of John Spencer Bassett." *North Carolina Historical Review* 25(4):427–441.

Tamale, Sylvia and J. Oloka-Onyango. 1997. "Bitches at the Academy: Gender and Academic Freedom at the African University." *Africa Development* 22(1):13–37.

Tap, Bruce. 1992. "Suppression of Dissent: Academic Freedom at the University of Illinois during the World War I Era." *Illinois Historical Journal* 85(1):2–22.

Thelin, John R. 1982. *Higher Education and Its Useful Past: Applied History in Research and Planning*. Rochester, VT: Schenkman Books.

Tiede, Hans-Joerg. 2015. *University Reform: The Founding of the American Association of University Professors*. Baltimore: Johns Hopkins University Press.

Tiede, Hans-Joerg. 2014. "'To Make Collective Action Possible': The Founding of the AAUP." *AAUP Journal of Academic Freedom* 5, https://www.aaup.org/reports-publications/.

"Trinity College and Academic Liberty." 1904. *South Atlantic Quarterly* 3(1):62–72.

Weiler, Kathleen. 2007. "The Case of Martha Deane: Sexuality and Power at Cold War UCLA." *History of Education Quarterly* 47(4):470–496.

Wheeler, W. G. n.d. "Minutes of the Faculty, 1908–1920." Washburn University Archives, Mabee Library, Topeka, Kansas.

"Who Willed American Participation?" April 2017. *New Republic* 10(128):308–310.

Williamson, Joel. 1984. *The Crucible of Race: Black-White Relations in the American South since Emancipation*. New York: Oxford University Press.

Williamson-Lott, Joy Ann. 2018. *Jim Crow Campus: Higher Education and the Struggle for a New Southern Order*. New York: Teachers College Press.

Yudoff, Mark G. 1988. "Intramural Musings: A Reply to Professor Finkin." *Texas Law Review* 66(7):1351–1357.

CONTRIBUTORS

Patricia A. Adler is professor emeritus of sociology at the University of Colorado, Boulder. Her areas of interest are qualitative methods, symbolic interactionism, deviant behavior, socialization, and work and occupations.

Peter Adler is professor emeritus of sociology and criminology at the University of Denver. His interests include the sociology of sports, drugs and society, and social psychology.

Together, the Adlers edited the *Journal of Contemporary Ethnography* from 1986 to 1994 and were founding editors of the annual *Sociological Studies of Children and Adolescents*. They are the authors of over twenty books and anthologies and more than 100 peer-reviewed journal articles. In 2010, they were awarded the George H. Mead Award for Lifetime Achievement by the Society for the Study of Symbolic Interactionism, and in 2006–2007, were the co-presidents of the Midwest Sociological Society. They currently reside in Maui, Hawaii.

Timothy Reese Cain is associate professor in the University of Georgia's Institute of Higher Education. His research explores academic freedom, the changing faculty workforce, unionization in higher education, student activism, and related issues. He is the author of *Campus Unions: Organized Faculty and Graduate Students in US Higher Education* (2017); *Establishing Academic Freedom: Politics, Principles, and the Development of Core Values* (2012); and, with colleagues at the National Institute for Learning Outcomes Assessment, *Using Evidence of Student Learning to Improve Higher Education* (2015). His current projects include a study of student protests in the 1960s and a history of faculty unionization from 1918 to 1980.

Dan Clawson taught sociology at the University of Massachusetts, Amherst. Over a long and distinguished career, he wrote on labor movements, as well as on higher education, and was active in his union, the Massachusetts Teachers Association. He wrote *The Next Upsurge: Labor and the New Social Movements* (with Max Page), *The Future of Higher Education*, and *Unequal Time: Gender, Class, and Family in Employment Schedules* (with Naomi Gerstel). He was co-chair of the American Sociological Association's Taskforce on Contingent Faculty Employment. Professor Clawson died unexpectedly as this book neared completion.

Joseph C. Hermanowicz, professor of sociology at the University of Georgia, studies the academic profession, academic careers, and universities as organizations. He is the author of *Lives in Science: How Institutions Affect Academic Careers* (2009), *The Stars Are Not Enough: Scientists—Their Passions and Professions* (1998), and *College Attrition at American Research Universities: Comparative Case Studies* (2003), as well as editor of *The American Academic Profession: Transformation in Contemporary Higher Education* (2011). He is also the author of articles and chapters on the sociology of higher education, including "The Professoriate in International Perspective," in *Higher Education: Handbook of Theory and Research.*

Philip Lee is a professor of law at the University of the District of Columbia's David A. Clarke School of Law, where he has taught Property I and II, Constitutional Law I, Torts II, Education Law, and Race and the Law. He received his bachelor's degree from Duke University, his law degree from Harvard Law School, and his master's and doctorate degrees in education from the Harvard Graduate School of Education. His research and writing center on academic freedom, diversity and educational access, school law (K–12), higher education history and law, and property law and race.

Gary Rhoades is a professor and director of the Center for the Study of Higher Education at the University of Arizona. He was formerly general secretary of the American Association of University Professors. His work focuses on the restructuring of academic institutions and professions. Among his publications are *Managed Professionals: Unionized Faculty and Restructuring Academic Labor* (1998) and (with Sheila Slaughter) *Academic Capitalism in the New Economy: Markets, State, and Higher Education* (2004). Currently, he is working on a book titled *Organizing "Professionals": Academic Employees Negotiating a New Academy.*

Laura Stark is associate professor at Vanderbilt University and associate editor of the journal *History & Theory*. She works on the sociology and history of science, medicine, and morality and the state from a cultural perspective. Her first book was *Behind Closed Doors: IRBs and the Making of Ethical Research* (2012). Her second book, *The Normals: A People's History* (forthcoming), explores how a global market for healthy civilian human subjects emerged in law, science, and everyday imagination. It is based on a vernacular archive Stark created, encompassing more than 100 "normal control" research subjects and the scientists who experimented with them from 1950 through 1980.

John Thelin is a university research professor at the University of Kentucky and studies the history of higher education and public policy. He is the author of several books published by Johns Hopkins University Press, including *Going To College in the Sixties* (2018) and a new, third edition of *A History of American Higher Education* (2019). In 2018, he teamed with Dean Emeritus Patricia Albjerg Graham of Harvard to present a congressional briefing on the Higher Education Act of 1965. He has received awards for outstanding research from the Association for the Study of Higher Education and the American Educational Research Association.

Hans-Joerg Tiede is director of the Department of Research at the American Association of University Professors (AAUP). His book on the founding of the AAUP, *University Reform*, was published in 2015. He served as editor of *Policy Documents and Reports* (2015), commonly known as the AAUP *Red Book*. Prior to joining the staff of the AAUP, he was a faculty member at Illinois Wesleyan University.

Gaye Tuchman is professor emerita of sociology at the University of Connecticut. Among her books are the ethnographies *Wannabe U: Inside the Corporate University* and *Making News: A Study in the Construction of Reality*. She was co-editor of *Hearth and Home: Images of Women in the Mass Media*, one of the first texts on gender representation in diverse legacy media. She was a co-founder of Sociologists for Women in Society and has served on the councils of national sociological organizations, the boards of sociology and feminist journals, and as president of the Eastern Sociological Society. She held a Fulbright/LaCaixa Lectureship in the Journalism Department of the Autonomous University of Barcelona and was a Fulbright Senior Specialist at the Institute of Communications and Image, University of Chile.

Stephen Turner is Distinguished University Professor of Philosophy at the University of South Florida, where he is also director of the Center for Social and Political Thought. He has been a visiting professor at Boston University, the University of Notre Dame, and the Virginia Polytechnic Institute and State University; a Simon Honorary Professor at Manchester University; and has held fellowships from the National Endowment for the Humanities and the Swedish Collegium for Advanced Studies. He has authored or edited thirty books, including, most recently, *The Calling of Social Thought: Rediscovering the Work of Edward Shils* (with Christopher Adair-Toteff), and *Cognitive Science and the Social: A Primer*.

Eve Weinbaum teaches labor studies and sociology at the University of Massachusetts, Amherst. She is president of the Massachusetts Society of Professors, the union of faculty and librarians that is affiliated with the Massachusetts Teachers Association. She is the author of *To Move a Mountain: Fighting the Global Economy in Appalachia* and currently works on organizing, collective bargaining, grievances, and equity in higher education. In addition to her work at UMass, she is president of the Pioneer Valley Workers Center and treasurer of the Western Massachusetts Area Labor Federation.

INDEX

MORE BOOKS in HIGHER EDUCATION

UNDERSTANDING ACADEMIC FREEDOM

Henry Reichman

Part of the acclaimed Higher Ed Leadership Essentials series, this book surveys academic freedom's history and its application in today's universities. **$27.95 pb/ebook**

THE FUTURE OF ACADEMIC FREEDOM

Henry Reichman

foreword by Joan Wallach Scott

Few issues are as hotly debated or misunderstood as academic freedom. Reichman's book sheds light on and brings clarity to those debates.

Winner of the Eli M. Oboler Memorial Award by the American Library Association

$29.95 hc/ebook

@JHUPress

@JohnsHopkins UniversityPress

@JHUPress

JOHNS HOPKINS
UNIVERSITY PRESS

ACADEMIC FAULT LINES

The Rise of Industry Logic in Public Higher Education

Patricia J. Gumport

How did public higher education become an industry? This unprecedented account reveals how campus leaders and faculty preserved the vitality and core values of public higher education despite changing resources and expectations.

$59.95 hc/ebook

THE FACULTY FACTOR

Reassessing the American Academy in a Turbulent Era

Martin J. Finkelstein, Valerie Martin Conley, and Jack H. Schuster

In an academy squeezed hard by formidable pressures, what is the future of the faculty?

$50.00 hc/ebook

UNIVERSITY REFORM

The Founding of the American Association of University Professors

Hans-Joerg Tiede

foreword by Michael Bérubé

How the AAUP fought to give voice to America's faculty and defend academic freedom. **$34.95 hc/ebook**

For more Higher Education books, visit **press.jhu.edu**